PRAISE FOR *Crossings*

Melissa Inouye demonstrates that no matter how closely scholars and historians examine the gospel of Jesus Christ, the true evidence of its power is seen in the everyday goodness of its followers. Inouye reveals to us her quiet moments, when the gospel works far deeper than cultural stereotypes and rote exercises to touch the most common part of humanity. If we know the gospel by its fruits, Inouye is at once a most treasured specimen and representative of so many who live close to Christ.

—NEYLAN MCBAINE, *Author of* Women at Church:
Magnifying LDS Women's Local Impact

With about ten pages to go I had the thought, "I can't wait to read this book again." Melissa Inouye's brilliant metaphors, her humor, her humility, her vulnerability, and her wisdom offer completely fresh perspectives on some of the most pressing challenges facing Latter-day Saints today. Her wisdom and generosity will resonate with people from many different backgrounds. You'll come away feeling like you personally know Inouye and her brilliant family, like you've personally experienced Hong Kong or Tainan or Auckland, and like you've personally had heartfelt conversations with Latter-day Saints around the globe. I think every reader will come away saying, "She just gets me. She sees where I'm coming from."

—J.B. HAWS, *Associate Professor, Church History and Doctrine,
Brigham Young University*

This thoughtful book is a beautiful example of how faith and scholarship can be brought together. Melissa Inouye's words are personable, powerful, witty, inspiring, engaging, thought-provoking, and real. She not only offers answers to challenging questions, but also models how to think through any number of questions, doubts, or concerns that may arise. She encourages readers to think beyond themselves and to consider the experiences, cultures, and worldviews of others—which is to say she highlights the need for greater charity, or Christlike living. Indeed, this book inspires the expansion and transformation of heart and mind, exemplifying conversion in its truest sense.

—RACHEL COPE, *Associate Professor, Department of Church History and Doctrine, Brigham Young University*

In *Crossings*, Melissa Inouye declares that "life is messy, terrible, wonderful, and hard." I agree! Her essays share the wisdom and strength she has gained living multiple roles—wife, mother, teacher, scholar, historian, missionary, athlete, and cancer survivor. She suggests that young people are the audience for her book. But as a much older woman, I found her life insights—from delights in her children's adventures, to her critical analysis of Chinese revolutions—equally meaningful to me. Melissa's writings are colorful, sometimes humorous, but always authentic. Reading her letters is like talking to a dear and treasured friend. She is not preachy, but instructive—never judgmental, yet willing to openly and honestly address concerns often raised by those confronting the complexities and imperfections of the Latter-day experience. It is a book I want to share with my daughters.

—RENATA FORSTE, *Professor of Sociology and Director of the Kennedy Center for International Studies, Brigham Young University*

crossings

A
Living Faith
Book

LIVING FAITH books are for readers who cherish the life of the mind and the things of the Spirit. Each title is a unique example of faith in search of understanding, the voice of a scholar who has cultivated a believing heart while engaged in the disciplines of the Academy.

Other LIVING FAITH books include:

Adam S. Miller, *Letters to a Young Mormon* (2nd ed.)

Samuel M. Brown, *First Principles and Ordinances:*
The Fourth Article of Faith in Light of the Temple

Steven L. Peck, *Evolving Faith: Wanderings of a Mormon Biologist*

Patrick Q. Mason, *Planted: Belief and Belonging in an Age of Doubt*

Ashley Mae Hoiland, *One Hundred Birds Taught Me to Fly: The Art of Seeking God*

Thomas F. Rogers, *Let Your Hearts and Minds Expand:*
Reflections on Faith, Reason, Charity, and Beauty

George B. Handley, *If Truth Were a Child: Essays on Humanities and Belief*

crossings

a bald asian american latter-day saint
woman scholar's ventures through
life, death, cancer & motherhood
(not necessarily in that order)

MELISSA WEI-TSING INOUYE

A
Living Faith
Book

DESERET
BOOK

BYU
Maxwell
Institute

All photos courtesy of the author except as noted below.

Throughout: MW 7976/Shutterstock.com and Attitude/Shutterstock.com; page 43: Diane Bowen; page 191: public domain/courtesy of the Metropolitan Museum of Art; page 196: Hugh Benson.

This book is the result of a joint publishing effort by the Neal A. Maxwell Institute for Religious Scholarship and Deseret Book Company.

Visit us at deseretbook.com or maxwellinstitute.byu.edu.

Library of Congress Cataloging-in-Publication Data
Names: Inouye, Melissa Wei-Tsing, author.
Title: Crossings : a bald Asian American Latter-Day Saint woman scholar's ventures
    through life, death, cancer, and motherhood (not necessarily in that order) / Melissa
    Wei-Tsing Inouye.
Description: Provo, Utah : Neal A. Maxwell Institute for Religious Scholarship and
    Deseret Book, 2019. | Series: A living faith book.
Identifiers: LCCN 2018059285 (print) | LCCN 2019009600 (ebook) | ISBN
    9781629737782 (ebook) | ISBN 9781944394806 (print : alk. paper)
Subjects: LCSH: Inouye, Melissa Wei-Tsing. | Asian American Mormons—Biography. |
    Mormon women—Biography.
Classification: LCC BX8695.I56 (ebook) | LCC BX8695.I56 A3 2019 (print) | DDC
    289.3092 [B] —dc23
LC record available at https://lccn.loc.gov/2018059285

Printed in the United States of America
Publishers Printing, Salt Lake City, UT

10 9 8 7 6 5 4 3 2 1

For Bean, Sprout, Leaf, and Shoot

CONTENTS

CONTENTS

INTRODUCTION

DEAR READER,

I've always been fuzzy about deadlines, but in May 2017, when I was diagnosed with colon cancer, everything snapped into focus: *Oh shoot! I'm going to die!* Suddenly, thinking about the Ultimate Question of Life, the Universe, and Everything seemed terribly urgent.[1] To be more precise, the project of *writing* about life and its conundrums seemed terribly urgent, because my children are young. With young (Primary-age) children, one does not discuss the meaning of life with a great deal of nuance.* Sentences and stories are short. After about five minutes, even "kid-friendly" family home evening lessons deteriorate.† I have occasionally written letters to my children and saved them in a filing cabinet for them to read when they're older. But when one contemplates the possibility of being entirely absent, a few letters do not seem like enough. This is why I began to think about writing a book: a literary form of food storage, a cache of meaningful communication, a stash of thought

---

* Primary is the children's organization, the children's Sunday School.

† Family home evening is the weekly family meeting, often including a lesson, songs, prayer, games, and treats, held by Latter-day Saint families around the world.

1

and memory that would outlast the board books, meltdowns, and fidgeting. Many months after my diagnosis, and on the other end of treatment, I have a more placid view of the future (including death, which is after all in everyone's future). I'm not out of the woods forever, but I'm not imminently dead. And, I now have a book!

My life hasn't been very long, but it's been extensive—as far as physical and cultural journeys are concerned. I am used to the feeling of being out of place. I was born in the United States to a Chinese American mother and Japanese American father but have spent the majority of my adult life in other places, including Taiwan, China, Japan, Hong Kong, and now New Zealand. I grew up on the West Coast, in laid-back southern California, but received my academic training on the East Coast, at Harvard University, among people who took themselves very seriously. In my professional life, I am a feminist scholar who researches Chinese history and global Christianity and rejects claims not supported by evidence. In my personal life, I'm a Latter-day Saint mom and Primary pianist who teaches her children to believe in miracles. In the United States and New Zealand, I'm identifiable on sight as a member of an Asian ethnic minority; in Asia, I'm an American expat who looks like most people on the street but thinks and acts in a foreign way. I'm bald, so I blend in with many bishoprics,* but stand out in most other social contexts.[2] I've been poor among the rich and rich among the poor. Wherever I go, it seems, I don't quite fit in, which is why I feel equally at home everywhere.

The writings in this book attempt to capture a Latter-day Saint life in its many possible iterations: as a child, parent, friend, disciple, and scholar in a variety of times and places. One's faith is present in the ways one encounters foreign cultures, reflects on the year, teaches students, addresses children, and responds to a life-threatening illness. I am not a Latter-day Saint only on Sunday morning, but in everything I do and in relation to everyone I meet—strangers, students, children, oncologists. A faith

---

* The bishopric is the three-person leadership unit (bishop and two counselors) that heads a local congregation, or ward.

tradition is not simply a collection of doctrines, but a distinctive way of engaging with the world and its people. Latter-day Saints' exceptionally long view of relationships creates a series of persistent entanglements, the peopled warp across which we must learn to weave our lives.

I suppose one of the reasons I am writing about my life is because I am aware that many people, including young people and perhaps, someday, my children, may at times wonder whether this is the sort of life for them. I am also aware that friends and family members of different religious or philosophical persuasions may sometimes wonder why on earth I have chosen to throw in my lot with the "Mormons."[3] I can't prescribe a life for anybody, but what I *can* do is share how I have found the fruits of this life to be worthwhile—costly, to be sure, but also rich and nourishing, a source of deep joy.

At times, we Latter-day Saints may feel that we are on the margins, variously defined, such as when our family situation does not fit the "perfect family" mold, or when we have felt like the only person with deep reservations among a sea of unqualified enthusiasm, or when we have felt the sting of discrimination because of gender, race, class, sexual orientation, nationality, and so on. At other times, we Latter-day Saints may believe that sisters and brothers who are feeling out of place may be indulging in self-pity, choosing to be offended, being unrighteous, or acting prideful and entitled. We may wonder why people who are on the edge can't just "get with the program" or "get over themselves." Yet all of us should remember that marginality is the purpose of God's plan of salvation. We are all aliens, exiles, sojourners far from our spiritual home. The purpose of life is to come to terms with the depth of this alienation in ourselves and *in others* and respond with charity—to seek, receive, and share the pure love of Christ so that we may be one amidst our differences.

Because we all inhabit multiple dimensions, physical and social, with multiple centers, we are all marginal in one way or another. People at the so-called margins have a unique and valuable perspective on the so-called center. In the scriptures, prophets and prophetesses often come from the wilderness, foreign lands, or those classes of people whose connections with mainstream sociality have been severed—the John the Baptists, the Samuel the Lamanites, the Annas in the temple.* I'm not blind to the fact that current church structures have yet to tap into the potential power of integrating the marginal center and the central margins. The real harm resulting from faulty institutional processes is deeply frustrating. I won't stop working to fix this. I get so tired, all the time. But I have deep faith in our collective potential to turn weaknesses into strengths.

Fix-it work isn't very glamorous, but it is the work of prophets, disciples, and Christ himself. The prophet Isaiah described people who have received spiritual strength as people who will make great construction workers—builders, repairers of the breach, restorers of paths to dwell in (see Isaiah 58:12). These images of filling in gaps and fixing walkways help me understand that the work of the gospel is to connect or reconnect people with each other. Often we come to the edge of vast divides that separate us from our fellow beings. But the discomfort we feel at the margins provokes growth and empathy. Christ suffered all things, many of them alien to his previous lived experience, in order to develop the capacity to heal others in their suffering. Having been a stranger, one is prepared to recognize other strangers and take them in. It turns out that all of us can and should find ourselves, and Christ, at the margins.

This theme of being strangers runs throughout my family's recent history. My ancestors on my mother's side were farmers in southern China. On my father's side, my ancestors were samurai, merchants, and farmers in southern Japan. In the early twentieth century, both my Chinese and Japanese ancestors made long migratory crossings that were very consequential for my family and me today. Their journeys across the Pacific determined the places we grew up, the language we spoke, and the people among whom we felt at home. My parents were raised as third-generation Asian Americans in places like Huntington Beach,

---

* John the Baptist and Anna the Prophetess are characters from the New Testament. Samuel the Lamanite is a character from the Book of Mormon, a member of the Lamanite ethnic group who ministered to members of another ethnic group known as the Nephites.

California, and Sigurd, Utah. They grew up speaking only English and listening to the Beach Boys. I didn't learn Chinese and Japanese until I was at university and in graduate school. These new languages, and the opportunities they offered, drew me westward across the Pacific. I have visited my Chinese family's ancestral village outside of Kaiping, Guangdong, and my Japanese family's *nashi* pear farm in Inaibaru, Fukuoka. I have burned incense at my Chinese great-great-grandfather's grave in a cemetery in Hong Kong's New Territories. I walk in the paths my ancestors walked and wonder that I have become so foreign to them. And yet, it was they who first traveled across the ocean, leaving friends and family behind.

My maternal great-grandparents, Gin Gor Ju and Gor Shee Ju, were young people when they left their villages in southeastern China and traveled to the United States. By the time I knew them, they were no longer vigorous farmers cultivating fields of celery, but frail chair-sitters in a small apartment in Los Angeles's Chinatown. Yet they had lived boldly. Because of their willingness to leave behind familiar places and people and make a new life overseas, their great-grandchildren grew up walking not the narrow dirt paths of Lianzhou, Guangdong, but the concrete sidewalks and sand-strewn bike trails of southern California. In 1999, as an undergraduate studying Chinese literature and language, I disembarked from the plane in Beijing and found a sea of people who looked like kin but whose words, gestures, and meanings eluded me. This trip to learn Chinese abroad was the beginning of my lifelong study of Asian language, history, culture, and religion.

Not all of my family's long journeys were chosen. For example, in 1942, shortly after America's entry into World War II, the American public gave full rein to their feelings of suspicion and resentment against people who looked like the Japanese enemy. My American-born grandparents Charles Inouye (a recent Stanford grad) and Bessie Murakami (the salutatorian of her high school class) were forced to pack up "all they could carry" with their two hands into suitcases. The homes, farms, and businesses they had worked so hard to build were lost. Soldiers escorted them and their families on the long train ride from their homes on the

West Coast to a prison camp at Heart Mountain, Wyoming. This particular forced crossing led to others, which brought my family and me into fellowship with the Latter-day Saints. After leaving camp, Grandma and Grandpa Inouye went to work as farmhands in Sanpete County, Utah. Eventually they bought their own farm in the town of Gunnison, where they grew melons, potatoes, and grass seed. Grandma and Grandpa were devout Buddhists, having become acquainted when they were teachers in the Buddhist Sunday School at Heart Mountain. They wanted their children to have some sort of religious training. There was no Buddhist temple, so they let the kids go with the neighbors to the local church. Eventually, these children chose to be baptized. Many years later, so did their parents.

My mother's family, the Chinese family, also encountered the Latter-day Saints in Utah. They grew vegetables on their farm at 2100 South and 400 East in Salt Lake City. Gin Gor Ju, an energetic and enterprising man, was known locally as "the Celery King" because of his bountiful celery crops and innovative methods. They were particularly close to one neighbor family, the Soderborgs. The Jus owned a cow; the Soderborgs milked it for the Jus and kept the cream. The Soderborg boys worked on the Ju farm, earning ten cents an hour, which eventually allowed them to earn enough money for their church missions. Other neighbors in Salt Lake were not so open to mutual friendship with a family that looked different. Some local kids threw rocks at my grandmother, Marjorie Ju, and her siblings as they walked home from school. These kids called them "Chinks" and told them to "go back to China." (Marjorie was the third of nine children, Mary, Fred, Lin John, May, Ken, Amy, Dorothy Jane, and James, all born in Salt Lake City.) Ken died at the tender age of eighteen months in 1936. My great-grandmother, Gor Shee Ju, eagerly absorbed Sister Soderborg's assurances that this child could be bound to the family eternally. Gor Shee agreed to be baptized, along with all her children. A neighbor transported them all from the farm to the Salt Lake Tabernacle in the back of his bakery truck. (Gin Gor Ju was not baptized because he said he had to work on Sunday.) Later, in 1939, the Ju family bought a thirty-two acre farm in Buena Park, California, where the growing season was longer. Because of the needs of the farm, they became less active. Eventually the ward missionaries and local members fellowshipped them again. My grandmother said that she and her husband Hall Lew (who was not a member, but who attended church faithfully and even held callings) went back to church "because of the children." After my mother Susan Lew graduated from Edison High School in Huntington Beach, she chose to attend Brigham Young University. There she met my father, Warren Inouye.

My parents raised my four younger brothers and me in Costa Mesa, California. As a child I played soccer but was never more than an average, placeholding sort of player who got swapped in and out according to "Everyone Plays" regulations. I rode my bike to school, to piano lessons with Sister Bastian[4] (the Costa Mesa First Ward's organist), and to the beach with my friends and brothers. My mother picked us up, dropped us off, and organized all manner of educational activities from art cooperatives to museum trips. My father filled our Saturdays with chores in the yard. On Sundays, we went to church.

We spent a lot of time at church, and not just on Sundays. The cultural hall of the Costa Mesa First Ward building is emblazoned permanently in my mind. I know well the deep storage alcoves for chairs and tables under the stage, the tiny dents in the wooden floors, the busy segment of hallway between the cultural hall's double doors and the kitchen. As a child, my Primary classmates and brothers and I knew which tree to climb to get onto the building's roof, where we scampered about and peered in through the skylights at the grown-up activities below. The feeling of the Costa Mesa Ward's metal folding chairs is part of my body's long-term memory. I can feel their cold smoothness against my back, from slumping during Sunday School, or "Mutual" activities, or early-morning seminary.* I know the exact weight of two chairs in each hand in the hustle and bustle of clearing away a ward social.

As a child in my parents' house, my general impression was that

---

* Mutual refers to the Church's program for young men and young women ages 12–17, historically known as the Mutual Improvement Association. Latter-day Saint teenagers in secondary school often attend scripture-study classes known as seminary.

anything involving church was a lot of work. My mother and father were always bringing food, teaching lessons, organizing youth activities, setting up chairs, taking down chairs, striking camp, and vacuuming the floor. They never attended just within the official parameters of an activity. Instead, they showed up early to pull out the long tables and left late to take out the last bag of garbage, turn off the lights, and lock the door. Sometimes my four younger brothers and I ran off to play in order to avoid setting up, taking down, and mopping up. But eventually we came to adopt our parents' ethic as our own: we worked together until all the work was done.

As engaged as our family was in the ward's social and pedagogical orbits, we also knew we were different from the other members of the Costa Mesa First Ward, whose ancestry was overwhelmingly European. We looked different. We were short and had dark, straight hair. We didn't turn bright pink with sunburn at Youth Conference service projects. We ate rice at dinner nearly every night. We regarded the buddy-buddy parent-child relationships within other ward families with suspicion but also some envy. At Christmastime, after singing Christmas carols and reading scripture, my Chinese grandfather, Gon Gon, distributed laycee ("lucky money") to the children in red and gold envelopes. We celebrated New Year twice (the Western solar date and the Chinese lunar date). In springtime, we observed the Tomb-Sweeping Festival, a traditional Chinese holiday dedicated to remembering ancestors and tidying their graves. We went to Forest Lawn Cemetery in Los Angeles to set boiled chickens before the graves of Gin Gor Ju and Gor Shee Ju. We burned sticks of incense and poured rice wine into the grass. It wasn't something that American church members usually did, but it was what our great-grandparents wanted us to do, so we did it with full hearts.[5]

So far this narrative explains my identity as an Asian American and a Latter-day Saint. Coincidentally, both of these identities are subjects I now research professionally, wearing another hat as a scholar of global history and religion. I first studied East Asia, including Buddhism and Daoism, as an undergraduate, then took two years off to serve a Latter-day

Saint mission in Taiwan. Most of my learning was personal and spiritual. I learned that philosophical discourses on truth and charity were in vain if I couldn't even manage to be kind and considerate to my companion. I became familiar with the powerful feeling of the witness of the Spirit and saw it moving others. And I also gained a working acquaintance with Chinese popular religion, as well as a sense of the promise and pitfalls of my own faith's global project.

In my final year of undergraduate studies, I signed up for a course in American religious history that covered the history of the early Latter-day Saints. Up to this point I had avoided formal study of church history because the potential collateral damage was frightening. Suppose my cherished faith could not stand up to the glare of rational scrutiny or was proved by historical records to have been irreparably flawed? This course was taught by Professor David Hall, a respected historian who was also, above all, a kind person with faith in Christ. Professor Hall's sophisticated but also generous approach to religious faith made a deep impression on me. "The question of whether Joseph Smith really had golden plates," Professor Hall said at one point during a lecture, "is fundamentally the same as the question of whether a virgin conceived and gave birth."

Professor Hall was pointing out that great religious traditions are at one point or another built upon certain claims or assumptions that go beyond the scope of critical reasoning. Many Christians accustomed to laughing at the "ludicrous" belief that an angel appeared to Joseph Smith and guided him to a golden book of scripture would not think to laugh at themselves for their firm belief that an angel appeared to Mary and that she, a virgin, became pregnant. In Professor Hall's religious history classroom, however, there was space for both kinds of knowing: understanding claims supported by physical or textual evidence and recognizing the value of things that could not be evaluated through such methods.

My first academic study of my own faith tradition opened my eyes to its distinctiveness and peculiarity. This appreciation has not prevented me from thinking critically about its evolving structures or lamenting ways in which we Latter-day Saints regularly fall short of our espoused ideals. Nor has it prevented me from seeing God at work through people of other faith traditions. However, being engaged in researching religion over the course of many years, including the history of world Christianity, I find myself still caught by wonder. I find my basic assumptions unchanged from what they were in Primary: God is real, and we are children of God. In a world torn by distress and alienation, Jesus Christ offers salvation and reconciliation. In Christ we can seek redemption not only from our individual sins, but also for collective sins that pollute the face of the earth. One consequence of our new reality as a global faith is that all the sins of the world are contained within the walls and stakes of Zion.* This is a tremendous burden but also an opportunity to do something really consequential. In the company of others, we learn to acknowledge our wrongs, to grieve and sorrow, to be accountable, to humbly seek atonement. Knowing and serving each other, we may come to know and serve Christ.

This book is a collection of writings that capture the particularities of a single Latter-day Saint life—at work and at play, as a student and as a teacher, as a child and as a parent, in health and in sickness. Some have been published previously, though most have not. These writings include letters, essays, lectures, and memoir. Interspersed between sections are several of the newsletters I wrote and illustrated at the end of each year, telling stories about the whole family, including my husband Joseph and (eventually) our four kids Bean, Sprout, Leaf, and Shoot. At the very end is a series of emails sent to family and friends in the midst of colon cancer treatments. My health challenges have certainly led to reflections on the purpose of life, the joy of human love, and the nearness of God. To connect the dots, I have included introductions at the beginning of every section and at the beginning of some individual pieces.

---

* Zion is a term with deep significance in Latter-day Saint scripture and discourse. It can be used, variously, to mean the Church, the city or place where God's people dwell, the kingdom of God on earth, the living community of faith, and "the pure in heart." The Latter-day Saint passage of scripture that always comes to my mind is Moses 7:18: "And the Lord called his people Zion, because they were of one heart and one mind, and dwelt in righteousness; and there were no poor among them."

I hope that this collection of "crossings"—writings that bridge gaps of space, culture, and generations—will illuminate the sacred space in which we connect with our fellow beings, even in seemingly mundane and non-religious contexts. I hope that these crossings will convey the meaning and power of a life among the Latter-day Saints. To me, the densely peopled quality of such a life is both what makes it problematic and also what makes it real and true.

It is through relationships with others, particularly those we behold on the other side of a large divide, that Jesus Christ calls on us to demonstrate faith in the first and second great commandments.* As we work to cross these divides, we will come closer to fulfilling the promise of Zion: one heart and one mind, no poor among us.

---

* "Master, which is the great commandment in the law? Jesus said unto him, Thou shalt love the Lord thy God with all thy heart, and with all thy soul, and with all thy mind. This is the first and great commandment. And the second is like unto it, Thou shalt love thy neighbour as thyself. On these two commandments hang all the law and the prophets" (Matthew 22:36–40).

PART ONE

going places

The Great Wall of China

The three essays in this section document consequential journeys made in earlier phases of my life. The first essay recalls my earliest experiences in the People's Republic of China as an exchange student. The second essay is a snapshot from the year and a half I spent in Taiwan as a missionary. The third essay recounts a process of working through faith and doubt from the time I was in high school to when I was finishing graduate school. All three of these stories are about encountering something new or unsettling and developing familiarity.

I first began studying Chinese in my second year at Harvard College. In my first Chinese class I didn't learn as much as I should have because I was often asleep. I was running on the cross-country team—training mornings, afternoons, and on Saturdays—and it made me tired. I was a better student when I studied Chinese at Tsinghua University in Beijing in 1999. I had a better motivation for learning—namely, learning all about Chinese street food. I still ran. I did 400-meter repeats on a red clay track outside the foreign student dormitories and went on long meandering runs around the Old Summer Palace. Sometimes I stopped to watch old men playing Chinese-style chess, slapping round wooden pieces onto the board between bites of watermelon (and spits of watermelon seeds).

On some hot summer evenings, when my friends and I explored the city, we sometimes stopped at a watermelon-seller's truck to buy a whole watermelon. In the light of electric bulbs clamped to the high sides of the truck, moths drifted back and forth. The vendor pulled a melon from the bed of the truck and brought it over to a small table surrounded by plastic stools. With a few zigzagging cuts from a long knife, the watermelon separated into two jagged halves. Each of us broke off a chunk. We sat around the table, taking huge bites, cool juice dribbling onto our fingers. In July or August, a whole watermelon could disappear in five minutes.

Between my third and fourth years of university study, I took two years off to serve a mission in Taiwan. I met my husband Joseph as a missionary (I always hasten to say that in Taiwan, we never served in the same area). I learned many things, but the most important thing I learned is that love is the power that allows you to be useful to others. I also ate a lot of scallion pancakes and drank a lot of papaya milk. In the city of Tainan, my companions and I regularly frequented a shaved ice shop known as the "Canaan Fruit Store," which served large platters of snow-shaved ice covered with chopped mango and rivulets of sweetened condensed milk.

One of the reasons I married Joseph was because his Chinese was so good. I know that sounds like a funny reason to be attracted to someone, but in the Kaohsiung Mission culture, good Chinese makes you a rock star. We interpreted for a mission conference together once—I interpreted the first half and Joseph the second half. He started learning Chinese as a teenager and has a great listening ear, so his Chinese has always been much better than mine. (Very attractive!) His Mandarin abilities also helped him win the approval of my Chinese American grandparents.

China, the land of my mother's ancestors, was not familiar to me when I first encountered it as a university student. But now it feels like home—now, one of many homes. I have been to my mother's family's village near Kaiping, in Guangdong Province, and gazed at the rows of names and statues in the Ju (Zhou 周) ancestral temple going back to the Song dynasty (960–1279). On one visit, my children and I walked through the narrow paths between the village houses and came to my great-great-grandfather's two-story family house, now abandoned. My great-uncle unlocked the door. The ancestral altar was still in a place of honor. On the side of a rough wooden cabinet in an upstairs room, someone had scrawled Cultural Revolution–era slogans.

When we were living in Hong Kong, on Tomb-Sweeping Day in the spring of 2013 and 2014, Joseph, the kids, and I traveled to a large graveyard in Hong Kong's New Territories, to the grave of Zhou Zaili (周在禮), my great-great-grandfather whose Kaiping house we had previously visited. We cleaned the tombstone, set down oranges and burned incense, and ate a picnic lunch. As a courtesy, we also burned incense before the tombstones of Zhou Zaili's immediate neighbors, who had no visitors that year. Perhaps their descendants, like the descendants of Zhou Zaili (including his son, my great-grandfather) had crossed the sea to find work and had never returned home.

Now I feel at home in many places: Orange County, California; Cambridge and Boston, Massachusetts; Provo and Spanish Fork, Utah; West Los Angeles, California, especially at the gymnastic ring apparatus at Santa Monica Beach; Taiwan; Beijing, Shanghai, and Xiamen, China; Hong Kong; and Auckland, New Zealand. I also feel a close connection to my grandparents' farm and old home in Gunnison, Utah, where my aunt and uncle still live. Every summer the extended family returns to Gunnison for the Fourth of July holiday. My children think the

At ancestral grave in Hong Kong

Fourth of July in Gunnison is heaven on earth, with the hot, dry sun, saltwater taffy scattered from floats, carnival games in the park, and the cool concrete of Auntie Jeannie's back patio.

Wherever home is, it's always nice to be back.

LONG DEPARTURES, LONG RETURNS

1999
Beijing, China

When I was nineteen, my parents let me go to China without much of a fuss. They'd long gotten used to the feeling of their oldest child's leaving the nest for one reason or another. When I lived at home, the call of the world outside drew me irresistibly. I would sit at our living room computer and pour my soul into correspondences, go on long runs from the house to the ocean and gaze hard across the inviting Pacific. Part of it had to do with the usual adolescent struggle for freedom and independence—the ability to come and go when I pleased, to move in my own spaces. And part of it had to do with the fact that I could never be truly free or truly independent—nor do I ever want to. I am bound to my family with ties of great strength. Wherever I go, I will always feel them pulling me back. Thus, I send myself to far-off places always with a feeling of security, knowing that the journey away from home is just a long return.

When I first went to China, I was a stranger—or worse. In some ways I felt like a spy. My mother was Chinese American, my father Japanese American. As long as I didn't open my mouth, I looked like any Chinese girl. In Beijing, a fairly international city, other Euro-American-looking foreigners could be easily spotted. But little did the Chinese know that the girl rolling by on the black bike with squeaky pedals was also a foreigner in disguise who had not grown up with the same set of allegiances and claims, who did not speak their language fluently. I had come to China not because I felt some deep cultural affinity for the place, but more out of a sense of curiosity: Who were these people who looked as if they shared my world, but whose context was so different from mine? I felt this way not only with regard to the Chinese population, but also with regard to my own great-grandfather: ninety-nine years old at the time, an immigrant from Kaiping, living in a tiny apartment in Los Angeles, and almost as much a stranger to me as anyone halfway across the world in China.

All that I know of my family story on my Chinese side begins three generations ago, when my great-grandfather Gin Gor Ju arrived in America in 1919. Like me on my first trip across the Pacific, he was nineteen years old. He originally came as a sojourner, sending a good part of his wages home to his family in Canton and intending to return someday, but after a number of years he found he liked America and decided to stay. Born in the early twentieth century, he lived to be 103. The earth was how he supported himself and his family, farming celery, crookneck squash, and Napa cabbage. Throughout his life people had known him as a strong, shrewd, and independent man. While World War II was raging across the Pacific and the Japanese were occupying China, Gin Gor Ju built and tested several small model submarines on his farm in the hope of helping to liberate his homeland. But I only knew my great-grandfather as the silent old man in a navy blue cap and blue sweater who slept—first in an armchair, and later in a wheelchair—during crowded family gatherings in his tiny apartment in Chinatown.

My great-grandmother Gor Shee Ju always sat next to him, sleeping less, but not saying much more. She, too, had lived life with great determination and ingenuity. She worked long hours in the fields. She sewed yards and yards of sheeting on her treadle machine to cover the hot house seedbeds. At Christmastime she cooked a turkey and filled the children's stockings with nuts and an orange. For special occasions, like my grandmother's wedding, she prepared hoi tom soup, featuring sea cucumbers. She taught her children to work hard and work together. Her business acumen was the stuff of family legends. Yet I can't recall ever hearing my great-grandparents respond directly to my greeting beyond a nod and a wave of the hand. When they

With Susan Lew Inouye, Marjorie Ju Lew, and Gor Shee Ju at Gin Gor Ju's eightieth birthday party, 9 June 1980

spoke to me in long sentences, perhaps I was too young to remember, and when I grew old enough to want to know them better, they had aged beyond my reach. Now there are only stories, and the lives and personalities of their children, to tell me who they were and how they went about their lives.

A couple of months before my twentieth birthday, I arrived in Beijing and began an intermediate Mandarin summer program at Tsinghua University. On the first day of classes, we were given a list of Chinese dishes in English and Mandarin and encouraged to work on our food-ordering repertoire: egg-and-scallion pancakes, steamed buns with red bean filling, ma po tofu, chicken and cashews, ants-climbing-the-tree noodles, knife-sliced noodles, hand-pulled noodles, noodles with fried sauce, noodles with bean sauce, thin noodles, rice noodles, spinach with garlic, lightly caramelized morsels of apple and banana . . . No assignment could have given me more pleasure.

My greatest discovery was the world of Chinese popsicles. The Chinese had found a way to turn every sort of carbohydrate imaginable into a popsicle—from grapes to corn to watermelon to sweet rice. White freezers like treasure chests protected them from city dust and heat and opened to reveal a mouth-watering array. My favorites were the red-bean-and-milk popsicles, cold sweet creaminess that melted in the mouth on a hot day. I ate a popsicle with every lunch and dinner, budgeting them carefully into my daily living allowance. Most popsicles cost two kuai, or about a quarter. Then there were expensive popsicles made by foreign companies like Nestlé, the kinds of popsicles that were advertised on TV. The Nestlé Magnum was an overdesigned chocolate-and-vanilla monstrosity that cost three kuai—one normal popsicle plus half of a second, and the Magnum didn't even taste that good. I could buy three red-bean pops for the price of two Magnums.

I began to calculate all expenditures in terms of popsicles. A subway ticket was one popsicle. A basic battery-operated tape player was eighteen popsicles, or around four and a half dollars. A Big Mac combination meal at McDonald's was about twenty-one popsicles, or around five dollars. For a little over twice that price, four people could enjoy a feast at a Chinese hotpot restaurant—forty-four popsicles, or about eleven dollars. I began to think with horror on the prices I'd paid for food in the United States—a bagel sandwich, for example, was five dollars or more! Why, that was nearly twenty popsicles!

I felt some guilt for estimating values with such a frivolous measure. The beggars on the street displayed their twisted limbs like expressionist statues and held out their cups for a pittance of coins and small bills. What amounted to their daily living was my fund for frozen treats. As I ate at cheap roadside stands, dressed in generic lightweight clothing purchased at Chinese markets, and rode my squeaking black bike amidst the crowds of countless others who looked so much like me, I couldn't help but feel like a bit of a traitor. My scrimping and saving was all a game, but to so many others it was the real thing, a desperate struggle to stay afloat in a tumultuous society where money provided the only promise of security. The amount of money I was used to spending on a CD in America would feed a poor family in China for a week. My physical similarity to the Chinese made my foreignness seem even more acute. How far away I sometimes felt from these people—these workers and beggars with the faces of my aunts and uncles, grandparents and great-grandparents.

One day I decided to make a trip to Tiananmen Square. I had been to the square before, but this time I was trying out a new mode of transportation: a large air-conditioned bus. It was a sweltering hot day in the city of dust. I was grateful for the respite from the sweaty intimacy of the Three-Seven-Five, the minibus to the subway station that was my usual transport into the city. Someone at the school had recommended this bus because it was air-conditioned, went straight downtown, and had a stop at the southern edge of Tiananmen.

Fare for the Three-Seven-Five minibus was two kuai, or one red-bean popsicle. It was a crowded ride. Plastic stools in the aisles accommodated as many people as possible. Riders touched fellow riders on every side, all silent and sweating in the stuffy heat. This air-conditioned whale-on-wheels that now carried me into the city cost three kuai, or the price of a Nestlé Magnum. Reclining against the padded plush of the seat in the shiny monster, I reflected: What would Chairman Mao say about me right now? He'd probably call me a bourgeois capitalist. Watching the flow of people in the bike lane next to the bus, I wondered idiotically for the hundredth time that there could be so many of them. The bus merged and turned its way through the city arteries as it made its way toward Tiananmen, the heart of Beijing.

Tiananmen Square had caught my imagination ever since I was in fourth grade, when I saw the pictures of the tanks and protesters on the news. Later I watched documentaries on the events of 1989 in university film classes. The images were astonishing. Clearly, those many people had gathered into that one place for countless different reasons. Did they want an entirely new political system, or did they just want a life with more possibilities for things to buy and places to go? Could their lives really be so different from mine?

Fellow foreigners who had lived in Beijing for years had told me of the darker sides of the city: glimpses of policemen beating beggars in the alleys, reports of people who disappeared without warning, or the black market that trafficked women and children. As I'd prepared to go to China, my parents had pleaded with me to be careful, knowing I wouldn't take all the prescribed precautions but hoping I would be more conscientious than usual. My parents did not only see China as the motherland, or as a bargain shopper's paradise, but also as a place of violence and enigma. They had seen the footage of the massacre at Tiananmen, and knew the square in no other context. "China is very far away," my father told me as I packed my bags the night before my departure. "There'll be nothing we can do to help you. Don't do anything stupid."

Since coming to Beijing, I had spent many hours at Tiananmen. The sky above the square was always occupied by high-flying kites: silken eagles, butterflies, dragonflies, and carp straining against their cotton-string tethers. The string was so thin and the kites so high, I marveled at the unrelenting connection between the person on the ground and the object in the sky. The tension in the line was what powered the flight. If the string were cut, or the reel dropped, the wind would catch the kite broadside and send it cartwheeling wildly down. The kites wheeled so far overhead, one could barely make out their shapes. The pull on the reel, the tautness of the line—this was what it meant to know that the soaring silhouette above was yours, was in your hands.

Only when I went to China did I begin to understand the thrill and terror my parents must have felt, letting their daughter out like a kite—watching the thin string spin itself out until there was nothing left but the simple knot around the reel, holding it in their hands and feeling the tug of currents high above. Living on my own in a foreign country, I finally began to realize that my parents' loving me and praying for my safety weren't enough. Although I'd never been particularly rebellious, I had a habit of ignoring parental warnings. But in China, I found myself frequently choosing a path of greater caution over a path of greater adventure, out of deference.

I began to understand the enormity of a parent's leap of faith: to send your own child somewhere far away to do some growing up, all the while praying that they will return to you still safe, still innocent, and still your own. Year by year, my interests drew me further and further from where my parents were. Yet I always knew they loved me. This was the reason I belonged to them, and why I always tried to make sure I came back.

The bus continued to stop, start, and belch oily black exhaust as it rumbled through the city toward Tiananmen. The current of people and vehicles flowing around the bus was ceaseless. Suddenly I imagined all the lives being lived around me: on my right and on my left, to the front and to the rear, here in China and off in America, begun many years before me, and continuing long after. *How small I am*, I thought all of a sudden. *How young and small and far away.*[1]

I thought of my great-grandfather, nineteen years old, alone among strangers on a ship bound for a new world, feeling the power of the waves that surged and split beneath the steel prow. I wondered how he felt as each day's sailing brought him closer to the other side of the Pacific and made him more and more a foreigner, one whose face would stand out and whose speech would not make sense. Did he dream of wealth, or land, or just an opportunity to do something consequential for his family? Did he intend to find a place for himself in the new society, or did he see himself as a lifelong sojourner, an immigrant stepping-stone? Could he have imagined the extent of his family's immersion in the foreign culture, his descendants' spliced and patched identities, their material and social comfort in American society?

Outside the bus, the city smog was saturated with late afternoon sunlight. A yellow glare lit the scene outside the window. I pressed my forehead against the plexiglass to watch tiny red cabs stealing in and out of the bicycle lane, old men slowly pedaling three-wheeled carts with loads of yellow peaches, slender young women riding home from the market. Vehicles in a hurry screeched, honked, and swerved around slower traffic.

My gaze fell upon a man of medium height, not young and not old, pedaling his bicycle through the chaotic lane. On the crossbar rode his infant daughter, her head of black hair still soft and wispy. His slender body bent around hers, sheltering her beneath his chest and fencing her inside his arms. She was so small and fragile, yet her expression was almost serene. He looked quiet and careful, his chin slightly lowered over the top of his daughter's head, his eyes focused steadily forward. Then the bus turned a corner, and they were gone.

As if a shutter to my soul had opened and shut, the image of the two of them moving through the noisy traffic burned into my consciousness. I was stunned by the simplicity and ancientness of the scene. How could there be so many people? And each of us somebody's son or daughter?

The bus lumbered through the city streets. The nimble minibuses pounced for passengers at the side of the road. The tide of bicycles surged and flowed through the grimy streets, carrying people away from the day's work and back to those who waited for them to return. The light was strong and hazy in the dusty afternoon, and on the other side of the world, where it was night, my family slept in beds in rooms in the house that is my home.

MORNINGS AND NIGHTS

Tainan, Taiwan/Costa Mesa, California

First published in *Irreantum* 12, no. 1, 2010

Dawn broke with a vengeance over the city of Tainan. The Taiwanese summer made us early wakers. The sun flared over the horizon around 5:00 a.m., and soon the city was a full-blown sauna. When it got that hot, there was no solace in sleep. I said my prayers, then unzipped my mosquito tent and spilled out sideways into the room. My roommate, Sister Alton, rose from her bed. We exchanged glances in silent greeting. Another morning.

Before my mission, as a university student in Boston, I had been a lover of solitude. My favorite was the peopled kind: sitting invisibly at the window of a café as throngs of strangers streamed past. My mission, however, had begun the moment I opened the door to my dorm room at the Missionary Training Center (MTC) and found myself facing my first companion, Sarah Faulkner, a distracted-looking girl with short brown hair and green eye makeup.* Her eyes snapped up to meet mine, both of us

---

* Missionaries of The Church of Jesus Christ of Latter-day Saints work in "companionships," usually consisting of two (but sometimes three) missionaries.

asking silent questions: *Will you break down into hysterics? Are you a zealot? Will you be a slacker? Will you exercise with me in the mornings? Will it be a pleasant thing to be with you twenty-four hours a day or will it be hard?*

"Hi," I said, extending my hand. "Are you Sister Faulkner? I'm Sister Inouye. We must be companions."

The MTC: a huge complex dedicated to the intake of nineteen year-old boys and twenty-one year-old women from all backgrounds and to the output of missionaries who would say the same sentences with the same pauses while wearing the same clothes, each day brushing their teeth in the same half hour of the morning and switching off the light at the same half hour at night. Together Sister Faulkner and I poked fun at the Orwellian aspects of the MTC, and together we knelt on the floor at night to pray, wrestling with the desires of our hearts.

We shared much in common. As university students, we had learned to relentlessly apply critical reasoning to every argument. When we scrutinized the tenets of our faith under this lens, they seemed absurd: a man named Jesus was God's son who came back from the dead; a man named Joseph Smith was a prophet who saw God and Jesus; every individual has the potential to attain God's perfections and powers; God hears and answers prayers. There was no way to prove these claims through experimentation or argumentation. Our faith also contained internal tensions, such as the teachings that each individual should rely on direct personal revelation from God but that members should also obey the directives of church leaders. And yet in our experience, our religion inspired us to be better people and had been the source of much happiness. Both of us were still searching for a way in which the world of objective rationality could exist separately from the world of subjective faith, a way in which one could lay claim to both of them and not be torn asunder.

"You know what I think?" asked Sister Faulkner one day between classes.

"Sister Faulkner," I responded, grinning, "this is the MTC. We don't think."

She smiled. Then her eyes grew earnest again. "I think I came on a mission ready to make some sort of sacrifice, but I don't know exactly what it should be or how to make it."

"Hm. Do you mean the intellectual sacrifice of not making snotty comments when someone says something stupid, or the psychological sacrifice of following all the hyper rules, or the emotional sacrifice of being away from your family, or what?"

Sister Faulkner paused for a moment.

Then she said, "All of them, but especially something about faith. All the people I know who possess true spiritual maturity have very simple faith. I can't figure out how to have simple faith without it seeming mindless."

"I suppose there aren't many shortcuts to spirituality. Lopping off lobes of your brain is a bad way to get simple faith. Maybe it's all a process of time, and doing things."

It was 5:37 a.m. as Sister Alton and I stood just inside the front door of our missionary apartment, about to pray as we did every time we left home. The official day began at 6:30 in the morning and ended at 10:30 at night, with eight hours allotted for sleep in between. Both Sister Ding, my companion, and Sister McCoy, Sister Alton's companion, preferred sleep to exercise. So every morning Sister Alton and I woke up early and went out together to run.

Sister Alton had played softball in high school. She was tall, big-boned, and strong, with blue eyes that blazed against her tan skin, and blond-brown hair pulled back in a ponytail. At university she'd majored in something that wasn't math and wasn't English and wasn't science. Maybe I just remembered the subjects she didn't study (the nerdy, academic ones) as opposed to her actual major because I sensed that she didn't associate with nerds and academics and was thus unlikely to have a natural association with me.

Sister Alton looked at my T-shirt, the armpits stained with dark brown circles from months of use with only a weekly washing in cold water and cheap detergent.

"That's disgusting," she said. Then she bowed her head and folded her arms to say our customary going-out-the-door prayer.

"Father in Heaven," said Sister Alton in Chinese, "We're going to go outside and exercise. Please bless our bodies so that through this exercise we'll be strengthened in our work. Please help us to become better missionaries. We ask these things in the name of Jesus Christ, Amen."

"Amen," I said. I clanked the door handle open, and we stepped out into the thick heat of the morning. We trotted down the stairs, hit the blacktop, and were off.

My calves seemed to emit little squeals of pleasure. The settled feeling in them started to pump itself out. My quads stretched and yawned. They snapped into every stride, feeling the shock that ran through my legs from the blacktop. My back straightened and my shoulders tensed slightly to gauge the swing of my arms. *This is what we do best!* chirped every muscle in my body. *This is the fun stuff! Much better than riding a bicycle in traffic and sitting on chairs while you talk about God. Couldn't we go a bit faster? Couldn't we go out for a little joyride?*

But missionaries must always stay close to their companions. I jogged slowly at Sister Alton's shoulder. This morning, like every morning, Sister Alton and I headed for the road that led away from our apartment and ran along the Tainan Canal. We ran at an easy pace, lost in the miscellaneous thoughts that were the luxury of early mornings. Early morning time was time in which we could act more like young twenty-something-year-olds and less like religious ministers. It was a time in which we could spend some thought on the inward self, without feeling guilty for not "contacting" everyone around us.

Leaving the MTC and heading for Taiwan meant entering a new routine of "contacting" and "teaching": knocking on doors or talking to people on the street, meeting with investigators at the chapel or in their homes. We wore collared shirts and long skirts that were occasionally mangled by the bike chain as we rode from one appointment to another.

Going door to door, or "tracting," was always a bit of an adventure because you never knew what kind of person would open the door.

"What!" yelled the Taiwanese amah* when she heard Sister Ding's knock one night. She opened the red iron door a few inches, glaring through the crack with narrowed eyes. Anger hardened the wrinkles in her face.

"Who are you?"

"Hello, Grandmother," said Sister Ding, addressing her respectfully. "We're missionaries, and tonight we're sharing a message about the purpose of life."

BAM! The amah slammed the door. A heavy bolt thunked across.

Sister Ding looked at me.

I shrugged.

We moved to the next door. Inside we could hear the TV—some Qing dynasty-themed soap opera. I rapped lightly on the red iron with the cap of my water bottle. It saved the knuckles on a long night of door knocking. A middle-aged man opened the door.

"Hello," I said. "My name is Sister Inouye, and this is Sister Ding. We're missionaries from The Church of Jesus Christ of Latter-day Saints. Have you ever heard of it?"

"Oh, I know," laughed the man, "those tall Americans on bikes in twos. The Mormons, right?"

"We're sharing a message about the importance of families and how families can be together forever." I handed him a tract.

I looked over his shoulder at his wife, who was shaking her hand at us in irritation. "No time," she called. "We're busy."

"No time right now," said the man. "Come back some other day and speak English to the kids, why don't you?"

The door closed. The bolt thunked.

We moved to the next door.

---

* "Grandmother" or "old woman."

5:39 a.m. We reached the canal and turned north. At noon the water was drab and brown, but the morning sunlight made it almost lively. For an instant, my thoughts were transported to other rivers I'd run alongside in other mornings, in other places and as another self.

The paths along the Charles River are narrow but smooth, worn down by the feet of countless runners—in the spring, the feet of distance runners training for the Boston Marathon. In the fall is the Head of the Charles Regatta, and all the college crew teams in New England come to race. The crews skim across the surface of the water, the boat leaping ahead from stroke to stroke, the angles of dipping blades and stretching backs all in perfect alignment. As one they slide forward, arms and backs stretching out, and then shove with their legs and slide back, the motion smooth but explosive. Their limbs and lungs are powered by strength borne of solidarity, their individual pain arrested and transformed by the laces at their feet. Tied into the boat, tied into each other, conforming to the stroke count shouted out by the coxswain, there is nothing to do when everybody else is rowing but row. Like a live thing the boat leaps across the water, drawing swiftly away into the distance.

People in America and Taiwan alike often asked why I had decided to take time off from university studies to spend eighteen months in a foreign country at my own expense, riding a bike in a dress, working sixteen-hour days, for a church whose hierarchy and patriarchy seemed to them to be at odds with the values of a smart, educated woman. The answer was simple: I believed that the simple things I taught were true, that they had enriched my life, and that the world would be a better place for their sharing.

"How do you feel about God?" I began almost every presentation. "Do you believe that God or gods exist? And what characteristics does God have?"

That question elicited a different reply every time: "God is a spirit." "God is a power." "God doesn't exist, but people use God as a heart-crutch." "If God exists, why do all these bad things happen?" "Your Western god is different from our Eastern gods, but they're all the same thing." "I can't believe in something I can't see." "I saw God the other day; it was really amazing!"

We would discuss broad concepts like the nature of deity, trying to establish some common ground. I would assert that most people believed in the existence of some Supreme Being, though they might call this being by different names. I would tell the investigator that we were God's children, created in God's own image, that God was not some impersonal spirit but a Father and Mother in Heaven who give us parents' love.

The words used in the discussions were simple. At the right time in a person's life, they had great power. They were most powerful when it was not the missionary who spoke them. Missionaries talked about "the Spirit," meaning the spirit of God, and prayed that God would send this spirit to descend upon the discussion and change its tenor. Investigators, members, and missionaries alike described it as a feeling of calm and clarity that, when present, spoke to the heart and confirmed the truth of what was being said. It was the element of the extraordinary that we didn't possess ourselves, but for which we hoped to qualify.

How was one to invite the Spirit? As missionaries our standards of personal conduct ranged from the loftiest to the most quotidian: one, keep God's commandments, and two, obey the mission rules. What were God's commandments? Love God; love your fellow beings. What were the mission rules? Don't watch television or read newspapers. Get up at 6:30 and go to bed at 10:30. Stay close to your companion. No physical contact with members of the opposite sex. Read six pages of the Missionary Handbook each day. "God's commandments" were obvious to the naked eye, as it were. "Mission rules" set out to capture truth under a microscope, in a petri dish.

At first I had scoffed at those who seemed fixated on executing the mission rules, no matter how minute. Would going to bed at 10:34 instead of 10:30 really detract from my spirituality? Obedience to God's greatest commandments ought to be the only standard that mattered, not conformity to a rule book. But with time I came to realize that both were ways to be good. They both required a certain sacrifice. The former, like "loving others as oneself," required the adjustment of one's priorities in being less self-centered. Still, it was fairly abstract. It was also a long-term project. The latter, like "staying close to one's companion," required the immediate sacrifice of constant attention to everyday details. This was the line to be toed in missionary life—willingness to sacrifice not only big things like school, time, and money, but also small things, like running fast, resting for a few more minutes, and enjoying solitude. In my desire to be obedient to even the little things, God would gauge my desire to be God's instrument, not my own. With time I also learned that God required different sacrifices of each person because only then could these sacrifices be made in the right spirit.

It was 5:42 a.m. as we bounded along the placid canal. The water of the canal had a cooling effect on the air around it, but it also bred mosquitoes and fermented garbage.

Sister Alton wrinkled her nose. "That is just *rank*," she said. "They say that even when you get back home, your clothes still smell like Taiwan."

At the end of the canal road was a rice distributor's shed, a great high tin structure with a wide-mouthed entrance that opened onto the street. One-hundred-pound bags of white long-grain rice were stacked several layers high against the corrugated walls. Here Sister Alton and I began to step with care. This was the part of the road splattered with rats.

In the summer, the shed attracted droves of rats. They would gnaw holes in the rice bags and eat to their heart's content. Unfortunately for the rats, this road running between the canal and the distributor's shed was heavily trafficked. Perhaps, too, after their nightly gorging they were less nimble. Almost every morning there would be a new dead rat. As the day's traffic increased, the rat would expand and flatten. By the end of the day it would have grown cardboard-thin, though the body, paws, and tail still retained their basic shapes. Even long coils of intestine would be flattened into perfect wiggly silhouettes. Finally, after a few days the dried-out rat would start to peel up off the hot blacktop. After that, someone would usually scrape it off the street and throw it away.

"You would think that they would learn," I said, as we bounded over a well-flattened rodent. "Why don't they post a crossing guard or something."

"This place is disgusting," said Sister Alton.

"Well," I said, "there are rats in America too."

She laughed, shortly. We said nothing for a while, legs and feet falling in a steady trot.

It is easier to be scornful of a place if the place is scornful of you. How often had I been tempted to find solace in disgust when a person or group of people mocked a set of truths that I had found precious. How desperately had I fought to make my love for others independent of the way they treated me. It was never easy.

At 5:51 a.m. Sister Alton and I arrived at the City Government complex and started laps around the grassy plaza. Many others were also out. China is always at its best in the morning, alive and bustling. Middle-aged women in sweats walked rapidly, slapping their palms against their hips and thighs. Silvery-haired men twirling long red-tasseled swords whirled in slow and intricate patterns.

The real action, however, was taking place in the breakfast shops across the street. Steam billowed from bamboo steamers containing mantou and baozi (steamed breads). Sweating pots of freshly cooked dou jiang (soymilk) dominated the stainless steel counters. At tables, customers dunked fat soup-filled pork dumplings called "little steamer buns" in chili sauce before popping the entire package into their mouths, where it burst and scalded the mouth with delicious ginger-and-scallion broth.

Mornings in Taiwan were an unapologetic mix of fragrant and fetid. The scent of frying oil and brown-bottomed dumplings on cast-iron griddles competed with the stench of open sewers and the brackish odor of betelnut spit drying out on the street. Chewing betelnut (the leaf of the areca palm) was largely a male habit. The juice stained the teeth brownish-red. Betelnut was sold by girls dressed in bikinis who sat in glass booths and rolled the leaves while they waited for customers. At nightfall, the booths lit up with revolving neon lights, the glass encasement illuminated like a fish tank in the darkness. The girls' thickly painted mouths pouted and their mascara-crusted lashes hung over their eyes as they sat in the booths, vulnerable to the outside gaze but defiant in their surly sexuality. Men pulled up in cars to buy bags of ten or a hundred, their mouths red as if with blood, the road outside dyed with splatter after crimson splatter.

I loved the mornings because they were so lively, decent, and leisurely. But in the morning air there were also reminders of the stifling heat of the coming day, the smell and stains of last night's garbage, and the demanding schedule just a few minutes into the future.

After three laps around the plaza, it was 6:12 a.m. I began to do the warm-up exercises from high school track workouts: skipping, bounding sideways, high knees. I fell slightly behind Sister Alton but caught up periodically in bursts of speed. My body began to feel purged, all of the stickiness sweated away and all of the restlessness run out.

"What time is it," said Sister Alton.

"6:14," I said. "Better head back."

We trotted off the field, across the sidewalk, and back onto a street that led back to the long homestretch along the canal. I put my legs on automatic pilot and began to arrange my thoughts in orderly piles. I took the morning's nonmissionary thoughts such as premission memories and sensory absorption in sights and smells and shoved them off to the side in a heap that would be stuffed into a mental drawer as soon as we walked through the door at 6:30.

My feet fell in steady thumps that paced the ever-tightening rhythm of my thoughts. I began to sort through the business of the day in my head—which investigators needed to be contacted, who was going to meet with us today, and the places where we had to be—and plan our routes through Tainan's crowded streets. We had two appointments in the Southern District of the city at 9:00 and 10:30. We'd take lunch down there and go contacting in the Central District for two hours. Appointment at the chapel at 4:00, dinner at 5:00, then back down south for some more visits. These many details were connected to a single purpose, which made everything almost simple.

University study had taught me that important things were not simple but complicated. They needed to be analyzed, figured out. I began my mission trying to explicate Truth, trying to weave Daoist philosophy into discussions, trying to prove an intellectual ideal of righteousness through argumentation. It didn't work. I convinced no one this way, least of all myself. I learned, later on, that the most beautiful and sophisticated presentation of an idea was found in its simplest form. I could only speak the things I myself believed to be true and rely on the Spirit to make them true to others.

It was 6:23 a.m. as we swung back onto the canal road, retracing our route back toward the apartment. The sun was higher and hotter. The sweat on my cheekbones started to sting. The cars on the road were more numerous, sweeping around us in arcs of exhaust and noise. Curtains of pollution draped the fragrant smells of steaming buns and frying dumplings in an acrid overlay.

What an odd combination of good and bad smells: not entirely pleasant, and not entirely revolting; not always comfortable, but memorable in an unapologetic way. Taiwan as a cultural entity was all one pungent whole. Breakfast oil and ratty rice. Steaming soymilk and dried betelnut spit. Old women who smiled at us in the morning and old women who slammed doors in our faces in the evening.

My own faith could be this way, too. Joseph Smith, the prophet called by God to enact a divine work, was the same person as Joseph Smith, the flawed and fallible human being. Radical and empowering Latter-day Saint doctrines on the divine potential of women and the existence of a Mother in Heaven coexisted with a conservative and patriarchal organizational structure. True obedience—not the mindless, Orwellian kind, but the self-conscious and deliberate kind—brought freedom from many harms, and true sacrifice brought great power. In the face of human reality itself characterized by contradictions, the Latter-day Saint tradition was not undone by contradictions, but reinforced by them. The tensions within itself were what made it vital, real, and—for me—worthwhile.

The thought passed through my head like a whiff of something familiar. I registered it, filed it away in the drawer of extraneous things, and continued to wonder why an investigator named Guo Ling-jun continued to meet with us and come to church, since she always seemed so bored. Did she just want to argue with us? Was she lonely? What did she hope for?

Suddenly, a freshly exploded mouse appeared in my path. I barely missed it. Recoiling, I leapt into the air.

"Ylehck!" I shrieked, looking over my shoulder at the mouse, a plump dumpling with hair and a tail. I fled with long steps, still looking backwards. I was thus completely off guard when I encountered a second exploded rodent—a great fat rat just before me.

"YAAAGH!" I yelled again, hurdling over the rat and running several paces ahead. "Ew! SICK! Lllegh!" I jumped several times into the air to distance myself from the road. Each time my shoes hit the pavement, I imagined the feeling of a juicy rat oozing beneath my soles.

Sister Alton jogged, lost in her own thoughts.

We reached the apartment and shucked off our shoes. I leaned on the door handle and the sliding bolt retracted with a heavy clank. Our companions were up. Sister Ding was cooking a Taiwanese egg-pancake for breakfast and Sister McCoy was in the shower, singing hymns in her lovely light vibrato.

It was 6:30 a.m., and our working day had officially begun. We went about the morning preparations of planning, study, and prayer. At 9:30 a.m. we would walk out the door. On the way to each appointment we would speak with as many people as the time would afford. During the course of the day we would teach some people to pray, invite some to be baptized, and ask others to change their lives in specific ways, such as giving up alcohol or fasting once a month. We would pray constantly as we rode our bikes along the street, asking to be guided to those who were searching for the teachings we had to share. We would not return to rest until 9:30 p.m., when, exhausted, we'd clank through the door and sling our shoulder bags to the floor. Together we'd plan the next day's activities and kneel on the tiled floor to pray. Then each would rise and attend to the individual rituals of getting ready for bed.

Around 10:20 every night, the humid skies around Taiwan began to hum as missionaries all over the island knelt beside their beds and poured out their hearts in silent prayer. Their supplications rushed heavenward through the muggy night, up through the roofs of the apartment buildings and past the smoggy, low-hanging stars. They raced on through the part of the sky that was cool and clear, and high above the earth the eternal One who comprehends all tongues and hears all petitions listened and answered in softness.

At 10:30, the bedroom light flicked out. Darkness descended. We fell almost instantly into grateful sleep, while outside the smells and sounds of night eased across the city, and the rats once more scampered blissfully in the great mountains of long-grain rice.

FAITH IS NOT A STRING
OF CHRISTMAS LIGHTS

23 January 2012

Earlier version published online for Mormon Scholars Testify

Is the Church true? Are its teachings correct?

These are the questions I asked as a teenager. I was fairly diligent and nonrebellious. I worked hard to please my parents, church leaders, high school teachers. I practiced the piano, I memorized scriptures and studied for tests in history and chemistry and calculus. I wasn't just going through the motions to please others, either. I loved learning about the world; I wanted to learn to know God.

And yet at that time, I felt there was tension between the two major tracks of learning in my life (learning how to interpret the world as an educated person and learning how to become a mature member of the Church). For instance, my biology textbook talked about the theory of evolution as the widely accepted view of how human life came to be. But when I questioned my Sunday School teacher on evolution, he gave me a dismissive look and said, "Melissa, do you really think that we came from monkeys?"

Now, this Sunday School teacher was—like all church members at the local level—doing his job as a volunteer. Actually, he was a conscript. A local bishop appointed him to the job. This Sunday School teacher wasn't a scientist, either. So I didn't see him as the final authority on whether the claims of our faith could harmonize with the claims of science.

However, it troubled me that contradictions seemed to exist among "the things I knew" as an educated Latter-day Saint. I was aware that some of my Christian friends had "Mormonism-awareness lessons" at their church youth groups. The derision in my friend Jessica's voice when she said, "We learned about your church on Sunday," was unmistakable. Another friend told my brother that "as a Mormon, you are living a lie."

Therefore, to my high school self, the questions, Is the Church true? Are its teachings correct? were important and also rather terrifying because the validity of so many other things seemed to hinge on these questions. I knew I would have to figure this out, but at the same time I didn't want to. I feared there was a zero-sum contest between my religious truth and "everybody else's truth." What if the Church lost? And then what could I believe, and who would I be?

"There are a lot of stories in the world, but the Mormon story is the one that I want to be true. To the extent that it is not, I will make it true."

For help, I turned to my "crazy Uncle Charles," as he called himself: my dad's little brother, a Stanford-and-Harvard-educated professor of Japanese literature at Tufts University. I told him my doubts about Latter-day Saint claims. In the sort of long, belabored emails that high school students with Big Questions write, I laid them out: What about evolution? What about Blacks and the priesthood? What about polygamy? What about Joseph Smith saying there were five-foot-high Quakers living on the moon?

Uncle Charles replied that long ago, when he was an undergraduate, he, too, had had doubts. He had gone to another Latter-day Saint professor for help. This professor had said, "There are a lot of stories in the world, but Mormonism is the story that I want to be true." Uncle Charles concluded his message to me with the statement, "There are a lot of stories in the world, but the Mormon story is the one I want to be true. To the extent that it is not, I will make it true."

At the time, I read this as a sort of well-meaning self-deception, kind of like the Santa Claus story. Santa Claus doesn't really exist, but for kids who believe in Santa Claus, he does. Wow! He flies around the sky in a sleigh drawn by reindeer! He fits down the chimney and magically leaves presents with tags signed in parents' handwriting! That's great for, say, five-year-olds, but for everyone else (and for those five-year-olds whose parents have let them in on the secret) it's just another tender falsehood. To say something like, "to the extent that it is not, I will make it true" sounded foolish and also a little arrogant. You can't make a religion "true" in the same way that you can pull off the Santa Claus act. There had to be "a right answer" that was definitely and completely right.

At the same time, I wasn't really sure what "right" answers looked like. As a second-year university student, I took a moral reasoning class that pitted the world's great moral philosophers against each other on the question of whether a belief in God was necessary for the formation of moral laws. Everything I read sounded about right to me, even when the readings were set up to directly attack each other. I read A and agreed with A. Then I read B and agreed with B.

Despite this ambivalence, I was ultimately comforted by Uncle Charles's endorsement, incomplete as it seemed at the time. Maybe there were some things about religion that weren't clear to me at the moment, but Uncle Charles was pretty smart. I still knew the key to what I loved most about my wonderful extended family was the common faith we shared in the gospel of Jesus Christ as interpreted within The Church of Jesus Christ of Latter-day Saints. I had felt the Spirit's powerful witness—not all the time, but enough times to make a difference. I decided to stick around and keep an eye out for answers.

I testify that this message is true. Will you follow Jesus Christ and be baptized?

I turned in my mission papers and was called to Taiwan. I had just finished my junior year as an East Asian Studies major with a specialization in Chinese literature and I hit the ground running in terms of language. At the Missionary Training Center (MTC), my teachers assigned me to study

Chinese with Elder McMullin, a missionary with thick, owlish glasses and a generally nerdy demeanor, who had previously been an exchange student in China. For the sake of propriety, our teachers had us move our desks into the hallway. We memorized discussions and waited impatiently for the opportunity to leave the MTC for Taiwan. I must admit that my eagerness to leave arose partially from narcissistic self-assurance: *I already speak and read Chinese! I've studied the Confucian classics as well as the Bible and the Book of Mormon! Taiwan needs me! The Lord needs me! Here I am, send ME!*

I arrived in Taiwan, was assigned a trainer, and found I had much to learn.* In the first place, my knowledge of Chinese religion and philosophy was not a secret conversionary weapon, but actually a hindrance. I would try to talk to people about the Dao (the Way) or about the bodhisattva's ultimate sacrifice and draw connections to the conclusion that the investigator should join my church. However, I soon found that while comparative philosophy was interesting, it didn't ask that anyone change anything about their lives—myself included. My companion and I invited many people to be baptized, and some accepted, but I didn't feel a sense of certainty about the presence of the Holy Spirit in my work. I worked hard, studied hard, prayed hard. But in many ways, despite my "successes" in terms of logging hours and baptizing converts, during the first part of my mission I was actually missing the point.

Create in me a clean heart, O Lord; and renew a right spirit within me (Psalm 51:10).

After a while, my many failures and shortcomings as a missionary and as a person became more apparent to me. I'm not quite sure how this happened or how long it took, but I do recall one event from this period of self-reflection. It was the day I picked up a new companion from the train station in Tainan. She was a "green" missionary who had only been out for six weeks. On the bike ride home from the train station—hauling suitcases strapped to our back racks with bike inner tubes as motorcycles and giant

---

* A "trainer" is a veteran missionary who works with a newly arrived missionary.

trucks rumbled past in clouds of black exhaust—I learned she hated riding a bike in a skirt, disliked Chinese food, was struggling with Chinese, and didn't like doing missionary work. My response was something like, "Tough. We're missionaries, we work hard, and we love it. So just get over it." Shortly thereafter, as we prepared to leave the apartment and paused at the door to pray, I looked up and saw my companion with tears streaming down her face. I thought to myself: How can someone who is supposed to be representing Jesus Christ to the world fail to take care of the person right in front of her, in need of love and support?

I decided that of all things, being a better disciple of Christ, and not racking up high statistics, should be the measure of my success as a missionary. As I rode my bike from appointment to appointment, I repeated in my head a scripture from Psalms: "Create in me a clean heart, O Lord; and renew a right spirit within me" (Psalm 51:10).

I had the good fortune to spend the last nine months of my mission in the western district of the city of Tainan. The members of the Church there were so dedicated and generous. I came to know the families and individuals in the ward well, to be aware of their hopes and trials. I thought about them constantly.

I also became well acquainted with Tainan's neighborhoods and cultural institutions, including its religious institutions. Every week, my companion and I went to a home for the elderly run by a Catholic convent and helped the nuns do the laundry. We climbed up to the rooftop and hung damp sheets and adult-sized cloth diapers in the sun. Sometimes we helped iron the priests' collared shirts. The nun with whom we worked most often, Sister Joan Ann, told me how she had been called to serve God at about my age, when she had been engaged to be married. She was an American woman, cheerful and hardworking as she labored in this part of God's vineyard. I felt certain God appreciated and accepted her sacrifices. I was also beginning to feel certain God also appreciated and accepted the sacrifices I was making. I experienced the good fruits of the Spirit in the joy and love that welled up in me like a miracle, like a superpower, like a fountain of living water.

When I returned from my mission and resumed my undergraduate studies, I found I had become a better student. I was less easily swayed by first this and then that forceful argument. I was able to think critically and exercise judgment. I was more invested in the work of studying and less easily distracted. I decided to apply for a PhD in Chinese history and was accepted to the program in East Asian Languages and Civilizations at Harvard University.

Hanging bedsheets on the roof of the Catholic convent and home for the elderly in Tainan with Sister Argyle

Church history has some sticky spots, and the Church sure is a patriarchal, conservative institution, but I really love my husband.

I deferred PhD studies for one year because I ended up engaged to Elder McMullin, the nerdy, skinny elder who had been my Chinese study partner in the MTC. During our engagement, I participated in a summer research seminar at the Smith Institute for Church History at BYU. It was the first time I had ever studied our history in depth.

Over the course of the summer, as I delved through history books and primary sources, I was alternatively inspired, impressed, intrigued, and shocked. I began to see that the early Saints had been flawed human beings like all of us. I learned that early leaders such as Joseph Smith and Brigham Young had made missteps in the course of their leadership. I learned that church culture, organization, policies, and even doctrines have been subject to shifts over time. I learned more about the Church's nineteenth-century practice of plural marriage, which is a very difficult subject for nearly all Latter-day Saint women, no matter how orthodox. Finally, I confronted the reality that in terms of its formal doctrinal and administrative structure, the Church was a patriarchal and very conservative organization. This was a challenge for me as I prepared for marriage in the temple and anticipated having to submit to the various aspects of the temple liturgy that reinforced this patriarchal order (changes to the liturgy in early 2019 have improved this somewhat).

At the same time, I was in love with my fiancé Joseph, the former Elder McMullin. He was intelligent, whimsical, even-tempered, and generous. We had many shared interests, including an interest in China and the Chinese language. He was supportive of my plans for pursuing a doctorate and later a professional career while also raising a family. He was deeply committed to following Christ, serving in the Church, and being a responsible husband and father. He was in love with me. Intellectual concerns about patriarchal liturgies notwithstanding, I couldn't think of anything more wonderful than being married to Joseph for time and all eternity. I was sure that our marriage would be a partnership of equals. Furthermore, I knew that so much of what I valued about who he was, including why he valued who I was, was directly linked to his upbringing as a Latter-day Saint.

So, I decided to marry Joseph in the temple. It was a good decision. My marriage has been wonderful—everything I hoped marriage would be. I don't mean for this to devolve into a husband-testimonial. The point is that the formal structures of a religion can be very different from its everyday practice. Focusing on the formal structures alone yields an incomplete picture.

There are a lot of stories in the world, and they all have sticky spots.

In the course of my PhD studies, I researched Asian religions and the history of Christianity in China. During seven years of taking classes, preparing general examinations, conducting field research, and writing my dissertation, I learned about religious movements from the great world traditions of Christianity, Buddhism, Daoism, and Islam. I discovered these religious traditions have also had leaders who made mistakes, that religions have transformed over time, and that all the large world religious traditions have historically been patriarchal and conservative.

In the context of other religious movements, I didn't see anything exceptionally problematic about the Latter-day Saint tradition, although I knew many had been terribly disillusioned by historic or contemporary blemishes in the Church's institutional structures and people. For instance, some might say: "Joseph Smith lied to his rank-and-file followers and most importantly to his wife Emma about his practice of polygamy—therefore he wasn't a prophet, and therefore the religion that he founded is all bogus." Or others might say: "The Church's structure is patriarchal, and patriarchy is oppressive to women—therefore the patriarchs are not called of God, and the Church is all bogus."

There was a time in my life when I would have thought about religion in this same uncompromisingly syllogistic way, as if a religious system were a string of cheap Christmas tree lights. If one light broke, the whole string was out. This is how I felt when as a high school student I asked my Uncle Charles, Is the Church true? Are its teachings correct? In my mind, just one flaw, such as a teaching attributed to Joseph Smith that the moon was inhabited by short people dressed like Quakers, could set off the whole chain reaction that ended with my faith being bogus. To me at the time, Uncle Charles's response was small comfort: "To the extent that [the Church is] not [true], I will make it true." If something is bogus, how can you do anything to make it true?

This faith-unraveling syllogism (Joseph Smith was a fraud, therefore the religion that he founded is bogus, therefore one's entire faith as a Latter-day Saint is bogus) is actually just the reverse of a faith-promoting syllogism often circulated at church on Sunday. If the Book of Mormon is true, the syllogism goes, then everything Joseph Smith did or said was divinely inspired. If Joseph Smith was divinely inspired in everything, then everything about the Church is just how God wants it.

I now have a different perspective on this issue of religious claims. Both Christmas-tree-light syllogisms, the faith-unraveling and the faith-promoting, are flawed. They demand that "light" leap from one point to another along a single string of connections. They argue: "If one junction along the string is flawed, then the whole string is dysfunctional; or If the whole string is functional, then every single junction must be perfect."

Like its namesake, the Christmas-tree-light view of religion is easily manufactured and easily broken. As a young girl in Sunday School, just hearing a tear-jerking story about how some hardy pioneer family pushed a handcart across the Great Plains filled me with religious certitude. Yet the Christmas-tree-light perspective makes faith quite fragile. All you have to do is knock out a single light, and kaplooey—the whole project is bogus.

Instead of a string of Christmas tree lights, perhaps a better metaphor for how I see the Church is a sourdough starter, which I sometimes use to bake our family's bread. Artisan sourdough with a reddish-golden crust that crackles and a creamy interior with large, irregular holes and complex flavors doesn't just happen. Enzymes break apart large, tasteless starch molecules so wild yeasts can unlock sugars and create bubbles of carbon dioxide that stretch strands of gluten. Strains of bacteria compete for dominance in creating an acidic environment.

All of this is a process of fermentation—what we normally call "food going bad." It begins with the starter—a riotous, resilient colony of wild yeasts and bacteria swimming together in starchy soup. There is nothing pure about sourdough starter. Its exuberance makes it sour on the verge of stinky, fermented bordering on decayed. Yet when introduced into a properly balanced supply of flour, water, and salt, the starter is a catalyst for producing a complex set of interactions that make heavenly bread.

Religious traditions are like artisan sourdough. They are complex, living things, both organization and organism, created and sustained by many processes and actors, shaped by time and their environment. They can be naturally subject to corruption. And yet they are also susceptible, through this same process of leavening, to producing goodness.

Maybe when Uncle Charles said, "I will make it true," he was simply making the effort required to exercise faith, to swim within the starchy soup and let natural processes work over time. Perhaps he was also speaking of Latter-day Saints' responsibility to exercise initiative in addition to faith—to do our part to bring our culture and everyday practices into harmony with our highest beliefs and values, to doggedly keep our covenants to follow Christ and be known as his people.

There are a lot of stories in the world, and many overlap with the Latter-day Saint story.

I wrote my dissertation on the history of the True Jesus Church, a Chinese Christian church with a founding story that sounds familiar: A man considered himself a Christian and read the Bible, but he looked at the numerous existing Christian churches and wasn't sure that any of them resembled Jesus's original church. One day he had a vision in which Jesus appeared to him, baptized him in a river, and commanded him to "correct the church." Therefore in Beijing in 1917, Wei Enbo founded the one true church: the True Jesus Church. Same story, different punchline.

During my research, I became personally acquainted with many members of the True Jesus Church who were moral, intelligent, and in many cases impossibly kind to me, the "gentile" researcher. I was certain they were truly striving to follow Christ. I heard their testimonies of God's love and care. In the course of my research on religious experience in the True Jesus Church, I heard and read many stories of miraculous healings, divine intervention, and guidance given in answer to prayer. I was certain that church members were not lying when they recounted miraculous or life-changing manifestations of God's power in their interviews. Why should they be? These were people of faith, and they saw the Holy Spirit at work in their lives.

The resemblance of True Jesus Church tradition to my own tradition, along with the respect I felt for the True Jesus Church members' faith, provoked much reflection. If the Latter-day Saint story is not entirely novel, what makes it different? What makes it matter? What makes it true?

Religions are more than just stories—so is truth.

One thing I have learned as a scholar of religion is that religions are more than just stories and doctrines. That is, a religion is much more than simply scriptures, recorded teachings of religious leaders, institutional policies, commandments, and so forth. Religion includes what people do, what people eat, when they pray and what material objects they use to pray, how they decorate their houses, and how they build sacred places.

Religion is how people feel, what they see in visions no one else can see, how they make friends and what they do to make amends to those whom they have offended. Religion is people's lived experiences, which are impossible to represent with a single list of doctrines or a single narrative. To understand religion, a scholar must encounter a movement on its own terms and according to the understanding of its believers, although understanding, of course, is not limited to this alone.

Doctrinal teaching is important, but I don't think any story we try to tell about God can be complete as a "truth" in itself. To me, the way truths become manifest in lived experience is a more valid measure of what is real or divine. Who cares whether something is "true" by any abstract measure, including intellectual or theological argument, if it cannot be realized in our daily work, bodies, or, most importantly, relationships with fellow beings? In the Sermon on the Mount, Jesus said that what people did was more important than what people said, and that people could be known by their fruits. The ultimate responsibility for whether someone grows into the measure of a disciple of Christ lies with that individual herself, not her religion. However, religions teach us what is possible, what is expected, what we can become. They set parameters and create conditions for our growth.

As I have matured as a scholar and have gained a deeper knowledge of religions and religious believers, especially global Christian movements, I've gained a deeper appreciation for how Latter-day Saint beliefs, practices, people, and institutions created a religious system based on compelling ideas and organized in a powerful way. I see how people at church learn Christianity not only through prayer and study of the scriptures, but through continuous opportunities to yield, serve, and express gratitude. I see how my faith has shaped my values and expectations.

As a group, Latter-day Saints are probably no better than other people, be they Jews or Buddhists or atheists, who are committed to doing what is right even though it is hard. I have friends who belong to other faiths or who have left the faith traditions within which they were raised. They are moral, kind people who make the world a better place. I can't speak for them. I *can* speak from my own experience. Here, within this church, I find evidence of God at work, the prophetic nature of Joseph Smith's founding revelations, and the divine validity of the covenants we make in our sacred spaces.

O then, is not this real?

Throughout my life I've been blessed with opportunities to feel the active presence of the Spirit: the transforming awareness that God exists and is mindful of us. I believe in the patterns and the commandments set forth in the scriptures. I have witnessed the Spirit working in people's lives, giving them words of comfort and blessing, expanding their capacity to be humble and generous, transforming enemies into friends. I am grateful that my life as a Latter-day Saint has helped me want to follow Christ and has defined the scope of my relationship to deity in such marvelously limitless ways. I am grateful for the discipline we learn as Latter-day Saints, including the laws of the fast, the Sabbath, the Word of Wisdom, tithing, and cooperation to get the job done. I know that today, as in days of old, prophets moved by the Spirit of God can still exhort us to repent and become better.

There are still many things I don't completely understand and many problems we must yet figure out. And yet my experiences have led me to treasure the fruits of the restored gospel as rare and valuable. As the prophet Alma says in his sermon about a seed that is planted, that grows, and that bears good fruit, "O then, is not this real?" (Alma 32:35).*

---

* Alma is the name of a prophet and a book in the Book of Mormon.

PART TWO

staying home

Shoot tops up while Sprout, Leah, Mama, and Bean wait for the Durango train

Slinging the Shoot around

Swimming in Clearwater Bay, Hong Kong

This section, which covers the years of my life in which I was not working and was the primary caregiver for my very young children, is clustered into groups of four. I didn't do that on purpose, but maybe it happened subconsciously because I have four children, botanically nicknamed Bean, Sprout, Leaf, and Shoot. They are lively and joyful human beings. They eat and grow like crazy. They play and fight and are incredibly noisy.

First, there are four letters to my kids. I first started writing these letters when I was pregnant for the first time in 2006. Often I write when I'm away from home, but I don't post the letters. I just come home and stash them in a filing cabinet. Second, there are four annual newsletters. These give overviews of the years from 2010 to 2013, when we lived in Hong Kong. Third, there is a selection of four songs that were a regular part of my family's life during this period. In Los Angeles and Hong Kong, women from church who had young children organized early childhood music classes, also held at the church building, called "Musicmakers." I have such fond memories of Musicmakers classes. In the first place, they were free. In the second place, they provided great opportunities for hand-me-downs and good advice. In the third place, I just loved being with my sisters and their beloved children. I never used to like babies before I had my own, but now that I've had my own, I love all babies. Luckily the same does not apply to cancerous tumors.

I learned so many things in the company of my Latter-day Saint sisters when my children were very young. After spending so much time with babies and toddlers, I was hungry for adult conversation and interaction. Once, some women in the ward and I convened a "Mormon-Muslim Interfaith Group" that met in the evenings. We talked about commonalities and differences in our traditions of prayer, fasting, and service. Our Muslim sisters read surahs and we sang Primary songs. When my hair fell out due to an autoimmune condition, my Muslim friend was the first person to whom I went. She lent me several headscarves. During that painful time, in which I came to terms with the fact that I would never again be beautiful—yes, yes, I hear you, but do you hear me?—it was comforting to look like Fatima, because she always did look beautiful. Eventually I got hot, and lazy, and comfortable. Bald is now my sporty, bedtime, casual, business casual, and formal look.

In another ward, we organized a "Park Day." Once a week, the women with babies and young kids got together at a local park. Occasionally, we organized a "Park Day Plus" in which one of us taught a lesson in her area of expertise, such as singing with the proper posture and muscles, learning principles of interior design, or making dumplings. One of the most beautiful and memorable things to come out of those Park Days was a collective poem, which we wrote for Mothers' Day, 2011. The diversity of perspectives and voices in this poem exemplifies the beauty of Latter-day Saint women coming together and captures the awesome spiritual power of the uniquely female experience of giving birth. Some of us who were expecting babies used this poem as a calming script for relaxation and meditation exercises in preparation for labor. I share the poem, and the introduction that accompanied the poem, here with permission from Segullah.org, where it was originally published.

"Mothers' Poem" was collectively written by twelve women from the Santa Monica California Stake on the occasion of Mothers' Day, 2011. The genesis of the poem occurred at one of the Westdale II Ward's Friday "Park Days" (moms chat, kids play). On one of these days, the topic of conversation was the article on Latter-day Saint women's ritual healing that had been published in a recent issue of the Journal of Mormon History.[1] *We discussed the nearly century-long legacy of Latter-day Saint women laying on hands to bless the sick. We were especially touched to learn about the beautiful ritual of sisters coming together to wash, anoint, and bless women about to give birth. One of the sisters in*

our group, eight months pregnant at the time, mused about how powerful and meaningful it would be to receive such a blessing from sisters who shared the experience of birth as a physical and spiritual passage. We wanted to draw on this rich spiritual legacy while showing deference to the Church's existing policy governing blessings and hit upon the idea of writing a collective poem.

Each section of the poem represents the contribution of an individual woman. This poem contains the words we would say if we lived during a time when Latter-day Saint women regularly performed such rituals, or the words of a prayer we might offer today on behalf of a sister among us preparing to cross the threshold into motherhood.

By Marcella Capasso, Darin Epperson, Melissa Erekson, Rachel Gee, Lori Hulbert, Melissa Inouye, Neesha McKay, Leslie Paugh, Tanna Romero, Donna Simon, Kim Wilson, and Gwendolyn Wyne. Edited by Melissa Inouye.

Mothers' Poem
As sisters in Zion, to cheer and to bless

Dear Sister:
As you prepare to birth your baby, we stand around you, united. May you feel our love and support as women who have crossed over the same threshold into motherhood, and as women of faith who offer prayer on your behalf and know that God will hear.

We rejoice with you in this time of celebration, as you prepare to reap the reward for the hard work of many weeks and months. Finally, your baby is coming.

Remember how pleased Heavenly Father is with your desire to give birth to His spirit children in a world in which a growing number of women choose not to become mothers. Cherish the special spirit that will fill your home with this new child who just left the presence of God. We are sure that ministering angels will be at your side and the side of this new infant as it gets accustomed to its new existence.

We release you from your everyday concerns: from professional, church, and family responsibilities, and even from your obligation to interact socially with people around you. Feel free, instead, to focus entirely on yourself and on your baby, to get comfortable, to preserve your strength.

We pray that your mind, heart, and body will be one as you prepare to birth your little one. Remember that this is a means to an end. The moments of pain are nothing that time won't mend. Think of your baby's tiny hands, feet, and face, and the beautiful spirit that you are bringing into the human race. May God grant you strength and peace of mind preceding his gift of the greatest joy you'll find.

We bless you with strength through your faith and Divine Nature, with the knowledge that you were chosen by Heavenly Father to fulfill this beautiful role; and may you feel honored to do so.

We invite you to be filled with peace, that you will welcome this wonderful time of motherhood. Understand that your body has been divinely designed to birth your baby and that you are doing so beautifully. As your birthing continues, allow your mind to be at ease knowing that your body and baby are working in harmony. We ask that you receive patience to pass through time as your baby descends.

We bless you with our diverse experiences and perspectives. We remind you that our babies came in many different ways, sometimes in ways that we did not expect or see as ideal at the time. We assure you that courageously adapting to changes as your birthing progresses does not make you any less important, committed, or successful as a mother.

We give you assurance that even when things seem to be going "wrong," you are entitled to seek and receive the Spirit's confirmation that God is mindful of you and that all things will work together for your good.

We say to you: be strong; have no fear.

56

We bless you that pain will help you understand how much the Savior values you; that just as the pain of this pregnancy and birth has taught you how precious your child is, so the pain of the Atonement must make you more precious to the Savior than you can possibly imagine.

Once your new little one has arrived, we bless you with the patience and endurance to make it through each new day having had little sleep, and a fair amount of frustration. It will all be worth it as you watch that precious little baby sleeping quietly and loving you unconditionally.

We bless you that in your birthing and new motherhood, when the time comes to search for courage and grace, you will remember us, your sisters. You will remember that we have felt what you feel, that we walked with God through the shadow of the deep valleys, that we laughed and cried for joy when at long last our baby came.

TO THE BEAN

4 May 2006

Harvard Yard, Cambridge, Massachusetts

Hi Bean (in utero),

I'm sitting here on the steps of Memorial Church. The 1:00 bells have just begun to ring. The pungent smell of cedar mulch is in the air. The crisscrossing paths flow with a steady stream of people. How young they seem to me now.

You seem like a pretty little guy too. It's hard to tell exactly how little because you're in my tummy. You just kicked me under the ribs. Sometimes I play a game: I find one of your feet and poke it. Sometimes you poke back. Sometimes you wiggle your foot away. It feels funny.

You'll be born in Cambridge, Bean, but we're going to move away before you'll have time to remember much. Too bad you can't remember today. It was a beautiful morning—I told you this as we stepped out onto the front porch to go to school—made all the more beautiful because of the two gloomy days of rain that preceded it. All of the trees in the Yard have awakened. They wear leaves of tender green and blossoms of white and pink. Cambridge is so joyful and lovely in the spring. All New England bursts back into life after the long winter. Maybe you'll get a chance to grow up in a place with seasons, and then you'll understand too.

My shoes and socks are off. The stone is cool beneath my feet. I have perched barefoot on these steps many times before. I have been almost a child here. And now I will be a mother. I hope you feel okay about that. I hope you're a good bean (and that I don't mess you up).

You know what, Bean? (You're moving around again. It must be cramped in there.) I think I already love you. I hope you're a healthy bean. I hope we take good care of you without making you spoiled and wimpy.

I suddenly remembered something. A couple years ago, I stood on these steps and gave a speech in front of a lot of people. It was about "Choosing Good Beginnings."[1] I was about to marry your father. It

58

seemed like a pretty good beginning then. It still seems pretty good now. I guess we're about to have another beginning, Bean, you and me. Did you choose this one or did I? I guess we'll find out someday.

Well, Bean, maybe I'll do my Japanese homework. Even expectant mothers have to turn in assignments at the end of the term. I just want you to know we can't wait for you to come out—after you're done doing your thing in there—and hang out with us. Probably you won't think it's very fun at first. Probably you'll think we just don't get it. But you know, everyone has to start out as a bean. And the world can turn out to be a very pleasant place.

See you later, I guess—
Me

The Sweaty Sprout

May 2009
Shanghai, China

Dear Sprout:

The following is an email I recently wrote to our family, reporting on the trip you and I took from Nanjing to Shanghai, along with all of our household possessions. You were a main character in this meteorologically sultry drama, though you were asleep most of the time. I'm passing it along as a little memento from your childhood.

Love,
Mama

Today I traveled by train from Nanjing to Shanghai with the Sprout, a rolling suitcase, and a big black zippered bag I bought from a market stall owner, in the following manner: "I need a big bag with wheels. The cheapest you've got." The bag was 60 kuai ("chunks"—a slang for renminbi, the Chinese currency) and it met all of these conditions. The "great deal" reminded me of our latest family maxim, developed over the past few months of delights and difficulties in our life overseas: "China giveth, and China taketh away."[1]

We filled the big bag with our cooking pots, our knife, some linens, and some toys to store at a friend's house in Shanghai, so we don't have to buy them again when we return to China for dissertation research in the fall. Together everything in the bag would probably cost about 400 kuai to replace, which is a lot of popsicles. The rolling suitcase was nearly 23 kilos (50 pounds) and the big bag with wheels was huge, top-heavy, and generally poorly designed and manufactured. But hey! The price was right! China giveth!

At the Nanjing train station, I had the Sprout in the chest carrier,

60

the rolling suitcase in one hand, and the big bag in the other. The big bag's wheels were small and didn't track well. The bag lurched and zoomed all over the place, banging my ankles or trying to flop over on its side. I dragged it down staircases and shoved it onto escalators and finally got onto the train. It was pretty tricky. And hot. 34 degrees Celsius (93.2 degrees Fahrenheit).

We didn't have a seat on the train because all the seats had been sold out. The Sprout and I plopped our luggage down in one of the doorway areas by the bathrooms and hung out there. The Sprout eventually fell asleep, flopping on me as I sat on the suitcase. An old man got on the train and kept on saying, "He sleeps so sweetly! He sleeps so sweetly! Look how sweet he looks, there on his mother's chest." This was all very nice of him, but the problem was that he kept on picking up the Sprout's hand and jiggling it, nearly waking him a number of times.

Finally we got to Shanghai. I strapped the Sprout up and began dragging the Stupid Bag by the left hand. The contents seemed to have shifted during the train ride and the balance of the bag was totally shot. I just started dragging it along the ground. The shoulder strap had already broken off. One of the top seams had already started to tear open. Of course, at this point I regretted buying such a cheap bag (a cheap bag even for China! why couldn't I have gotten something for 160 kuai [about 20 USD] instead of 60 kuai [about 8 USD]?!). Disgust for the worthless piece of junk raged within me as the Stupid Bag lurched this way and that, despite my considerable efforts to heave it upright with my left hand, all in sweltering heat, caught up in the surging sea of people, strapped to a sweaty Sprout. China taketh away!

At the top of a ramp leading off the platform, a lady offered to help me, and I gratefully gave her the rolling suitcase. Then a man walking behind me came up and took the Stupid Bag. These two strangers carried the bags all the way down the ramp, out of the station, over to the subway, through the subway station to Line 1, and through the interchange station to Line 2. They went down elevators and up escalators, down stairs and up stairs, waited for trains, pushed their way through thick crowds. Altogether they accompanied me, hauling the bags, for at least half an hour. The man carried the bags all the way to the train on Line 2, even though he was eventually going to take Line 8. He waited for the train to come and put the bags into the car. I thanked him profusely and he just smiled and said "Yinggai de" 应该的, which means something like "it's what one ought to do," or, less precisely, "I could do no less."

China giveth.

Dispatch from Dissertation Research

28 March 2010
Somewhere in southeast China

Dear Bean and Sprout,

Hello! I'm here in one of the "reception" guest rooms of the True Jesus Church in a village in southeast China. They have been gracious hosts, helping me arrange interviews and welcoming me at all of their church services. I may stay here another night because I'm getting great stuff in my interviews. This is too bad, in a way, because I miss you buddies and I miss Papa. But hopefully the dissertation will get finished. It hasn't been finished for many years now. Sigh. Some things take a long time to do right, especially when you are trying to do multiple things at the same time.

For us Latter-day Saint expats in China at this particular moment in time, church is on the phone. It is simply a big conference call, with clusters of "foreign nationals" participating from various locations around the country. Some unmute their phone to say opening and closing prayers; others unmute to deliver Sunday School lessons. I'll be honest: It's like listening to an excruciatingly long phone message. In our small groups, two or three families crowd together, straining to hear the voice coming out of a tiny phone. This is the price we pay for grand unity. But I suppose it also provides an opportunity to get together in person with the local families. We always share a meal afterwards.

I won't be able to call into church today because I am still in the middle of interviews. Later this morning will be the best time to visit a little village where the local True Jesus Church community met throughout the turbulent 1950s and 1960s, when most community religious activities were shut down. I have been reading scriptures instead. Yesterday I read the story of David, Bathsheba, Uriah, Tamar, and Absalom in 2 Samuel. I didn't find it uplifting at all (the text itself). I certainly hope you don't expect all parts of the scriptures to be uplifting. They're not meant to be a bunch of warm fuzzy stories. Rather they are a record of human beings' dealings with God, their covenants with God, and their attempts to live up to these covenants. Sometimes people fail spectacularly and tragically and abominably. The Old Testament can be especially tricky. At many points it seems clear the people who recorded those stories had a vastly different understanding of who God was and what God expected of them.

The True Jesus Church is interesting in that it prides itself in its adherence to the Bible (admirable but also problematic, in light of the above). "Whatever the Bible says, we do," church members say, "and whatever the Bible doesn't say, we don't do." I attended True Jesus Church worship services all day yesterday, since Saturday is their Sabbath. It was a lot of church. You can never have too much gospel, but there are definite limits to the amount of time you can spend sitting in church.

The True Jesus Church is like a Chinese version of our church.[1] It is a restorationist tradition, which means that they, like us, are a Christian movement teaching that the true church of Jesus Christ has been divinely restored after a long falling away. They believe their early leaders, including a farmer-turned-silk-merchant named Wei Enbo, saw Jesus in vision. They believe Wei was personally commanded by Jesus to restore the one true church. This was in 1917, in Beijing. Like the early Latter-day Saints, the early True Jesus Church members proclaimed that false Christianities abounded and that only their church had the complete, correct gospel. They pointed to members' frequent experiences of miracles of healing, exorcism, tongues, and visions to certify these beliefs. Wei Enbo even quoted the same verse (Isaiah 29:13) that Joseph Smith quoted to criticize the Methodist, Presbyterian, and Baptist establishment in upstate New York: "They draw near to me with their lips, but their hearts are far from me." They were quite successful, and to this day they are one of the major independent denominations in China. (Technically they are part of the nondenominational "Three-Self Patriotic Movement" churches, but in actual practice they maintain their own distinctive church tradition.)

The True Jesus Church members keep encouraging me to learn more about their church, the Holy Spirit, the truths and rituals that God has restored, and the "plan of salvation." They tell me if I learn to pray like them, in tongues, then God will give me my hair back. They are very kind and concerned.

This puts me into an interesting frame of mind. On the one hand, I genuinely respect their sincerity, devotion to their faith, and desire to be good and righteous people. On the other hand, I see the historical origins of their church, the ways in which their church is not as unique as they think it is (for example, I can see the larger context of other religious movements with Pentecostal, charismatic, or restorationist ideas, or of the history of global Christianity, etc.). To me it seems like one of many existing attempts to create a systematic interpretation out of something that fundamentally defies systematic interpretations. Explanations for why everyone should join the True Jesus Church make sense to them, but don't make sense to me. Now I understand how many people feel when they meet our missionaries, and the questions and answers the missionaries are so eager to supply simply don't strike a chord.

It's hours later, now. In the middle of writing all these detached observations about religion I have just learned, in a phone call with Grandpa, that our family friend in Shanghai died suddenly of heart failure a few days ago. She was in her midthirties, just a little older than I. She was a warm and vibrant person. You've both spent the night at her house. She kindly received us when the Sprout and I traveled from Nanjing to Shanghai. She made a place in her house to store the Stupid Bag (that big flimsy bag full of household things like cooking pans and duvet covers). She has four little children. The oldest is eight. The youngest is a year and a bit. What an inexplicable and terrible thing this is. I couldn't believe it when I first heard it.

It's at times like this, when you face the reality of death and all we don't know about the meaning of life and life after death, that you start thinking about what we know and don't know and how we ought to live our lives. One goes beyond trying to make distinctions between different forms of Christianity and simply asks: If God is real, then why is *this* (whatever it is) also reality? I don't understand why a God who cares enough to help someone find their keys, or to help a missionary find someone to teach—to use two frequently cited scenarios—doesn't take up the task of saving a mother of young children. Clearly, the world is full of stark injustices and terrible atrocities, many directed at "the very least of these," the children, whom God so loves. This is a status quo that God allows. I suppose it has to do with God respecting the laws of human agency and the laws of nature. But at other times, it seems God does allow these laws to be bent. When? How? Why not in this instance?

I also don't fully understand why, if there is God who created all things and who loves all creation, God has not helped everyone to fully realize this truth in the same way. If it is so important, why are there different ways of knowing? Why does God allow people to be born into environments that dramatically shape their receptivity to certain ideas about the meaning of life or the existence of the divine?

I wonder whether "the happiness the gospel brings" is the happiness of avoiding things that make us unhappy or the happiness of learning to live with things that make us unhappy. Probably a little of both. Some things lie within our control (not drinking, not smoking, not being promiscuous, not seeking fights, etc.), and some things lie outside our control. Regarding that which we ourselves cannot control, God will sometimes help us (for reasons we don't fully understand). At other times, what happens, happens. There may be some grand design in this, but I don't know.

It's a day later, now. I'm about to depart on a bus bound for home. I'm excited to see you again. Hopefully I can get back in time for Papa to go kitesurfing. The ticket lady is striding up and down the aisle, yelling at people and demanding to see their tickets. This is a combined performance of professionalism and tyranny. Because of people's habit of not sitting in assigned seats, we need someone to boss us around to get the bus on the road. There is a certain security in knowing someone forceful and competent is in charge. Everyone will get a seat; the bus will leave according to schedule. This is why some people think of God the way they do: controlling everything, dictating every outcome, running the universe like a well-oiled machine. This sort of God does not seem likely to me, personally. I've seen the kinds of mistakes people make, including errors in our own church history, and declaring that God has willed or caused these mistakes or errors to occur is really throwing God under the bus. We who believe in free agency should take responsibility and own our mistakes, as well as our repentance.

I suppose the reason I thought to write this letter to you is because I knew I would be missing our Latter-day Saint worship services in order to understand the Christian faith of the True Jesus Church. Although in these few days I have gotten lots of Sabbath-keeping, Bible-reading, hymn-singing, and faith in Jesus Christ, and although the events of these few days have raised difficult questions to which I may never find satisfactory answers, I wanted to write to affirm my peculiar identity as someone who believes in God, and who is a Latter-day Saint. Why, you ask, if there are so many deist and Christian outfits out there, am I so loyal to this one in particular? Latter-day Saints are Christians like many others who stake our hopes on Christ the Redeemer, but we go about our Christianity in a particular way. There is indeed a particular set of questions that is very important to us, for which the restored gospel supplies particular answers.

Who are we? We are children of God. By God, I mean our Heavenly Father and Heavenly Mother, who created all things, who love us, who want us to have joy—joy deepened through sorrow and trial. What is the purpose of life? It is to become better and better until we learn to be like our Heavenly Parents themselves. I have faith in Jesus Christ, the Savior who atoned for our sins and made this spiritual growth possible. This atonement sets us free to improve every day, to serve our fellow beings, and to love without fear. Many voices in the scriptures, and the lives of many people, speak up to bear witness of the truth of Jesus's example and atonement.

How are we to undertake this project of spiritual cultivation and exaltation? I am thankful for The Church of Jesus Christ of Latter-day Saints, for inspired women and men who have come together to establish God's kingdom on the earth. Not all Christians go about their Christianity in such an organized, systematic—some might say corporatized and bureaucratic—way. Some might say it is hard to find God in a crowd. I sympathize with this point of view. And yet, it is also hard to follow Christ in isolation. To be a Latter-day Saint is to be the kind of Christian who sees salvation as a collective project and doesn't mind things getting a bit grandiose (prophets, apostles, temples, revelation, inspiration, very long church name), though sometimes bumbling. Even as an amateur—we Latter-day Saints are professional amateurs—it is a privilege to volunteer in such a world, full of sweeping vistas and multiple dimensions, open heavens and warm hearts.

I have seen the Holy Spirit at work in this Church and in our lives, and know this Spirit will lead us to do good and to be good. I promise as we obey God's commandments, honor our covenants, and live always in thanksgiving, we will meet with joy. We will grow in wisdom and ability so that we become more like our Heavenly Parents. As a people, we Latter-day Saints do not have a monopoly on wisdom, righteousness, or godly sorrow. But we share the belief that these things are real and valuable, and we work toward them together.

Finally, I tell you plainly of my great love for both of you, as your mother. You, Bean, are a squirrelly, bright-eyed boy who likes to carry sticks in your hands and round things in your pockets. You carefully enunciate all of your words in a musical, chirruping way. You, Sprout, are a fuzzy-headed little guy. When I put you to bed, you always say—in a low, husky toddler voice—"Goopy kiss" and keep saying it until I have given you several goopy kisses on your plump, dimpled cheeks. The two of you, and your father, are the most precious and beloved people in my life. It is selfishness, of course, that I love you because you are mine. But this is also God's design. Be well, be good, be happy!

Love,
Mama

To the Leaf

July 2010
Huntington Beach, California

Dear little Leaf:

It's 1:00 a.m. on Saturday morning. You, my little daughter, are officially four days and one hour old. We are here at Bak Po's house (my grandmother, your great-grandmother) in the back bedroom. We are here because of your brother's strange, red, possibly infectious rash. "Could be chickenpox," the pediatrician said, "and if she gets it, she'll have to be hospitalized because she's so little." At home we were all sleeping in the same bedroom. So you and I came here to Bak Po's house to escape the plague.

Tonight we went to bed around 11:00 or so. Now I lie awake, inspecting you by the light of the bedside lamp. You sleep peacefully beside me, the sound of your breathing sweet and faint and rapid. Every once in a while your one free arm—the other is swaddled—waves in the air. From time to time you sigh and stir.

I lie here thinking about how you came to me. It took a long time. It started last Sunday night. I was up all night with contractions that came and went every ten minutes or so. Then they disappeared Monday morning. On Monday afternoon I walked for about ten miles or so to try to get them to return. Finally on Monday evening the midwife went ahead and induced labor.

As the contractions began to be more frequent, to exert more force, and to be more painful, I welcomed them. This meant that they were finally doing the work of labor. I lay on my side, breathing slowly, trying to relax, while the contraction began with a slight tightening and quickly ramped up with incredible power. It felt as if my womb were wringing itself out.

When the pain was especially bad I thought about Mom, your grandmother, who was in agonizing, constant pain for the last several months of her life due to a rare cancer of the bile duct. When I had this thought the contraction would suddenly feel less painful. Then it would subside completely, and I would rest.

There is a point in labor when the entire process becomes completely overwhelming, when the pressure feels unbearable, when you don't know what to do or how you are going to cope for another second. The surges feel like thousands of pounds of pressure smashing down, all at once, with no sign of relief or escape. In these most intense moments one feels despair and begins to believe that perhaps the baby will actually never be born.

I yelled as your head came out. The rest of you soon followed.

All of a sudden there was no more pain. It had been so very difficult, so overwhelming, and then it was over. What an absolutely amazing contrast. I was so pleased to hold you in my arms, to see that you stopped crying almost immediately, to smell your hair and put you to my breast. I almost couldn't believe that it was all over, that the hard work of hours and months was done and that I finally had you, my baby, in my arms.

Still sleepiness has not come to me. Still you sleep, stirring occasionally.

Another person who lay sleepless for hours in this same room, in this same bed, was my mother, whose name we've given to you as your middle name. For a period of a few weeks, when her cancer was in its late stages and when she was in severe pain all the time, Mom stayed here while her sister, Auntie Nancy, and her mother, Bak Po, took care of her. It was a more relaxing environment for Mom partly because it was her childhood home, but mostly because Auntie Nancy was Mom's very best friend in the whole world.

Sometimes during this time my brothers and I would take turns sleeping here at Bak Po's house in order to give Auntie Nancy a break at night. Mom was on massive doses of heavy-duty opioids at the time. Every three hours she needed a new dose of pain medication. Sometimes in between these intervals she needed additional doses to deal with breakthrough pain. The medication didn't take away the pain, but something was better than nothing.

I remember lying on the floor of Bak Po's living room with your brother, the Sprout. He was just a few months old. In the middle of the night, Mom's call button rang near my pillow. I wrenched myself out of sleep and hurried down the hall to this back bedroom where Mom was staying. The bedside lamp was on and she was sitting up in bed with a tight, drawn look on her face.

I gave her a dose of morphine under her tongue with a medicine dropper. Seeing her suffering, I wanted to stay up to keep her company. But although my spirit was willing, my flesh was weak. I was tired and sleepy. In the midst of her utter loneliness, Mom sent me back to bed. "Get some sleep, honey," she said. "Take care of that baby." "Thank you." I returned to my spot on the living room floor, both relieved and ashamed to be relieved, and dropped instantly back into sleep.

Mom became patient and accepting as her body lingered on and on in this terrible path. As my father, brothers, and I gave her medicine and tended her in her bed, we became more aware of the many ways in which we had often taken Mom's love and care for granted. I deeply regretted that I didn't have more time to return to her my appreciation and service in fuller measure. And yet, I prayed daily that her ordeal could end soon.

Mom passed away at home, early in the morning two weeks before Christmas. As I sat next to her bed, stroked her cold forehead, and looked long and hard at the vacant look in her half-open eyes, I discovered that I believed with absolute certainty in life after death. I felt sure that she had not ceased to be, but had gone elsewhere. It was an interesting realization. I feel that at least occasionally, perhaps in times when we need her most, Mom is looking after us. I thought of her during my labor with you, and in this sense, she was a presence with me throughout the pain, a presence that helped and healed and gave perspective.

It is a true principle that there must be opposition in all things, or else there could be no real meaning in life. The best things are achieved or experienced through contrasts. I was so very happy to see you. You were worth all the pain, and because of you, the pain itself has become a deeply meaningful experience. It is part of how you came to me and it is part of the blessing.

I lie here in the bed thinking about your birth and Mom's death and how pain was a hallmark of both experiences. In the case of your birth, it became a source of triumph. Perhaps, when we meet again, I will learn that

Mom's pain, too, became deeply meaningful to her. I wonder if in a way, the involuntary pain and anxiety of death reprise the involuntary pain and anxiety that were also part of birth. I believe that on the other side of death, the side we can't see, there is also peace and happiness in equal measure. Death, like birth, is simply another great spiritual passage, and this transition is marked by great contrasts that make it meaningful, solemn, sorrowful, and joyous all at the same time.

It is good for us to be here, my little daughter, you and I together in this back bedroom and in this bed where your grandmother spent those lonely and trying hours at the end of her life. It reminds us that life is full of contrasts and changes, and that as we move through it—through places, through time, through relationships—we are never the same, but always growing and always being made anew.

This room is the same room, this bed the same bed, but this night it is you and I who sleep, a joyful and thankful mother and a peaceful and angelic little baby. I already feel so much love for you: the way your cheek smells, the way you smile goofily in your sleep, the way your entire forehead wrinkles when you furrow your brow, and the way you flop on my shoulder after I've filled your tummy with milk.

I will take care of you, little Leaf. As you grow older, you will learn wisdom through your own experience of life's contrasts. You, too, will soldier through these contrasts and in the process learn to more fully realize the divine nature within you. Someday, God willing, you will have a daughter of your own. And then you will know how I feel about you, just as I now understand how my mother felt about me.

Sleep well, little daughter.

Love,
Mama

ing
pparatus
at →
Santa
Monica
beach

Annual Newsletter

December 2010
Los Angeles, California

Dear Friends:

At the end of this year we find ourselves in a state of shock. After literally decades of both being either students or teachers and arranging our schedules according to classes, winter breaks, and summer vacations, we have now come face-to-face with the World of Normal People. It is not pretty. We plan to pay off our student loans and relocate to a rural village in Inner Mongolia. We will teach English and raise sheep. Our children will gallop horses across the steppes like the horde of Genghis Khan. We will call you on Skype. In the meantime, however, we are really enjoying our little family.

The Leaf arrived early in the morning on July 20. The whole process started a week earlier, when Melissa's water broke while on a backpacking trip on the Washington coast. Although "Hello, Starfish!: Woman Delivers Baby in Tidepool" would have been a great story to relate in a holiday letter, the Leaf apparently reconsidered and the leak resealed itself. A couple of days after returning to our home in Southern California, the Leaf once again broke Melissa's water, and once again got cold feet. Melissa walked miles trying to restart the labor. As she walked, she sometimes sang a song:

Life in the tummy's no fun
Just come on out in the sun
Out here we walk and we run
Out here we say that our life has begun

[Chorus]
You don't have to fall very far from the tree
But please, Little Leaf, fall out of me
You don't have to fall very far from the tree
But outside is where Little Leafs were meant to be

Eventually the Leaf did come out. We named her after her Japanese great-great-grandmother and her Chinese grandmother (Melissa's mother). She is now five months old. She has a crazy lotta hair. The boys call her The Leafy-Chan ("Cute Little Leafy" in Japanese). Joseph calls her Leafy-chu. Melissa calls her Shrieking Shack.[1]

The Sprout is two and a half. He likes to eat and drink and do whatever the Bean is doing. He is also the most injury prone of our children. This is because—we think—he has such a big head and it's harder for him to balance. Just recently, when we were hiking in Malibu, the Sprout started running down a steep part of the trail. He went faster and faster. We watched with mounting feelings of self-pacification ("it's okay, he's got to learn the natural consequences of risk") and anxiety ("ah! Ah!!! AAAHH!"). Just as Joseph observed, "He's out of control," Sprout stumbled, fell forward, and whacked his head on a big rock. It gave him two deep puncture wounds, as if he'd been bitten by a big snake. Head injuries aside, he is happy and cheerful most of the time, except when acting tragically because he is being teased by the Bean. We are working on this (on the tragedy, and on the teasing). If anyone has any magic solutions for intersibling harmony, do share.

The Bean is four and a half. He is proving himself to be his mother's son in that he really likes to make schedules and write lists of things to do, including things like "Eat Artichokes" and "Play with Blocks" and "Clean Bathroom." Sometimes Melissa requests that he schedule in a "Mama's Nap," which he does very obligingly. He also likes to draw little smiling people. One little smiling person fits all—Mama, Papa, whoever. He just identifies individual people with labels. He likes to make (and eat) poached eggs on toast. He attends a local cooperative preschool, which Melissa really likes because it gives her the chance to observe him in his social habitat and to get to know his little friends. He loves learning capoeira, an Afro-Brazilian martial art, because it involves a lot of scampering and jumping and cartwheeling and singing. Sometimes he makes up his own silly songs. One of them goes like this:

Kai (stoic, post-head-whacking expression)

The wise man built his house upon the rock
The baby mouse came and ate it all up
A bear came and ate the baby mouse
Daba dooby dab dab doob

Melissa finished her dissertation and should graduate in March of 2011, insha'Allah ("God willing"). The next project is to turn it into a book, but for now she is taking a break. She spends a lot of time reading a book called *Cookwise*, written by a chemist-cook to whom she refers as "My Person."[2] Because of My Person, Melissa goes around spouting interesting food facts. Did you know, for instance, that postharvest vegetables are breathing (engaging in respiration by taking in oxygen and releasing carbon dioxide)? That over the course of one hour at 59° F (15° C), one kg of green beans produces 250 ml of carbon dioxide, while a kg of potatoes produces only 8 ml? That this respiratory difference is behind why certain fruits or vegetables spoil more quickly than others?

On Mondays and Fridays, while Bean is at school, she takes Sprout and Leaf for a run toward the ocean along Ballona Creek. Along with the usual mallards, coots, stilts, and seagulls, they occasionally spot something really wonderful. The other day they stopped to watch a great blue heron hunting in the tall grass. It stood still as a statue, its neck set in a muscular curve, its long beak poised. All of a sudden it struck. Its neck muscles rippled as it snatched and tugged at something on the ground. It came up with a fat brown gopher swinging from its beak. Then the heron calmly spread its wings, flew to a tuft of marsh grass on the other side of the creek, and ate the gopher. It was the coolest thing (though not so cool, alas, for the gopher).

Joseph just started working at his new lawyer job in the bankruptcy practice group at Skadden Arps. He bought a bunch of new lawyer clothes for the occasion. Unfortunately, we are still struggling to adapt to Joseph's new corporate reality. For instance, you know those little plastic stiffeners that go inside the collars of dress shirts? Melissa saw a pile of them on the counter, saw that one had a recycle symbol on it, and recycled all of them. Now he just has two left, which he transfers from shirt to shirt. Joseph frequently commutes to work via folding bike and bus. One night, he had to stay late and missed the last bus. So he decided to spend the night on the floor of his office. For a pillow he scrounged up the Bean's jacket, which happened to be lashed to his bike's rear rack. When he got cold around 2:00 or 3:00 a.m., he crumpled up a bunch of contracts and proofs of claim from the recycle bin and stuffed them into his clothes, which worked like a charm. He is quite a good sport about his job despite the really long workday that often keeps him prisoner until the kids are already asleep. Another exciting thing that happened to Joseph this year is that he got stung by a stingray. Apparently Long Beach, California, which has ideal conditions for kitesurfing, also has ideal conditions for stingrays. One third of the stingray stings in the United States occur at Long Beach. But, kitesurfers really like to kitesurf.

The juxtaposition of pleasure and pain in "The Kitesurfer

In the left margin, handwritten notes:

Natural proteins

denatured proteins

(proteins heated or exposed to air or acid)

Coagulated proteins

(denatured proteins hook together in a mesh that holds water)

The longer you heat the proteins and the higher the temperature, the tighter the bonds of the protein mesh become, squeezing out the water. p.197

of Cookwise, Shirley Corriher (New York: William Morrow & Company, Inc. 1997).

and The Stingray: A Cautionary Tale" reminds us of the impermanence of many of the things that make life enjoyable: well-behaved children, satisfying professional opportunities, and, most of all, good health. When we have these things, we are so thankful. We also recognize that from time to time, all of us struggle with significant challenges. We are so grateful to you for your friendship and pray that God will bless us all with a measure of grace as we persist in our shared journeys of learning and growth. In this season of thanksgiving we also celebrate the birth of Jesus Christ, who, we believe, made this journey possible, and who shows us the way to be good.

Round
Stingray
Urobatis
halleri

With love,
Melissa, Joseph, Bean, Sprout, and Leaf

Annual Newsletter

December 2011
Causeway Bay, Hong Kong

Dear Friends:

We send this year's greetings from Hong Kong, where it is freezing cold. That is, people are dressed in scarves, hats, and ski jackets as if it were freezing cold. It's actually about 60 degrees Fahrenheit (15 degrees Celsius). We suppose when you compare this temperature to the sweltering heat and humidity of the summer months, the drop in the mercury does seem more precipitous. It's all about contrasts.

Here's a brief synopsis of the major developments of the year, followed by a longer version:

1. Melissa graduated, finally.
2. Joseph is still a lawyer who wears lawyer clothes.
3. Children are growing up.
4. Hong Kong is growing on us.

Melissa graduated in March but is still working on the history of the True Jesus Church, revising her dissertation for publication. She's currently doing research in the archives of the London Missionary Society at Hong Kong Baptist University. Melissa was so excited to be browsing through London Missionary Society missionary reports for the years 1904–1906 and to stumble upon references to a man who must be Wei Enbo, founder of the True Jesus Church (no name given, but all the details check out). Just so you can share in the geeky thrill, here is an excerpt from the report for 1905:

> One of those mentioned in last year's report as hav-
> ing joined the church was a seller of cotton cloths, which
> he exposed on a stall on one of the principal streets.
> Owing to street improvements by the government, all
> these small businesses have had to remove elsewhere.
> This man rented a shop, and from the outset did not
> open on Sundays. The customers could not under-
> stand opening a shop only to close it after a few
> days, and then open it again, and there was a danger
> that his trade would suffer. He therefore posted up
> a notice that he did no business on Sundays, but on
> Mondays he would sell all goods at a cheaper rate.
> The result is that he has as many customers as he can
> deal with. Formerly on the street he had one assistant,
> now he has four. He ascribes all his success to the good-
> ness of God.

Isn't this so wonderful!? Archives are the best! Thank you, London Missionary Society, for saving all of your random papers for over a hundred years! Thank you, HKBU Special Collections!

Joseph recently completed his first year at Skadden Arps. Like visiting a prisoner in jail, Melissa and the kids go to visit him and have dinner at his office in Central every evening between 5:00 and 6:00. Sometimes we talk about "going to Papa's house." He brought his in-office sleeping bag from Los Angeles, and he has used it a couple of times. He is slaving away—er, getting lots of experience—and learning all about the thrills of initial public offerings, Lehman Brothers debt, and late-night Egg McMuffins. In the spirit of using primary sources (as above), we considered sharing an excerpt from an IPO prospectus, but then he might lose his job and you would certainly lose interest. He also does quite a bit of work for the Los Angeles bankruptcy practice as their Asian Time Zone Monkey.

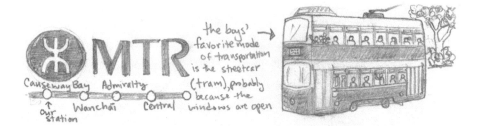

The Bean and Sprout are fortunate to be able to attend Suzhe, a Mandarin-language school in North Point. The school's motto is "Orderly and Strict." Yikes! It is the polar opposite of La Playa, the positive-discipline, child-directed-learning co-op preschool that Bean attended last school year. However, we've found a lot about the school to like. The kids' Mandarin is pretty rudimentary thus far, but a good foundation is being laid. Bean likes writing Chinese characters. Sprout is kind of clueless most of the time, but he is great at spouting Chinese kid-songs, complete with hand motions, like the one about the little dog standing at the gate that wants to eat meaty bones.

We like Suzhe so much that we are willing to jump into the crazy-competitive world of Hong Kong schools. Hence we have started prepping the Leaf for her kindergarten admissions interview a year from now: body parts, colors, scissor skills, front handsprings, and Shakespearean sonnets, all in English and Chinese.

If only kindergarten admissions interviews tested one's ability to make things disappear (the Leaf's great talent). She has turned our small three-bedroom apartment into a black hole. She lost one shoe from three different pairs of shoes in one week. She lost one of Bean's shoes and one of Sprout's shoes in one day. She is always chucking things into the trash. She may have thrown Melissa's cell phone down the toilet. She scribbles on walls, floors, and furniture with indelible markers. She is the best of babies, she is the worst of babies. We're sure you understand. Hopefully our landlord will as well.

We originally thought of Joseph's six-month stint with Skadden in Hong Kong as a mere jumping-off point for China, but the place and the people have grown on us and we now hope to be able to stay here for a while. These are the best things about Hong Kong:

1. lots of green, wild space and beaches just a short hop from the urban jungle
2. food: fresh coconuts in the fridge, shrimp dumplings at the local dim sum joint, mung bean popsicles after a hike in Tai Tam, vegetable pakoras at restaurants in the infamous Chungking Mansions (home to over 120 nationalities and the SARS outbreak), and ji-dan zai (waffles in a round, egg-like pattern, crisp and shattering on the outside, warm and chewy on the inside)
3. bus and subway connections to everywhere, cheap taxis, 41A (Sprout's favorite bus)

These are the worst things about Hong Kong:

jidanzai
雞蛋仔

1. insane housing prices
2. narrow sidewalks, relentless traffic, jostling crowds of people swinging bulky, heavy things precisely at the level of the boys' heads
3. wenzi (evolutionarily advanced, super-stealthy Asian mosquitoes)

How TO EAT A FRESH COCONUT

① punch hole in shell through eye with Sharpening Steel

② Drain Coconut juice into Cup for drinking later

③

It's all about contrasts, right? Joseph's work with Skadden in Hong Kong comes to an end on February 3. Where will be living after this, you ask? We don't know. Why? It's complicated.

In this season of thanksgiving and celebration, we are so grateful for family, for friends old and new, and for traditions that link the generations. We are thankful for the life and teachings of Jesus Christ, whose disciples we strive to be. As the various stresses of each day force us to confront our weaknesses and move us to try to become better, we draw inspiration from your friendship and your good lives. Warmest wishes for a happy new year!

Love,
Joseph, Melissa, Bean, Sprout, and Leaf

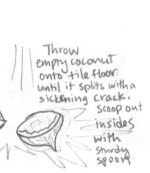

Throw empty coconut onto tile floor until it splits with a sickening crack. Scoop out insides with sturdy spoon.

Annual Newsletter

December 2012
Sai Wan Ho, Hong Kong

Dear Friends:

Greetings from Hong Kong! This year our family hit a milestone with the birth of our fourth and—we anticipate, though one can never be sure—final installment, the Shoot. We are happy that with the addition of the Shoot, aka Hanbao (漢堡 "hamburger"), our little tribe has finally reached what seems like a critical mass. The only downside is that our house is now in a constant state of critical mess. Of course this is hardly surprising. Actually it is nice to have a grand and noble excuse for what has always been a structural weakness in the Melissa-Joseph configuration.

Last year when we wrote this letter, we had no idea where we were going to be living in the next month or so because Joseph's temporary Hong Kong gig with Skadden Arps was set to expire in January 2013. He was lucky enough to land a job with a different firm, Kirkland & Ellis, in time for us to avoid deportation. We signed a two-year lease for a flat in "Yat Sing Mansion"—a dilapidated apartment building facing the ocean on the northeastern side of the island. We are becoming more and more like proper Hong Kongers.

One of the ways in which we have become thoroughly initiated into local culture is by sweating through the stressful process of getting our kids into school. Our six-year-old has already been rejected from first grade three times. Our two-year-old has already flunked her kindergarten admissions interview. In the process, however, we became open to the idea of sending Bean to a local (i.e., public, Cantonese-language) school instead of to the private English- or Mandarin-language schools that most expat children attend. After some looking around, we have found a little school close to our home that seems like a really good fit. It's Buddhist. It has "small" classes of no more than twenty-five. It has a lion dance team and a Chinese musical instrument class and numerous interest groups. It has a meditation room for the kids who misbehave. The catch is that Bean will have to learn Cantonese. He's currently looking forward to speaking a language that Mama and Papa don't speak. The Leaf may also end up "going Cantonese" because of her "performance" in her admissions interview at Kiangsu Chekiang School, where the boys are currently enrolled. During her interview, she refused to say anything and simply shook her head "no," squirmed, and glowered at the examiner. The verdict is out in February.

We've had over a year to become acquainted with Hong Kong's hiking trails and natural landscapes. Joseph's favorite place is Cheung Chau, a small island with a fishing village and a cave that was historically a pirate hideout. The pirate who lived in this cave was named Cheung Po-tsai. This name happens to sound like "pickled cabbage" in Mandarin, so Joseph subsequently spun a long and elaborate yarn—which the kids completely believe—about how the pirate treasure stored in this cave was actually jars and jars of pickled cabbage. Joseph tells the kids a lot of stories because he spends a lot of time with them on buses and subways.

Melissa likes to go running in the morning. One of her favorite runs starts at our apartment at the edge of the harbor and winds south past the MTR (subway) station and through a wet market that bustles with life (and death). Produce sellers set out piles of bok choy and baskets of guavas, breakfast shop customers slurp up fish ball noodles, butchers pull flapping chickens out of cages and saw their throats with methodical strokes of a serrated knife.

THINGS
WE LIKE
TO DO:

① Eat shrimp dumplings and ginger chicken steamed buns from the local dim sum shop

② Boulder-hop in mountain streambeds

On the other side of the wet market is a cluster of apartment buildings through which a series of escalators ascend. On the other side of the apartments is a sloping water maintenance road that runs up the mountain and joins a clay-and-sand track. The path threads first through ferns and then through pine forest up to a mountain peak with a breathtaking vista of Victoria Harbour and the Kowloon peninsula. Getting to this point takes about thirty-seven minutes.

The kids' favorite trip involves taking the ferry from the dock in front of our building across the harbor to the fishing shantytown of Lei Yu Men, where there are tanks full of giant lobsters and squirming langoustine and elegant abalone and sharks and geoduck and all sorts of live seafood. The kids also enjoy climbing around on a rather gritty beach with big rocks and crabs and a lot of glass bottles and junk. If they're lucky, sometimes the fish merchants let the kids toss shrimp into the tanks holding giant groupers as long as the kids are tall. The groupers' mouths make a heavy, hollow sound (and an epic splash) as they snap up the shrimp at the surface of the water.

③ Kayak in Sai Kung

④ Take the ferry from the pier in front of our house to the fishing village across the harbor (Lei Yu Men) ⑤ Push buttons

Now that we have four kids, we are discovering all of these interesting sibling combinations, i.e. Bean + Sprout = Eight Minutes of Hysterical Laughter and Then Loud Wail; Bean + Leaf = Most Likely to Result in Cooperative Daughter; Sprout + Shoot = Laughing Baby; Leaf + Shoot = Mama to the Rescue; and so on. The Shoot is turning out to be extremely good-natured. You can just wedge him into the vertical crack in the couch cushions and he stays there for long periods of time with a slightly bemused, patient look on his face. He also has this great Pac-man smile. Recently the kids have gotten good at making him laugh in response to their silly antics, which is really the best. People should bottle baby laughter and sell it as an antidepressant.

We are deeply grateful for the many blessings that have made this year so wonderful. And yet, through-out this year, we have been acutely aware of the fact that life comes to us in equal measures of joy and sor-row. In times like this we are also grateful for sacred texts and personal spiritual encounters that have affirmed our deep belief in life's purpose as a passage in the midst of an eternal journey. We recall the words of the biblical text of Ecclesiastes: the race is not to the swift, nor bread to the wise, but time and chance happen to us all. We draw on memories of times in which we have felt with certainty that God was mindful and gave strength in times of need. We are grateful for our faith, which teaches us about the worth of experiencing both good and evil, dark and light, health and illness, and other opposites that enlarge the dimen-sions of being human.

In this season we celebrate the birth of Jesus Christ, whose disciples we strive to be. We are grateful to you, our friends and family, for your influence in our lives. In good times and bad, friends and family are the richest blessing. Merry Christmas! Happy New Year! May you feel love and joy this holiday season.

With love and appreciation,
Melissa, Joseph, Bean, Sprout, Leaf, and Shoot

Annual Newsletter

December 2013
Sai Wan Ho, Hong Kong

Dear Friends and Family:

Here we are again on the cusp of a new year and the threshold of a great adventure. After three wonderful years in Hong Kong, in June 2014 we will be moving to Auckland, New Zealand. We are very excited—life is short, the world is large—but we will miss our friends and family in Hong Kong.

To make a long story short, because we were fed up with Joseph's terrible corporate lawyer hours ("early" = 8:00–10:00 p.m., "normal" = around midnight, and "late" = 2:00–5:00 a.m.), we decided to do a job swap. Melissa applied for professor jobs this fall and just accepted a position at the University of Auckland. Joseph is going to be a full-time dad for at least a year or so. Joseph is looking forward to being loosed from the manacles of his Blackberry and spending more time with the kids. Melissa is looking forward to more balanced parenting and more time for teaching and research. The kids are looking forward to everything and anything. This is because they still have such wiggly brains.

Shoot, the youngest and wiggliest at sixteen months, is loved by all. One evidence for his general popularity is the burgeoning collection of nicknames (like "Shooty," "Shootworth," "Kapoots," "Ootifer Rootifer," and "Hanbao" [Hamburger] to name just a few) given to him by goo-ing and gaa-ing family members. He says a couple of things, like "cracker" ("ga!") and "mama" ("MA!"). He is a happy baby. He forages happily in the garbage and splashes happily in the toilet. He likes wearing other people's shoes. He likes chewing on other people's shoes. He is soft and squirmy, scoopable and kissable.

[Update from last year's letter about Hong Kong schools:] To get your two-year-old accepted into Kiangsu Chekiang School (KCS) after a hostile, completely silent admissions interview performance, follow these easy steps: (1) write a letter to the headmistress explaining how the Leaf's interview occurred during her naptime and so she was not her usual *angelic* self; (2) have a real Chinese person edit this letter, adding key colloquialisms such as "the Leaf is usually such a happy 'pistachio'"; (3) hand deliver the letter; (4) follow up with additional artwork and letters from your elder children saying how much they love KCS; and (5) make regular visits to the school office.

Thankfully, the Leaf (three years) loves school. Despite the advent of this promising new Happy Schoolgirl phase, she seems to have a strong ongoing affinity for Angry Toddler mode. She is charming, fierce, affectionate, and violent. As a girl with two older brothers, she has learned the law of the jungle and gets a lot of respect. She is very independent and self-entertained, which is generally wonderful—with notable regular exceptions such as the time we found her under the dining room table, busily snipping our passports into tiny triangular pieces. She is a block-building virtuoso. Maybe this means that she'll go into engineering someday. She would be great at demolition.

The Sprout (five years) is a sweet, generous boy, quick to apologize and hapless in his misbehavior. He is learning to play the cello. He plays a 1/16th cello so tiny that it's more like a large viola. It has been a joy to see how he has thrived when given the opportunity to pursue his own special talent. Every Wednesday and Thursday he and Melissa take the bus to cello lessons in Wanchai. Like so many routine journeys in Hong Kong, going to and from cello is a busy, jostling, sensory trip. On the way to the 2X bus stop, Sprout and Melissa take a shortcut along a small side street. There's a price to

FAVORITE FORBIDDEN ACTIVITIES

Foraging in the delicious trash can

Splashing in the delightsome toilet

Gnawing on the enticing power cord

pay for the shortcut: a shop along the way that sells "stinky tofu" 臭豆腐. The name "stinky tofu" really does not do justice to the real thing. It is super, super stinky. It fills the street with the smell of something that has gone badly wrong. (However, stinky tofu is an acquired taste; if you are willing to pay the price to acquire it, you will find it delicious.) After escaping the stinky tofu street, Sprout and Melissa cross the streetcar tracks and walk along busy Hennessey Road. Sprout loves to get treats from the vegetarian dim sum shop right next to the bus stop, which sells little fried vegetable triangles, spring rolls, sesame balls with red bean filling, and coconut mochi.

stinky tofu frying in a wok

Yet another amazing example of kids' wiggly brains is the way in which Bean (seven years) has adjusted to his new local primary school. He started the school year speaking no Cantonese at all and now is able to answer questions in class. One of the early milestones in his Cantonese-learning journey was the day he came home from school, laughing hysterically every time he got us to repeat a Cantonese phrase. Apparently—as he later gleefully informed us—it means "pee my pants." So far we have been quite pleased with the school's teachers and Buddhist teaching philosophy. The school motto is "Bright Wisdom Revealing Compassion," which is way better than the KCS motto ("Orderly and Strict"). Bright, sensitive, and focused, Bean is becoming a quality pianist.

vegetable triangle

sesame ball

coconut mochi

In the mornings when Joseph takes Sprout and Leaf to school, they always clamor for a story and insist that it follow a set formula. Any deviation from the formula is strictly spotted and shot down. The current formula involves Sprout and Leaf choosing one superpower and one magical animal. Sprout usually picks the ability to spontaneously create black holes (or sometimes pizzas) while he flies on a cheetah that can shoot laser beams out of its eyes. Leaf generally prefers to be able to spontaneously create "biting foxes" while riding on a blue monkey with butterfly wings. Each story involves them discovering and defeating a new villain (giant slugs, lightning lizards, rabid marshmallow bunnies). The stories make perfect sense if you are under five;

Buddhist
Chung Wah
Kornhill
Primary
School

otherwise they are complete nonsense. When Joseph no longer feels like telling the superpower story he will try to get away with other short stories. These short stories are really short. For example:

Once upon a time there was a fairy princess who loved butterflies, and there was a flower prin-cess who loved flowers. And they both kissed Sprout on the face. And he really liked it. The end.

Once upon a time there was a boy who forgot to say please. And a monster ate him up. The end.

In short, we have had a busy year and look forward to the coming year's adventures. We are grateful for our health. We are grateful for our children, our beloved eternal associates. We are grateful for Jesus Christ, whose teachings we strive to follow and whose atonement makes it possible for us to keep trying though we often fall short. Finally, we are so very grateful for you, the people in our lives from all faith backgrounds and all walks of life, who are such wonderful friends, teachers, and examples to our family. Happy Holidays!

With love,
Joseph, Melissa, Bean, Sprout, Leaf, and Shoot

FOUR SONGS THAT
NEVER LET YOU DOWN

All I learned about teaching, I learned from Primary or from doing early childhood music classes with other Latter-day Saint women. In my university classes, I make the students sing a Chinese History Song (written by me, summarizing major events and interpretive themes) to the tune of "Twinkle, Twinkle Little Star." It actually draws really positive feedback in student evaluations. On this page are four tried-and-true songs from Musicmakers.

Moon Magic

With thanks to Arvida Steen. Used with permission.

Good for quieting kids down, or starting off with something focused. Very simple melody. Sung in a round, it is beautiful and mesmerizing. If you have a glockenspiel or a piano, have a kid play a drone on E and B.

Where Is the Baby?

With thanks to the Hong Kong Musicmakers.

Helps the babies feel included (you need an actual baby, or multiple babies). The kid-baby interaction is a nice shift of focus. Also helps younger kids learn the names for parts of the body (feel free to improvise: eyebrows, fingers, etc.)

Each pair of call-and-response lines is sung on the same note, starting with DO, and up the scale to TI. Sing softly. The last line (the punchline) is a mock shout.

DO   C [Caller]: Where is the baby?
        R [Response]: Here is the baby [pat the baby]
RE   C: Where are its toes? [you can also say "his" or "her"]
        R: Here are its toes [wiggle toes]
MI   C: Where are its feetses?
        R: Here are its feetses [jiggle feet]
FA   C: Where is its tummy?
        R: Here is its tummy [pat tummy]
SOL   C: Where are its arms?
        R: Here are its arms [wave arms]
LA   C: Where are its ears?
        R: Here are its ears [gently wiggle]
TI   C: Where are its boogies?
        [Caller exclaims:]
        DON'T TOUCH THE BOOGIES!

Sleeping Bunnies

With thanks to Juliana Morgan and the Hong Kong Musicmakers.

The kids have to curl up on the floor like sleeping bunnies. When cued, they hop around. After bunnies, have the kids suggest other (initially sleeping) animals. Dinosaurs stomp, frogs jump, etc. This one tends to make kids boisterous—save for a bit of fun at the end.

See the little bunnies sleeping
   'til it's nearly noon
Shall we wake them with a merry tune?
They're so still . . .
Are they ill?
[Spoken:] No . . . Get up, little bunnies!

[Clap on bolded syllables]
Up little **bun**nies, **hop** hop **hop**
Up little **bun**nies, **hop** hop **hop**
Up little **bun**nies, **hop** hop **hop**
Up little **bun**nies, **hop** hop **hop**

This Is the Way We Wash Our Clothes

With thanks to the Westdale Ward Musicmakers.

This is a fun parachute song. Parachutes are simple to make, but if you don't have one, you can also sew old sheets together or use a single big sheet or tarp. The point is having a lot of material to swish, flap, and fold around the kids, who sit in the middle and squeal with delight. Caregivers do the singing, kids do the squealing.

[swishing in a circular, washing motion]
This is the way we wash our clothes,
Wash our clothes,
Wash our clothes,
This is the way we wash our clothes
So early in the morning

[flapping up and down to make breeze]
This is the way we dry our clothes,
Dry our clothes,
Dry our clothes,

This is the way we dry our clothes
So early in the morning

[bringing edges of the parachute in toward
the middle, covering the kids, then stepping
back, and repeating, with the rhythm]
This is the way we fold our clothes,
Fold our clothes,
Fold our clothes
This is the way we fold our clothes
So early in the morning

PART THREE

thinking things through

Preparing a book index at the kitchen table

This section is about thinking a lot, and thinking hard, while being a parent, scholar, and practicing Latter-day Saint. It intersperses essays about aspects of Latter-day Saint history and culture, lectures about Chinese history and philosophy, and three family newsletters in which we are moving to Auckland, New Zealand, settling in to new routines, and installing floors and laying tile. How do all of these things come together?

For three years in Hong Kong, while Joseph was working as a corporate lawyer, nearly every evening around 5:00 p.m. the kids and I packed food into thermoses and bento boxes, boarded a bus into Central (the downtown business district), and ate our family dinner in a food court below Joseph's law office. He was constantly tied to his work phone; sometimes he was called into the office on Sunday mornings as we sat in church. We decided to pursue a more family-friendly lifestyle. I went on the market for a full-time academic job.

At the time, I was teaching a class on American religion at the University of Hong Kong, but I didn't have an office. Therefore, during my Skype interview with the University of Auckland search committee, I sat in a sort of closet—a storage nook lined with bookshelves. Surprisingly, I was offered the job, but when the offer came I was sure I wouldn't take it. New Zealand was too far away. It was unthinkable. Joseph, however, had been googling New Zealand during his lunchtimes and read about cool caves full of glowworms. "We have to see the glowworms!" he said. So, we went to New Zealand for family life—and for the glowworms.

For the first year and a half, Joseph didn't work full time, but was home with the kids. They did a lot of hiking and grew a lot of things in the garden. Eventually he went back to work, and I became the kids' primary caregiver again. I was able to schedule my teaching so that I could leave the University by 2:00 p.m. and be home by 3:00 p.m., when the kids finished school.

This position at the University of Auckland was my first full-time job. At first I couldn't believe I was being paid to sit in an office and enjoy peace and quiet while reading and writing, every day. It seemed too good to be true. Now, although I am enmeshed in more administrative duties than I was when I first began, it is still wonderful, though with the usual challenges of managing time and expectations.

During this time I also began to be more involved in the community of people who write and think about The Church of Jesus Christ of Latter-day Saints and the broader webs of culture, theology, piety, politics, and relationships that surround it. The essays in this section reflect some of this thinking. One of the reasons I started to do more thinking and writing about faith at this stage in my life is that with the youngest kid finally potty-trained, and a husband freed from a hyperdemanding job, I had more time. But as I reflect on it further, I think the main reason is that my kids are growing up. I feel a sense of urgency. There are some things we've got to work on, now, in order to help them see the power and beauty of the restored gospel during this formative period of learning to think, speak, and believe for themselves.

My Latter-day Saint worldview informs my work at the University of Auckland. I was recently honored to receive the University's highest teaching award for early career academics. I felt a bit sheepish, however, to receive an award for simply teaching the way I learned to teach the Primary children. In my interactions with students at the University, I try to teach the way I would like to be taught, to value people, to cultivate caring relationships, and to create spaces for meaningful conversations.

In sum, the pieces in this section are written for different—though often overlapping—audiences, but they are all trying to get to the same place, which is a place of truth and integrity amidst coming-together. People often talk about the difference between "faith" and "reason," and the balance between "work" and "life." For me, there are no stark distinctions between these things. They all seem to blur into each other.

This must be why my house is so messy . . .

ANNUAL NEWSLETTER

December 2014
Auckland, New Zealand

Dear Friends:

Last Christmas we were in Hong Kong, trying to wrap our heads around the consequences of Melissa's accepting a job as a lecturer at the University of Auckland starting June 2014. We were huddling together in our uninsulated concrete apartment on the tenth floor, staring at the plastic Christmas tree we had purchased from the Shamshuipo wholesale markets, wondering what we had done to ourselves.

Now, nearly six months after our relocation, Auckland feels like home. It doesn't take much to make a place feel like home. We arrived with all four kids and the plastic Christmas tree. With us came the blender, the books, and Sprout's green sweater, which he now wears every single day. Even the hair-trigger tantrums, pre-bedtime delays, and potty-training accidents have carried over. Home is where the stain remover is.

There have been some significant changes, of course. Joseph is enjoying his new job as a stay-at-home dad and the Shoot's New Indispensable Parent. Melissa was mildly insulted by the speed with which Shoot switched his parenting preferences but also somewhat relieved after eight years of indispensability. Now instead of saying things like, "Sorry, I probably won't be home until after midnight," Joseph says things like, "I just want an hour to sit and read by myself and not deal with poop or have anyone jump on me." Joseph is the ultimate Superdad. He

transformations

99

bakes whole wheat bread for daily sandwiches, makes homemade kimchi, serves flourless chocolate cake with rhubarb strawberry sauce for special occasions, and stretches discs of homemade dough for Pizza Night every Thursday night. The secret ingredient for Pizza Night is crushed pineapple. You've got to try it. Crushed pineapple on a pizza has a completely different effect compared to chunks of pineapple. The ratios are transformed. It is a revelation.

Melissa is enjoying her new job as a full-time academic. She loves teaching even though it is quite time consuming. She takes a bike + train combination to work and then bikes home from central Auckland to Henderson Valley (about 20 kilometers, or twelve and a half miles, in total). Because of the bike commute, she has to change into professional clothes at work. It was too complicated to try to shuttle elements of this or that outfit back and forth in bike panniers, so during the entire semester when the weather was chilly she simply wore one of two pairs of pants she kept at her office. About half the time it was Black Pants Day and the rest of the time it was Grey Pants Day. She got this idea from Joseph, who in his Hong Kong lawyer days wore one pair of pants per month. Mind you, there have been some variations on this theme. For instance, when it was especially cold she wore wool-blend Bright Blue Pants all week. And when Black Pants somehow got worn home, every day became Grey Pants Day. Now that summer weather is slowly edging its way into Auckland, however, she is branching out a bit.

In our new green, spacious environment, the gardening genes Joseph inherited from his mother, a farmer's daughter, are expressing themselves with a vengeance. He has four garden beds planted full of everything from rhubarb to strawberries to spinach to garlic and everything is growing riotously—except the basil. He is having bad

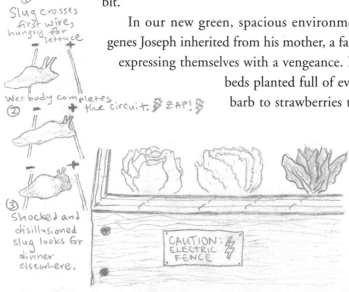

HOW THE SLUG FENCE WORKS

① Slug crosses first wires, hungry for lettuce

② Wet body completes the circuit. ZAP!

③ Shocked and disillusioned slug looks for dinner elsewhere.

CAUTION: ELECTRIC FENCE

luck with the basil. First there were the slugs. So he built a slug electric fence around the garden beds using twin wires and a 9-volt battery. Then there were the cats. So he sprinkled the garden with chili and began terrorizing them with a squirt gun. Now the basil is slowly coming back. Joseph is serious about his garden.

Joseph's "totally adorable" cucumber sprouts

So far we have only had to water the garden a few times because it rains all the time in Auckland. The local adage is "all four seasons in a day" and this can really be true. In the course of twenty-four hours we've experienced clear blue skies, blazing hot sun, rainbows and scattered showers, howling winds, and hail. When it's not raining, however, it's beautiful—so green and fresh feeling, the skies so blue and the sunsets fiery.

Bean (eight years) loves his personal garden plot, where he is growing roly poly carrots, bush beans, a tomato plant, and leeks. Sprout (six years) has recently gotten into reading comic books and playing soccer. Both boys work hard each morning before school at their piano or cello practice. We feel lucky to have found wonderful music teachers. Henderson Valley School, located on beautiful grounds surrounded by farms in the foothills of the Waitākere Ranges, is pretty laid-back. School starts at 9:00 a.m. There is a morning tea break, then a brain food break, then lunch, then afternoon tea break, and then they go home at 3:00 p.m. Just up the road is Leaf's kindergarten ("kindy"), called "Old MacDonald's Country Kindy." It's housed on the grounds of a farm, and the kids get to feed the animals, go on tractor rides, and play in the hedge maze.

In other words, the kids' educational experience is the polar opposite of Hong Kong, where Bean was often disciplined for running at recess and where Sprout and Leaf's school had no green space whatsoever. This is not to say we don't miss Hong Kong, or even those hard-core Hong Kong schools, because sometimes we do. It's hard trying to keep up their Chinese language learning, though Joseph is trying despite the circumstances. Leaf doesn't do Chinese yet because

SLOW Escaping Goats

Sign in the drop-off driveway at HVS —school has small herd of resident goats

she is learning how to read in English, and with Leaf one must conserve one's "instructional capital." When she does study an instrument, we've decided that it will have to be the piano because this is least likely to become dysfunctional when kicked.

Leaf (four years) is fearless, independent, and a prolific artist. She enjoys taking care of Shoot (two years) (and bossing him around). She's made friends with the little girl across the street who is her same age. Shoot is funny and amiable. He is particularly taken with the digital piano. The first thing he likes to do with the piano is to turn on the schmaltzy '80s demo song and dance. The second is to slide CDs into the piano's crevices until the keys get stuck. Like all youngest children, he makes his living through charm and manages to pursue regular sabotage without incurring too much wrath.

As diverse as their personalities may be, right now our four kids all have the same haircut—a close buzz. It happened on a Sunday morning when Melissa was braiding Leaf's hair and suddenly remembered Sprout's teacher had sent home a notice about lice. She then began checking the kids' hair, giving the expressions "going through it with a fine-toothed comb" and "nit-picking" new meaning. When Joseph discovered a real live louse trundling along through Sprout's hair, this was the last straw. Out came the clippers. This Licemageddeon fortuitously corresponded with the North American October 31, giving the kids and Joseph the opportunity to be Melissa for Halloween. Now all of our heads are barren wastelands in which no louse or its detestable offspring may find refuge. Melissa was originally going to spare Leaf's long black hair, which had taken years to grow, but then complied when Leaf requested the shave herself. After all, attachment is a source of suffering, as the Buddha taught.

One way in which we have failed to be proper Buddhists, despite our respect for Buddhist teachings, is in the great value

OUR FAVORITE AUCKLAND PLACES (SO FAR):
(A) Te Henga beach
(B) Anawhata beach
(C) Lake Wainamu
(D) Fairy Falls
(E) Auckland Museum

TOP 10 THINGS TO DO IN HONG KONG:
(1) Swim at Clearwater Bay beach
(2) Go hiking (take the subway or minibus to the trailhead)
(3) Take the Midlevels Escalator
EAT:
(4) shrimp dumplings
(5) shumai
(6) squid ball noodles
(7) flaky pastry egg tart
(8) fried sesame balls (jindoy)
(9) Hike to the Peak
(10) Chi Lin Nunnery

we place upon attachment to people we love. We believe that bonds with family members and friends are not illusory but are in fact eternal, the very essence of humanity's divine nature. We are grateful for Jesus Christ, whose life and teachings we remember in this season. At the close of the year we feel very grateful to have had the blessing of your friendship and good examples in our lives. Thank you! Happy holidays!

Bye-Bye, Braids...

    With warm wishes,
    Melissa, Joseph, Bean, Sprout, Leaf, and Shoot

HOW CONFERENCE COMES TO HONG KONG

4 March 2013

First published online at the Peculiar People blog, Patheos.com

The Church of Jesus Christ of Latter-day Saints is currently undergoing a period of dramatic change and adaptation. Once it was a religious movement with its heartland in Utah, populated by families of European descent with names like Bennett and Frandsen. Now it is a global religion that has grown roots all over the world, among Zhangs and Rajaratnams and Malabis and people whose cultures do not use surnames. What once seemed like "typical" or "ideal" patterns for a Latter-day Saint way of life are now just a few among a multitude of ways of living the restored gospel within a particular cultural context. Reorienting to our global reality is exciting, but also stretching.

Where does the gospel reside, after all? Can universal truths be separated from local culture? The Church is wherever the saints strive to follow Christ, and the prevailing beliefs, practices, and culture in a given locale are as authentic as anywhere else. Church culture in Provo, Utah, is every bit as exotic and shaped by local traditions as church culture in Taichung, Taiwan, or Likasi, the Democratic Republic of the Congo. Is there a way to bridge the differences and contradictions that exist between God's children in global situations without creating sterile conformity? There is a world of difference between universality and uniformity, but sometimes we conflate the two. The essays in this section explore what it means to cross over boundaries of space, time, experience, and culture in a Latter-day Saint context.

In one month, general conference will come again to the red brick building with the gray spire that sits on Gloucester Road, the east-west artery into Hong Kong's throbbing urban heart. By Hong Kong standards, the Wanchai building is a modest twelve-story low-rise, dwarfed on all sides by skyscrapers easily over four times as tall. But small as it may seem, it contains worlds.

Hong Kong is famous for its diversity and contrasts. Its tiny borders create a crowded space for the confluence of wealth, poverty, tradition, transience, centrality, marginality, urban, rural, East, West, and nearly everything else. Within Hong Kong, The Church of Jesus Christ of Latter-day Saints comes into focus as a dynamic global faith in which powerful forces of sameness and diversity exert themselves side by side. This productive tension is especially apparent during the Church's worldwide general conference broadcasts in April and October.

When conference comes to the Wanchai building, elevators are stuffed and stairwells fill with congregants tromping to and from rooms on floors of the building where the Salt Lake City broadcast is being streamed in Cantonese, Mandarin, Tagalog, English, and Bahasa Indonesian. There are so many languages zooming back and forth over the building's multimedia network that sometimes it goes haywire. In the middle of one English-language conference meeting in October 2012, Relief Society General Counselor Linda S. Reeves suddenly began speaking Korean, necessitating a flurry of tech-shifting strategies and some impromptu congregational hymn singing until she could be reacquired in English.[*]

It would be possible to see the multiple floors of the Wanchai building as a symbol of the stratified nature of Hong Kong society or the Church's highly regulated, top-down administrative hierarchy. And yet, in the Wanchai building one can also see the kind of democratic leveling effects produced by Latter-day Saint community structure. After the conclusion of one general Relief Society meeting (now the women's session of general

---

[*] "Relief Society" is the name for the Church's organization for women. The context for its name is that when it was first established in the mid-nineteenth century in the United States, female benevolent societies or charitable associations were a popular mode of women's organization.

conference), I watched with amusement as the vice president of operations at Hong Kong Disneyland and a professor at the University of Hong Kong (both white, well-to-do US expatriates) bent over a table, a wild look in their eyes as they frantically cored, sliced, and served Granny Smith apples to the intimidatingly long line of mostly Filipina domestic workers snaking back and forth across the gym.

The Wanchai building is a different sort of haven to different groups of Latter-day Saints. While most Indonesian and Filipina domestic workers in Hong Kong spend their day off in crowded parks and underpasses, sitting on plastic tarps, Indonesian and Filipina sisters in the Wanchai building make good use of the sofas, kitchens, and clean bathrooms as they socialize, engage in spiritual study, and recharge for the week. While most early childhood music classes in Hong Kong are expensive and commercialized, expatriate mothers use the second floor Primary room every Thursday to run a cooperative "Musicmakers" class and swap local knowledge.

The majority of church members view the Sunday session of general conference on a Sunday, but in Hong Kong this is not necessarily the case. Like deep-sea hydrothermal vents that sustain rare forms of life, the transient and fragmented nature of Hong Kong society has provoked unconventional forms of Latter-day Saint congregation. Domestic workers whose day off does not fall on Sunday attend the sabbath services on Tuesday, Wednesday, Thursday, Friday, or Saturday. Two senior missionary couples from North America are assigned to superintend these full three-hour-block weekday meetings. They get Sundays off to go shopping, go to Disneyland, and generally take a sabbath from the sabbath.

Another way in which the Hong Kong domestic worker units are unusual is in their leadership structure. Leadership positions in nearly all Latter-day Saint congregations worldwide are dominated by men, including the executive secretary and ward or branch mission leader; the highest-ranking local female leader, the Relief Society president, is seen as an "auxiliary" leader with special stewardship over only the portion of the congregation that is female. Yet in the overwhelmingly female domestic worker branches of Hong Kong, the Relief Society president exercises stewardship over nearly everyone in the congregation, and the executive secretaries and branch mission leaders are women. (When I asked a sister in the Island 1 Branch if the branch mission leader was really a woman, she gave me a blank look, as if I had asked whether Spiderman was really a man.)

When conference comes to the Wanchai building, the same talk on the blessings of paying tithing is broadcast in five different languages to people from over a dozen different countries whose incomes can range from 4,000 USD a year to 4,000 USD a month or more. When the Western expatriate branch and the Filipina branch watch conference in English together in the big chapel on the first floor, the two groups often respond differently at different points in the talk. You might hear an audible gasp from one contingent while the other is silent, or laughter from one while the other doesn't quite understand what was funny.

All of this difference and disjuncture comes together in a building in Wanchai that is a welcome place of spiritual, physical, and cultural refuge to Latter-day Saints from all walks of life. It works. By "works," I don't mean in the sense of "runs like a well-oiled machine," but rather that it relies on the sustained effort of many moving parts (i.e., people) in order to build the body of Christ, supply miraculous answers to prayers in the form of service, and fan the flame of faith against the suffocations of a dreary world.

This Hong Kong church culture where general conference is viewed is no less authentic or representative than the Salt Lake church culture where general conference is produced. In the global community, the homogenizing and heterogenizing impulses within the faith reinforce each other. The impulse to sameness stems not just from the church's centralized administration, but most profoundly from our shared faith in the teachings of the restored gospel of Jesus Christ. The impulse to diversity stems from our view of Zion as not merely an idea or a belief, but a real community. Not only in Hong Kong, but from Los Angeles to Lubumbashi, these forces of sameness and difference come together in Latter-day Saint congregations—demanding ongoing negotiation and innovation, but also imparting strength and value to the community of faith because of the effort they constantly require.

TOXIC RELIGION?
THE PARABLE OF THE PAN

12 November 2014

First published online at the Peculiar People blog, Patheos.com

On 12 November 2014, a new "Gospel Topics" essay appeared on lds.org, the Church's official website. Over time, the "Gospel Topics" section had been populated with thoughtful and candid essays on topics considered controversial or sensitive, including "Book of Mormon and DNA Studies" and "Peace and Violence among 19th-Century Latter-day Saints." This new essay, "Plural Marriage in Kirtland and Nauvoo," dealt with the often-murky details of the practice of plural marriage under Joseph Smith Jr. in early church history. Latter-day Saints who are encountering these difficult topics for the first time often experience dismay and disillusionment. The essay below, first written as a response to fellow Latter-day Saints wrestling with jarring new perspectives, expresses my view that by virtue of their being at least a partially human endeavor, all religious movements are prone to flaws, but also very precious, in their own way.

There are "winners and losers" in the wake of the public acknowledgment by The Church of Jesus Christ of Latter-day Saints that its founder, Joseph Smith, practiced polygamy. The Church itself is a clear winner. This step in the direction of transparency signals the Church's maturity and adaptability in the twenty-first century. The acknowledgment is also vindicating for scholars who have worked hard to promulgate a nuanced narrative of church history that avoids the extremes of demonization on one hand and whitewashing on the other.

In spite of these gains, however, there is also a sense of real loss among Latter-day Saints used to thinking of Joseph Smith as a man beyond reproach. Even if one accepts some church historians' premise that Smith's polygamous marriages were in strict obedience to divine command, to learn for the first time that Smith concealed some of his additional marriages from his wife, Emma, for whom his polygamy was "an excruciating ordeal," can be jarring.[1] Given the Church's current emphasis on strengthening family relationships, especially trust and fidelity within marriage, the thought that such deceptive behavior could have played any part in the Church's founding story can be a bitter pill indeed.

More broadly, Latter-day Saints' wholehearted desire to share their faith with all can sometimes make it easier for them to see flaws in others' beliefs, values, or religious institutions, than in their own. Suddenly coming face-to-face with the same kinds of flaws or problems within one's own tradition can be very disorienting. It can feel sickening. It can leave a terrible taste in one's mouth.

The taste of religious disillusion is not a secret Latter-day Saint recipe but is in fact shared among many believers and former believers of various "organized" religious traditions. The institutionalization of the divine is a bold but fraught undertaking, conspicuously vulnerable to human error. I recall the struggles of a Catholic friend in Boston during the clerical abuse scandals of 2003 and the detachment of a friend in Auckland looking back on her former evangelical zeal and seeing it as misguided.

I first tasted this bitterness myself many years ago, as a university student.

A few months ago, I tasted it again when I boiled sodium bicarbonate in my favorite saucepan. Let's call it the Parable of the Pan, or Is Your Cookware Toxic?

The Parable of the Pan

My cousin was researching cookware online. Aluminum and cast iron were reactive (certain foods would trigger chemical reactions and form metallic precipitates). Nonstick pans emitted poisonous gases under high heat. Even stainless steel cookware, she told me, apparently "contained toxins."

I had always known about the risks associated with certain forms of cookware but had always believed that my stainless steel pots and pans were safe. Troubled, I googled "stainless steel toxins."

I found a website that stated that every kind of commonly used cookware was in fact hazardous. It suggested a home "toxicity test" that involved boiling one tablespoon of sodium bicarbonate (baking soda) in one cup of water in a pan for five minutes and then tasting it to see if any metals had leached into the water. For comparison, the taste of the "cooking-pan" water could be compared to the taste of 1 tablespoon of baking soda simply dissolved into hot water.

I went ahead with the test, using my favorite saucepan. After just five minutes, the water that had been boiled with baking soda had a suspicious tint. I first tasted the dissolved mixture to get a baseline: salty, but clean-tasting. Then I tasted the boiled pan water.

Phlegh! I spat it out. It tasted like a dirty bike chain.

I was shocked and disgusted. The trusty stainless steel saucepan I'd been using for years was actually leaching toxic chemicals into our food! We could never use this toxic pan again. I chucked it in the trash.

Then further suspicions crept into my mind. What about the rest of our cookware? The stockpot, the sauté pan, the enameled cast iron Dutch oven? Were they, too, leaching heavy metals into our pasta sauce?

I conducted the test with each kind of cookware in our cabinet and laid them all out on the living room floor for a family taste test. I placed spitting receptacles at strategic intervals.

Even now, just recalling this taste test is provoking a physical response in my body. My mouth is watering in an attempt to defensively dilute the harsh, bitter tastes best described as "Scraped Nails," "Industrial Solvent," and "Magnet Tea." From enameled cast iron to hard anodized aluminum, the taste of the water boiled in these pans varied slightly but was over-whelmingly nasty. After the taste test we all rinsed our mouths several times. Despite these efforts, the bitter taste stayed in my mouth for the rest of the day.

What was I to do with these "toxic" pots? I considered throwing them all away. But then what? Would I put the whole family on a raw food diet of oranges, lettuce, and sprouted lentils? Would I sizzle sausages on a stone slab? Returning to the website that had recommended the "toxicity test" in the first place, I saw that this website sold (very expensive) titanium pans, which, unsurprisingly, did not react with sodium bicarbonate.

In the end, I thought: *stir-fried veggies are good.* I kept them all.

Let those with buds to taste, taste.

The metallic bitterness I tasted in the Parable of the Pan is not unlike my initial taste of disillusionment upon first encountering Joseph Smith not as a handsome, infallible superhero, but as a complicated, flawed hu-man being. One of my first reactions was to consider giving up altogether and either becoming a Quaker or going off to harvest my own raw spiri-tuality in the wild. And yet as I studied more about church history and about religious history from Buddhism to Pentecostalism, the more I real-ized that flawed, human elements are an integral part of all major religious movements. If you want to cook your food, the fundamental reality you will have to accept is that cooking pans are made in factories, out of alloys of nickel and chromium.

Organized religion is like that pan. Religious traditions provide the discursive and logistical vessels of communal religious experience. To be sure, these "divine vessels" can be so jarringly manmade in both their ma-terials and the methods by which they came to be. One does not simply pluck a Torah off a tree or peel a fresh-picked Communion. The mainte-nance of any distinctive tradition involves hardware, assembly lines, and the work of many human hands. Composed of such human elements, is it any wonder that under certain (shockingly commonplace) circumstances, a bitter taste can leach out? And yet these human alloys form tools for making good things.[2]

I can't speak for my friends whose experiences with religion have left them with a persistent bitter taste in their mouths. Nor, in the scope of this short piece, can I explain my experience of the Divine within this particular space of faith, practice, and relationships. But the Parable of the Pan suggests that when it comes to religion, being a pragmatist has its hazards but being a purist can mean missing out on a lot.

For myself, wrestling with uncomfortable aspects of my faith's history and administration is a liability I'm willing to accept, though it is sometimes bitter work. Through my faith, I've stood in holy places with people I love—people who have taught my children to want to be kind, people in whose service I have cooked food and preached sermons, people who have known my faults and forgiven me. Despite the loftiness of the divine aspirations that have inspired religious movements throughout history, it is the humanness of the project that is both most problematic and most inspiring.

CONVERSATIONS ARE LIKE CASSEROLES

DIFFICULT TOPICS AND THE SECOND GREAT COMMANDMENT

6 May 2013

First published online at the Peculiar People blog, Patheos.com

During conference in October 2007, at the end of Relief Society General President Julie Beck's now-famous talk, "Mothers Who Know," I made a derisive sound from my perch on the living room couch. Once again, began a commentator's voice inside my head, a talk for women that focuses largely on domestic roles: "nurturing," "homemaking," "cooking, washing clothes and dishes, and keeping an orderly home," and "Latter-day Saint women should be the best homemakers in the world."

My mother, who at that time was traveling through the eye of the storm of cancer that had begun in 2006 and that eventually took her life at the end of 2008, heard me and looked up wearily. After months of chemotherapy, just sitting in an armchair made her tired. I could see that my reaction had hurt her. She asked, "Do you have a problem with anything in that talk?"

My insides contracted, shrink-wrapped with a film of guilt. Here was my mother, acutely facing her own mortality and trying to make sense of her life, which had centered around precisely the kind of cooking, washing, and homemaking President Beck had described. Here I was, her daughter, saying "Pfftt."

I had intended to strike a blow against the impersonal forces of Gender Inequality, but somehow I had accidentally hurt someone I loved.

113

Somehow, I had drawn a battle line where one didn't properly belong. Actually, I didn't have a problem with the actual activities President Beck was asking people to undertake in her talk. I absolutely believe that the mundane physical chores of parenting are imbued with spiritual power. Now that I have children of my own, I truly appreciate the awesome investment of time, talent, and pure grit my mother and father made in the process of raising my four brothers and me. Call it nurturing, homemaking, or war, it is definitely not for the faint of heart. On this fundamental point my mother, President Beck, and I were all on the same side.

So what went wrong? How had I ended up reacting in a way that contradicted not only my actual views on motherhood but also my desire to express appreciation for my own mother?

Looking back, I think the problem was that I had responded to President Beck's talk as a partisan, or in other words, as someone who interpreted her remarks not on their face value but solely in their relation to an entire ideological "platform." This platform of mine included not only planks such as "Jesus atoned for my sins" and "Joseph Smith restored divine truths," but also "Church talks should be inclusive of a diverse membership" and "Thank you, O God, for prophets like Gordon B. Hinckley, who said to the young women of the Church, 'The whole gamut of human endeavor is now open to women. There is not anything that you cannot do if you will set your mind to it.'"[1]

When President Beck said "homemaking," my partisan ears heard "narrow—not the whole platform" and effectively closed to the entire talk. Such knee-jerk partisanship may be standard for electoral politics, but in the realm of real people and actual relationships it is a blunderous and bludgersome instrument that "worketh not the righteousness of God" (James 1:20).

Current conversations in the Church regarding gender equality and sexual orientation are frequently characterized by such partisan approaches. In these wars of words, casualties occur on both sides. For instance, during the Wear Pants to Church Day event in December 2012, some Latter-day Saint women expressed the pain they feel because of their exclusion from most decision-making positions within the Church's worldwide administration. At the same time, some Latter-day Saint women and men felt hurt because they felt such activism constituted a personal attack on their beliefs and church participation.

The "passion" (i.e., zeal, contempt, and even death threats) attending such intrareligious exchanges signals that we must by all means keep working through these conversations on gender and sexuality within The Church of Jesus Christ of Latter-day Saints.

If you're a Latter-day Saint, these conversations are your problem. On the one hand, even if you feel that the current status quo is the best of all possible worlds, there is still a real possibility that your child, grandchild, or someone under your stewardship may leave the Church on account of these issues. In light of the current hemorrhage in church membership, especially among young people, it makes sense to address people's sincere concerns in an open and safe setting, instead of treating them as taboo or suspect.

On the other hand, if you feel that limitations on women's spiritual leadership opportunities are obvious and troubling, many other women do not share this view.[2] Gaining news coverage in major media outlets is not as important as starting grassroots conversations. Only the latter approach can replace the adversarial "aura" around women's issues with a spirit of cooperation and common sense.

Fundamentally, our willingness to engage these controversial issues of gender and sexuality is a test of whether or not we believe that the Second Great Commandment remains in force (Matthew 22:36–40). Loving neighbors, enemies, and friends-of-friends-on-Facebook does not have to mean compromising one's own beliefs or ignoring points of sincere disagreement. But it does require people to take the time to disagree respectfully. This includes understanding other people's views well enough to focus disagreement on a specific point or argument instead of entirely dismissing or condemning the people who hold those views.

Proven models for dialogue can be found at the Foundation for Religious Diplomacy (FRD, religious-diplomacy.org), an organization dedicated to inter- and intrareligious dialogue, with which I have been affiliated since 2009.[3] In 2010 and 2012 I worked with FRD and the City of Los Angeles Human Relations Commission to convene a dialogue of several local religious leaders, including Latter-day Saints, from both sides of Proposition 8 (a controversial ballot measure that proposed banning gay marriage).

In these dialogues on Prop 8, I saw that FRD's model, which emphasizes trust, not agreement, really works. I believe this model can stand up to the even tougher test of intrareligious contention over issues of gender and sexuality. In a nutshell, FRD's approach to dialogue, called the Way of Openness, comes down to several potent attitudes and practices:

- Be Honest
- Be Kind
- Listen Well
- Share the Floor
- Presume Good Will
- Acknowledge the Differences
- Answer the Tough Questions
- Give Credit Where Credit Is Due
- Speak Only for Yourself
- Keep Private Things Private

Some people might feel as if chatting up "angry activists" or "ignorant reactionaries" at church is not worth their time. And yet, engaging someone in dialogue requires just the same generosity and gumption as any other sort of Christlike service. When someone needs a meal, we automatically volunteer to spend one to two hours of precious time washing greens, stir-frying chicken, cutting fruit, and delivering everything to the door. When someone needs to move, it's a no-brainer to spend half the day cleaning bathrooms, painting walls, and schlepping chests of drawers. So when someone takes a stance on a gender or sexual orientation issue that is completely opposite from our own and yet fundamental to that person's testimony of the gospel, we should be willing to give twenty minutes to listen.

In our conversations, when we hear potentially offensive comments like, "Those feminists just don't understand God's plan," or "People who oppose change in the Church are completely ignorant of church history and doctrine," our knee-jerk reaction should be active listening. The people with whom we disagree on a specific issue must be able to feel our love and respect for them as people who deeply desire to be part of the body of Christ. As we read in 1 Corinthians 12:21, this mutual awareness will save us from the delusion that we can simply say to another member of Christ's body, "I have no need of thee."

On far too many occasions, including after President Beck's 2007 conference talk, I have adopted a spirit of partisan dismissiveness instead of earnest engagement to express disagreement, and each time I have been the poorer for it.

And yet the more I practice, the more I learn: Be honest. Be specific. Be kind. The miracle of Zion's one heart and one mind was not that all members of the community had been born identical, but that they had chosen to love and serve each other despite—or perhaps because of—their diversity.

ELECTRIC (MUTUAL) JOY

10 November 2015

First published online at the Peculiar People blog, Patheos.com

On the 6th of November 2015, news broke of a church policy stating that Latter-day Saint children belonging to a household with same-sex parents could not be blessed as babies and could not be baptized until they reached adulthood. Upon reaching the age of eighteen, children could be baptized and join the Church, provided they disavowed their parents' practice of same-sex cohabitation or marriage and stopped living within the household. In a video, Elder D. Todd Christofferson explained that while the Church worked to protect "rights and employment and housing and that sort of thing for all," the Church also desired "to teach and abide by its own doctrines."[1] This policy provoked heated discussions within Latter-day Saint communities.

Sharp divisions make it hard to pinpoint "how people feel" about the policy barring children of same-sex parents from blessing or baptism in The Church of Jesus Christ of Latter-day Saints. But—thinking about electricity—these three things are true:

1. Our faith is charismatic (the electric current).
2. Our faith is organized (the insulated network).
3. Our faith is living—comprised of real human beings (the power within a living body).

By "charismatic" (from the term *charismata*, or gifts of the Holy Spirit, including visions, healings, prophecy, etc.) I mean that its existence as a religious tradition is predicated on certain miraculous stories being real: first and foremost, the wondrous birth and life of Jesus Christ, and later, the visions and prophetic calling of Joseph Smith. This live connection to God's power through prophetic and also personal revelation is like high-voltage current—a source of power but also a serious liability. On the one hand, the personal experience of the Spirit is truly miraculous—a blessed anomaly, a life-changing reorientation, a joy. On the other hand, in the history of religious movements, charismatic power inevitably leads to schisms because it provides an alternative basis for spiritual authority, independent of church hierarchies.

By "organized," I mean that religious life unfolds not only within an individual's inner spiritual progression, but within the context of a local community and the centralized, correlated, official hierarchy of The Church of Jesus Christ of Latter-day Saints. Handbooks prescribe exactly how to perform rites, capitalize words, and define acceptable and unacceptable community behavior. Layers and layers of institutional structures have been built up—and continue to accumulate—with the intention of channeling what is beneficial and insulating against what is potentially destabilizing in the Church's charismatic claims. These highly bureaucratized structures are like insulation around the wire—limiting the directions in which power may flow, rechanneling energy, guarding against shock. For example, if a Latter-day Saint bishop hears a congregant proclaiming that God has commanded him to sacrifice his young son on an altar with a kitchen knife and start a new Church of Jesus Christ of Latter-day Abrahams, the bishop will intervene (with the backing of a section in the Handbook that states that abuse of a child cannot be tolerated in any form).

By "living" I mean that our faith is made up of individual Latter-day Saints who are producers of religion just as much as they are consumers of it. Our faith is not defined by creeds (standardized expressions of core doctrine) but by councils (groups of Latter-day Saints acting together). Those who currently occupy the highest levels of leadership were all originally chosen from the ranks of weekend Sunday School teachers and youth leaders and asked to spend more and more time (and eventually all their time) sitting on church councils. In this sense, the distance between the Church's top leadership and lay members can be quite close in terms of everyday experience and shared culture, although of course there are wide variations globally between the experience of members in, say, Spanish Fork, Utah, and the experience of members in Mitaka, Japan. Our religious tradition is not a monolith—not its top leadership, not its culture, and not its people. It is a living body, animated by electric impulses, comprised of many diverse systems, organs, and cells.

Those who view the policy as evidence that all Latter-day Saints are homophobes or that church leaders are entirely unsympathetic to sexual minorities are mistaken. Many Latter-day Saints are passionate advocates for the rights of minority groups, including the LGBTQ community. The Church has supported civil rights legislation for LGBTQ persons in Utah and donated substantial funds to support programs for LGBTQ youth. In an official video in November 2015, Elder D. Todd Christofferson attempted to show good faith and integrity as he explained the Church's approach to a complex and sensitive issue. To me, in this video he came across as sincere—though clearly uncomfortable because he anticipates that many will doubt his sincerity—when he said that if you believe that a person's behavior is grievously wrong and contrary to God's commandments, you do that person no favors by pretending her behavior is acceptable to God. According to the dialogue conventions of the Foundation for Religious Diplomacy, here he would be "answering the tough questions" as he shared his deeply held beliefs with integrity and candor.

Those who think that Latter-day Saints who feel consternation at the new policy simply lack faith, are wrong. Despite the compassionate intent Elder Christofferson expressed in his video recording, the policy has created or reopened deep emotional wounds in LGBTQ Latter-day Saints and their family members. As described by Tom Christofferson, Elder Christofferson's gay brother, in an interview shortly after the policy was announced, the policy perpetuated "the problem of treating people as groups instead as individuals," without making clear allowances for various compassionate and pastorally sensible arrangements.[2] Baptisms eagerly awaited on the following weekend were canceled. Children sent to Primary by parents in mixed-orientation and same-sex marriages now stand to be stigmatized and, even more significantly, barred from receiving Christ and developing sensitivity to the companionship of the Holy Ghost in their formative years. Many struggle to understand how it is in keeping with the second article of faith, or helpful for the formation of children's spiritual identity, to exclude children from baptism because of their parents'—or one parent's—choices.[3] The deep pain felt by LGBTQ Latter-day Saints and their children is cause for sorrow among all who have covenanted to mourn with those who mourn.[4]

This sharp disagreement over the Christlike course of action has been confusing for many. We are a worldwide church held together, despite vast cultural divides, by common emulation of Jesus Christ. In his earthly ministry as recorded in the scriptures, Jesus never said anything about marriage except for a comment on divorce, but he is much better known for declaring that the greatest commandment after loving God was to love others as ourselves. The power of Christ's love is real, and the reason why people become and remain Latter-day Saints is because they have felt it—through the Holy Spirit, and through people. Living this second great commandment brings the Spirit and gives life joy. This is why many people's reactions are so raw. They perceive a conflict between Christ's charismatic pattern of ignoring religious rules to embrace social and spiritual outcasts, and the organizational boundary-keeping set out in the policy.

These three elements—charisma, organization, people—exist in a state of dynamic tension and have shaped Latter-day Saint life for close to two centuries. In their various combinations they have brought about numerous doctrines, practices, policies, and ways of life, including temple ordinances, polygamy, worldwide evangelization, women's healing blessings, the cessation of polygamy, the cessation of women's healing blessings, the exclusion of Black Latter-day Saints from the temple and the priesthood, the Church welfare system, the inclusion of Black Latter-day Saints in the temple and the priesthood, video recordings of temple ordinances, translations of temple ordinances into dozens of languages, humanitarian wheelchairs, and wells for clean water.

If we look beyond the bounds of religion and define the charismatic more broadly as compelling, universalistic moral ideology, the productive tension between charismatic and institutional impetuses drives nearly all large human organizations: Pope Francis's Catholic church, the government of the United States of America, the Chinese Communist Party. Like the grinding forces in an electric generator, it is this tension between extraordinary ideals and everyday rules that keeps the power flowing. Both are essential. You can't just have divine love, and you can't just have handbooks.

This policy has brought to the fore divisions over core interpretations of church community. People have taken to social media, email, and Sunday School to declare support or dismay, to report personal divine revelation both for and against the policy. They have ranted. They have wept. They have taken their concerns to God. How does it all work? How do our Heavenly Parents feel when their children fight over how to be good? I have no idea. Fortunately, as is the case with all eternal relationships—and as my Uncle Dillon would say—"the first million years are the hardest."

One certain thing is that the rhetoric of church leaders and members on same-sex attraction has evolved in the direction of greater understanding and sympathy, considering where we were twenty years ago, and will continue to evolve. Since the policymakers have claimed that they intended it as a compassionate measure, I am hopeful that they will diligently seek to understand how it has affected Latter-day Saint families and take measures to repair the torn fabric of our community. I anticipate that future actions will be more effective in demonstrating love and understanding. This is not about political correctness, but about protecting the religious community's very life. True, at various points in a religion's existence, people are asked to simply "get in line." But over time, long queues do not make for thriving charismatic movements, and charisma is the Church's lifeblood. Without the electric joy that flows from a mutual experience of the love of Jesus Christ, we will struggle, limited in our ability to succor those in need.

Of the three statements with which I began this piece, the last is most important: Our faith is living. We Latter-day Saints live our religion within a dense network of relationships, vertical and horizontal. With the vitality and intimacy of these relationships comes real responsibility—more than a citizen owes to an elected official or vice versa, more than a midfielder owes to a team. Our practice within a lay leadership structure gives us familiarity with the refining processes of leading and being led, making mistakes and making amends.

The key to moving forward as a church that desires to be defined by common faith in Jesus Christ is to reach out to each other, to speak candidly and humbly in councils and in private, to bind up wounds and to apologize where unintentional hurt has been inflicted. We have stood shoulder to shoulder in holy places and covenanted to love and serve one another, with God as our witness. The Church of Jesus Christ of Latter-day Saints is not an organizational machine of cranks and cogs that are easily replaced, but the body of Christ, powerful and electric, sensitive and fragile, with limbs and organs we cannot afford to slough off. To either bring to pass the compassionate intent or mitigate the hurtfulness of this policy, we must each do our part within our own families and congregations. Here, we must find the charity that will help us keep our covenants and restore our mutual ties.

WHAT ANA SAID

30 May 2018
Auckland, New Zealand

The other day my cousin in Colorado emailed me to ask how to a respond to an eleven-year-old girl, who, in the middle of a sharing time lesson on the blessings of the priesthood, blurted out, "But girls don't get the priesthood" and "The men are in charge of the women."

"How would you respond?" my cousin asked. "I didn't know what to say."

I'll talk through possible responses below, but first I would like to acknowledge that Latter-day Saint family members and friends would answer this question in different ways, many of which would be starkly contradictory. For various reasons, the gender topic is a can of worms. This essay will probably offend and annoy many of my fellow Latter-day Saints in multiple ways. Nevertheless, I am writing it, because the eleven-year-old in Colorado—let's call her Ana—has raised a heartfelt concern, and I feel like I owe her the best answer I can come up with.

I have tried to think through a range of various responses according to my experience as a mother, Primary leader, Young Women leader, and university professor who frequently interacts with bright, energetic young women. I have given all of these responses at one point in my life. Regardless of how we grew up thinking about gender, if we want our children to desire to nurture the seed of faith in the twenty-first century, we have to start doing some things differently.

Kids these days

When I was growing up, I never paid attention to the issue of gender. I was the oldest of five children, with four younger brothers. I feel like I was basically raised as my father's oldest boy. He was the ward Scoutmaster, so I accompanied the boys on a number of scout hikes and campouts. When I didn't go on the hikes and campouts, it was no big deal. I liked Young Women activities, which were less structured than my brothers' Boy Scout activities, but gave me a chance to hang out with the girls my age. We didn't hang out at school—the other girls were all way more popular than I—but we had grown up together, and we were friends. I also loved my Young Women leaders, warm and lively women who were willing to show up for us.

As a kid and as a teenager, I never noticed that female leaders always had to ask male leaders for permission or knew that the ward budget was controlled exclusively by men. I never looked at the chart in the *Ensign* showing portraits of all the top church leaders and wondered why none of them were women. In my childhood, men doing the work "on the stand" and women doing the work "behind the scenes" was the water in which I swam.

Now, in the twenty-first century, girls and boys are being raised with a strong, clear message that girls are just as capable as boys. We are teaching them to recognize and question assumptions, deeply embedded in our culture, mistakenly suggesting that women are inherently weak or less competent than men, such as the phrase "throw like a girl" to describe a feeble throw. We explain studies on unconscious bias showing that when musicians auditioned for professional orchestras, men tended to be selected at much higher rates than women, but after the introduction of screens to conceal the musician's gender from the selection jury, these "blind auditions" increased the likelihood of women being selected by 30 percent.[1] We coach girls on how to push back against coercion and sexual harassment. We teach boys that respect for women means not engaging in intimate contact or sexual acts without consent. We point to the female prime ministers, presidents, Olympic athletes, Supreme Court justices, astronauts, doctors, and CEOs who are role models for strength, leadership, and perseverance.

These teachings are not evil propaganda or trendy falsehoods but are truthful and inspired. They embody our Latter-day Saint beliefs that "every person is a beloved son or daughter of Heavenly Parents, with a divine purpose and destiny," [2] and that "all are alike unto God" (2 Nephi 26:33). They help our children see beyond the crass and false teachings of the world that objectify women. They empower young people with empathy in the project of following Christ's commandment to love others as ourselves, and to see strangers as neighbors. They help reinforce our girls' understanding that they have the potential to become as God, beings of infinite power and wisdom.

And yet, this new and welcome awareness of the strength and capability of women can be a liability at church, where the official institutional roles for defining religious orthodoxy, making final decisions on behalf of the congregation, allocating budgets, and administering sacred rites are filled primarily or exclusively by men and boys. Our daughters and sons now notice this. Indeed, as shown in Jana Riess's recent study of American Latter-day Saints in their twenties and thirties, while only one out of four American Latter-day Saints of the baby boomer generation said they strongly or somewhat agreed with the statement, "It bothers me that women don't have the priesthood," six out of ten American Latter-day Saint millennials (a majority) said they were bothered.[3] No wonder, then, that eleven-year-old Ana exclaimed, "But girls don't get the priesthood" and "The men are in charge of the women."

Four possible answers

My cousin describes Ana as "pleasant and confident, curious and observant," a good artist who likes to do back handsprings when she's outside. Ana is about to move to a new town but is sure she'll be able to make friends because "I'm not afraid to talk to people." We owe her a response that will stick with her as she's growing up and searching for her own testimony. How might we respond to her expressed concerns? I thought through a couple of scenarios, all of which make very important points, but which I think are ultimately insufficient:

1. "You're right: boys get the priesthood, and the men are in charge of the women at church. But girls get to be mothers, and they get to be in charge of the kids at home."

As a mother of four children, who formed their bodies within my womb, labored to bring them into the world for their first breath, and nourished them for several months with just the milk from my breasts (the original superpowers), I absolutely recognize the power of mothers. This power, of course, includes but also goes beyond jiggling babies and changing diapers. When I think about my mother's lifelong influence in shaping my talents, values, and ability to believe in things I can't see, there is no way to quantify it.

Still, this response doesn't work for two reasons. First, the male parallel to motherhood is not priesthood, but fatherhood. Creating new life requires both a man and a woman. A male parent is called a father. A female parent is called a mother. True, only women's bodies can give birth, but they can't do it on their own. There's a reason why a virgin birth is considered miraculous. Hence, motherhood would be a more appropriate parallel to priesthood if women could generate babies within their wombs at will, without any external influences. Motherhood would also be a more appropriate parallel to priesthood if church callings, not fatherhood, were men's paramount sacred duty. "Priesthood for boys, motherhood for girls" completely omits the sacred role of fatherhood and the divine mission of preparing to be a father. My father's influence in shaping my talents, values, and ability to believe in things I can't see is also inestimable. David O. McKay said that nothing, not even church service at the highest level, is more important than one's work within the family, but this is the message sent by this false priesthood-motherhood dichotomy.

Second, currently in the Church, an eleven- or twelve-year-old boy can be ordained to the priesthood, but we do not want girls to become mothers at this age. Because of this, it makes sense to me that we should either ordain only mature, married men to the priesthood or give eleven- and twelve-year-old girls formal spiritual roles and duties throughout their teenage years and beyond that parallel the formal spiritual roles and duties that commence in the year a boy turns twelve. These parallels should continue throughout adulthood. Fulfilling sacred responsibilities with diligence is something over which both girls and boys, women and men, have individual control. By contrast, girls and women who desire to marry or have children nevertheless do not have full control over contingencies such as whether they will be able to find a suitable marriage partner, conceive, carry a pregnancy to term, and so on.[4] Saying to a woman who is unmarried, or who has not been able to have children, "After you die, you'll finally be able to fulfill your life's great sacred purpose" is a terrible idea. I hope I don't have to explain why.

2. "Well, men have the priesthood, so they sit on the stand on Sunday, but actually, women run the show—in the background, through activities, service, outreach, and ministering to one another and in their communities."

It is absolutely true that women shoulder a great deal, and perhaps even the greater portion, of the work of building Zion in terms of hours, sweat, and tears invested, and that this work is deeply meaningful. The Church as a whole could not function without the effort, leadership, and good ideas of women. Women serve as teachers, members of ward councils, Relief Society and Young Women presidents, and general officers. Moreover, living a Latter-day Saint life is much more than having a position within a church administrative hierarchy. It is about showing up to minister to people around us, to share their burdens, to consecrate our time and talents along with our experience and our pain to build up the people around us.

At the same time, this response does not adequately respond to Ana's concern. Ana's concern was not about whether women had influence. It was about who was ultimately in charge—who was at the top, and at the bottom, of the Church's hierarchical structures. At the local level, women are Primary teachers, Sunday School teachers, people in Primary, the Relief Society president, and so on. They all ultimately report to the bishop (or to the stake presidency if in stake positions). The bishop reports to the stake president. The stake president reports to an Area Seventy. The Area Seventies report to the Presidency of the Seventy. All the General Authorities report to the Twelve Apostles, who report to three members of the First Presidency. This entire vertical chain of authority—the authority to make decisions, to allocate budgets, to grant or withhold access to the temple, to discipline for spousal abuse, to excommunicate, to escalate concerns or relay ideas—is composed of men.

In April 2018, President Russell M. Nelson taught, "Good inspiration is based upon good information." He explained that he was not able to select two counselors for the First Presidency until he had first interviewed each apostle and prayerfully sought the Lord's will concerning who should serve with him. This principle that good inspiration is based on good information helps highlight the importance of information in decision-making. One cannot make a good decision with incomplete information. This teaching suggests ways in which we as a church can improve, by expanding the sources of information that shape decision-making to include women on par with men. Although church councils have recently been restructured in a way that includes more women, the authority to escalate matters and make decisions still rests primarily with men.

These men are largely good men, giving generously of their time, trying prayerfully to enact their considerable responsibilities to bless others' lives. But the very fact that they are all men, imperfect men, who are forming policy and staffing wards and stakes and adjudicating problems and church standing in the lives of men *and* women engenders some unintended consequences. Some of these consequences are even tragic. For instance, as recent church statements and ongoing news events have made clear, Latter-day Saint congregations, however admirable as a whole, are not immune from problems afflicting wider society. To choose an egregious example, we are not immune to the problem of spousal abuse, despite clear church policy condemning it. And we have the problem of women not always being taken seriously when they report such abuse to priesthood leaders. I am familiar with the stories of many of my Latter-day Saint sisters who have been denied temple recommends and callings because of opinions they expressed on social media or the internet, while men who have abused or been unfaithful to their wives, who are friendly with members of the bishopric, still hold temple recommends and prominent callings. When the abusers are themselves church authorities, women have little recourse. Men ultimately hold the keys of authority in the Church's governing structures at every level. The voice of higher spiritual authority is always male, and never female. These realities shape the dynamic between women and men within church communities and Latter-day Saint homes.

In his first talk as a new apostle, Elder Neil L. Andersen recalled a lesson that Boyd K. Packer once taught him about the peril of a culture of leader-worship. Standing at the pulpit, addressing the congregation, Elder Packer said, "I know who I am." After a pause, he continued, "I am a nobody." Then he turned to Elder Andersen, sitting on the stand behind him, and said, "And, Brother Andersen, you are a nobody too. If you ever forget it, the Lord will remind you of it instantly, and it won't be pleasant."[5] This story is refreshing because it provides a counterpoint to cultural conventions that proclaim clear distinctions in leaders' rank within the ecclesiastical hierarchy. The recipients of these cultural expressions of higher respect are overwhelmingly male. For example, in a local Sunday sacrament meeting, the highest-ranking priesthood authority (a man) is passed the sacrament first.[6] This would be the case even if the General Relief Society President, who is a general officer of our sixteen-million-member worldwide Church, came to speak, and the highest-ranking priesthood authority were the bishop, who is a local leader of, say, 250 of these members, in a set of neighborhoods. At the top level, apostles and members of the First Presidency follow the conspicuous practice of always entering and exiting rooms in order of seniority. This whole apparatus of ranks, orders of precedence, and titles sends a strong message of special respect for male church leaders and the hierarchy of the roles they fulfill. However, this apparatus is not currently used in a comparable way to show respect for female church leaders and women's roles. From General Relief Society Presidents to female missionaries with mission-wide leadership responsibilities, female leaders are addressed by the one title, "Sister," in contrast to the multiple tiers of male "Elders," "Bishops," and "Presidents." (This is a break from nineteenth-century practices, in which

Emma Smith was referred to as "President Emma Smith," local Relief Society presidents in Utah were regularly addressed as "President," and the General Relief Society President was called for life, like an apostle.) Ana, though only eleven years old, had imbibed this message about who should be shown respect in our institutional culture. It bothered her.

3. "Girls don't get the priesthood, and men are in charge of women, because this is how God wants it." This is a plausible answer, because I'm not God and I don't know what God wants, but we have to be ready for Ana's inevitable next question, which is "Why?"

I came up with some possible answers to that next question, but they're not convincing to me. "Because having a male body instead of a female body makes someone more like Heavenly Father?" It may seem impertinent to think too hard about this, but failure to do so allows a presumption to exist that may be neither true nor righteous. Clearly, when women are exalted and become gods, they do not acquire male bodies and become Heavenly Fathers. Our teaching is that they become Heavenly Mothers. We have no teachings that male physiology holds the key to exaltation and godhood.

Two other answers to Ana's "Why?" come to mind. Although both are a little extreme, I've heard versions of both of these viewpoints at church, implicitly or explicitly. "Because God created men to be more competent and spiritual than women"? (A common variation on this answer is "God wants women to follow their husbands' direction.") I don't think so. This is what people may have thought for thousands of years, including when men were writing ancient texts, including the scriptures. And it may have been what people thought more recently when they argued that women couldn't be trusted to vote. But such assertions now sound sexist, the product of human, not divine, thought. An equally implausible justification of gendered inequality might be phrased this way: "Because God created women to be more competent and spiritual than men, so God has to put men in charge so that it can all balance out." (A common variation on this answer is "Women are naturally spiritual giants, but men need to be in charge or else they'll go inactive and be immoral.") No. This speculation sounds too sexist—all too human.

Honestly, I don't have a good answer for Ana on this one. For behind her "Why" (does God want it this way?) lies a deeper query: *Does* God want it this way?

Probably you have been thinking about your own response to Ana. I don't think that any of these answers above will satisfy a smart girl in the twenty-first century over the long term, but what I actually said (i.e., suggested my cousin say) wasn't much better.

4. "You're right. That's how things are now, and I'm not sure why. However, we believe in continuing revelation, so we are always gaining more understanding, line upon line. Also, recently President Oaks taught that because the priesthood is the power of God, when both women and men serve at church, they are acting with priesthood authority."[7]

This answer, though the best I could come up with, is inadequate because it invites another difficult follow-up question from Ana or possibly her sixteen-year-old self, which is, "Why are men allowed to access all kinds of priesthood authority and to hold priesthood keys that allow them to direct and delegate this authority, while women are not allowed to access certain kinds of priesthood authority and are never given priesthood keys?"—put another way, "Why must women always have to ask to use someone else's keys?"

One good thing about acknowledging what we don't know is that such a response at least gives Ana room to think, grow, and have faith. The ninth article of faith—"We believe that God will yet reveal many great and important things pertaining to the kingdom of God"—has always been a source of faith and inspiration for me. Continuing revelation is cool. I felt energized to hear President Nelson say, in April 2018, that Jesus Christ still has yet to perform some of his mightiest works. I've always loved our unique teaching that the heavens are open, not just for individual help and comfort, but for inspiring big, important, organized work.

Of course, the Church is not just another big organization, interest group, club, institution, or system of democratic government. It is special. It is the kingdom of God on earth. It is the place where we are sisters and brothers, where we recognize each other's divine worth, where we honor truth and follow God's commandments. Although we aren't perfect, church is the place where we want to do things differently (better), in accordance with divine truth. Our church institutions should express our highest values and best practices.

This cherished expectation that The Church of Jesus Christ of Latter-day Saints should be special was perhaps why Ana could not withhold her outburst. If all are truly alike unto God, black and white, bond and free, male and female, why was there such a wide gap between men's and women's formal power at church? Church institutions should be noticeably better, or at least not noticeably worse, than secular workplaces, civic associations, and school environments, in terms of fostering organizational cultures that demonstrate respect for women on equal terms as men, and benefit from the rich perspectives and talents that women contribute.

Changing our culture to express our values

To be clear, in this essay I am not advocating that girls and women should be ordained to the priesthood.[8] Rather, I am advocating that we recognize the merit of Ana's concern (shared by women and men of all ages, but particularly poignant because she and others like her are the future of the Church) and do what we can, at all levels, to integrate girls and women into formal, authoritative structures and processes that make important decisions and receive visible respect. Even if some girls and women don't acutely feel a respect-deficit at church, many do. A close look at our institutional culture on the central and local levels shows that there are definitely things we could do to more powerfully express our values that women and men are equal partners in the work of God.[9]

Doing all we can to recognize and show respect for women's spiritual authority and work is important not because the purpose of going to church is to gain accolades—it's not—but because we do not want to be misunderstood. To paraphrase Thessalonians 5:22, we want to abstain from all appearance of disrespecting women. Some may think that it sounds "prideful" to say, "women should receive visible respect." Please consider the implications of negating or qualifying this statement. Would we say, "respect for women should be invisible" or "women should get respect, but not officially"? Clearly, giving and receiving visible respect are important aspects of our church culture. We just need to make sure that women are not excluded from this culture of authority and respect. Respect for women's divine nature and capabilities as full human beings should be clearly demonstrated in our administrative structures, policies, terminology, and culture.[10] We want to boldly proclaim, through word and deed, what we inwardly believe (another word for this is testimony).

Institutional culture, of course, is just one of many factors influencing our children to become and remain Latter-day Saints. Among the strongest of these factors is spousal and family respect and love at home. We cannot sit back and rely on the church institutions to make our children believers in God and disciples of Christ. At the same time, we cannot forget that when we teach our children to believe in God and follow Christ, we typically ask them to do so within the particular parameters of membership in The Church of Jesus Christ of Latter-day Saints. Because many of those baptized into the Church around the world eventually disaffiliate, it stands to reason that we need to do a better job of helping youth and young adults feel enthusiastic about this Church, specifically.[11] People's experiences at church, including the experience of respect and love, are bound to influence their desire to stay or go. In today's world, the language of respect and love is not "the women of the Church are so amazing," but the language of mutual power, expressed through titles and jobs and activities that are the same for peers, cutting across class, education, racial, and gender differences. Members of the rising generation—noticing that even when women are included on councils or invited to speak, ultimately the authority to make decisions and have the final word rests with men—may well observe this lack of formally shared power as a sign that love and respect are not equally given.[12]

Our own history contains indispensable resources for responding to Ana. In our past, Latter-day Saint teachings have included a robust doctrine of our Mother in Heaven. As explained in the Gospel Topics essay, "Mother in Heaven," in 1909, the First Presidency taught that "all men and women are in the similitude of the universal Father and Mother, and are literally the sons and daughters of Deity."[13] In their popular book, *The Christ Who Heals*, published by Deseret Book in 2017, Latter-day Saint authors Fiona and Terryl Givens point to the "familial pattern found in heaven": "As Elder Erastus Snow declared 'There never was a God, and there never will be in all eternities, except they are made of these two component parts; a man and a woman; the male and the female.'"[14] In premortal councils, they write, "our Heavenly Parents clarified precepts and instituted ordinances, along with a mortal educative process, for the purpose of establishing and eternalizing an endless web of familial relationships."[15]

In a 2011 article in *BYU Studies*, David Paulsen and Martin Pulido reviewed over six hundred references to Mother in Heaven in Latter-day Saint literature and concluded, "Several Church leaders have affirmed that Heavenly Mother is a fully divine person and have used reverential titles such as 'Mother God,' 'God Mother,' 'God the Mother,' and 'God their Eternal Mother,' and 'Eternal Mother' in referring to her."[16] For example, Paulsen and Pulido note, apostles like John A. Widtsoe and James E. Talmage declared, "[we have] a mother who possesses the attributes of Godhood,"[17] and "we are literally the sons and daughters of divine parents, the spiritual progeny of God our eternal Father, and of our God Mother."[18] Brigham Young taught, "We were created . . . in the image of our father and our mother, the image of our God."[19] The text of "The Family: A Proclamation to the World," first presented in September 1995, reads, "All human beings—male and female—are created in the image of God. Each is a beloved spirit son or daughter of heavenly parents, and, as such, each has a divine nature and destiny." Hence, we are children (sons and daughters) of God (heavenly parents).[20]

In recent decades, we've gotten somewhat out of the habit of including Heavenly Mother or Heavenly Parents when we talk about God, but all we need is some brushing up on this longstanding, powerful, and now extremely relevant Latter-day Saint teaching. On this score of giving respect and reverence to a female source of divine power, the Church has recently made significant strides, with increased references to "Heavenly Parents" and "Mother in Heaven" in official magazines and general conference.[21] If we take the cue from our leaders and embrace this renewed teaching, I believe it will make a tremendous difference toward a more balanced understanding of spiritual power in our culture.

Indeed, I am certain that leaders with authority to direct the Church are committed to addressing structural imbalances within our fellowship. Recently church institutions have taken small but encouraging steps to increase women's visibility, such as publishing the portraits of general female leaders alongside those of general male leaders, including general female leaders in some key governing councils, inviting women to pray in general conference, creating leadership structures for women within missions, encouraging young women to accompany older women in formally doing the ministering work of the Church, and so on. I am hopeful that ongoing revelation is in store. In the meantime, I will seek to lift where I stand.

Patriarchy is harmful for everyone

In an October 2017 address, Elder M. Russell Ballard boldly called on Latter-day Saints to "eliminate any prejudice, including racism, sexism, and nationalism."[22] Patriarchy (a hierarchical system in which the privileges of leadership and decision-making authority are reserved for men only, and in which men's voices and actions take precedence over women's) is inherently sexist. Without a doubt, the male-only quota system for formal church authority is spiritually damaging for men as well as women, for sons as well as daughters.

A culture in which only men can be in charge influences some boys and men to unconsciously believe that their opinions, preferences, and even well-being are automatically more important than those of the girls and women in their lives. It makes it harder for the cries of women and children in need of help, healing, and dignity to reach the ears of senior leaders. It inhibits people's ability to see and value others up to the full measure of how God sees and values them, leading to imbalanced relationships and even sinful disregard. It yokes women and men together unequally, hindering the work we must do together. Organizational structures that systematically privilege men's voices over women's voices inevitably bring forth the rotten fruits of abuse. Even one case of abuse is more than what should be acceptable, but the regularity with which abuse occurs within a Latter-day Saint context suggests that the status quo needs adjustment.

The negative unintended consequences of patriarchy are increasingly visible to many, though not all, among the younger generations. However, its negative effects on relationships between women and men can be experienced at all ages. My Aunt Mary[23] is a generation older than I and has served in many callings such as senior missionary overseas, stake Relief Society president, ward Relief Society president, Young Women leader, Primary leader, and so on. She is a cheerful soul, a stalwart member, and a pillar of her family. Speaking of the first time she noticed inequality as a woman at church, she said,

> I don't think this stood out to me as much until I was the director of an assisted living facility of 120 residents and noticed the difference in the way I was treated by men in that organization in contrast to the sometimes paternalistic and dismissive way some men in the church treated me as a leader. These are men that I worked with as ward and stake Primary president, stake Relief Society president and now as ward Relief Society president. They are men that I am very fond of personally and who treated me very kindly, though not equally.

Aunt Mary recalled how on several occasions, sisters went to priesthood leaders regarding their husbands' moral transgressions, but were not believed, "to the later detriment of the marriage and family." During her time as stake Relief Society president, she had dedicated considerable time and effort to working with the stake president to train bishops to not always take the man's side in cases of domestic abuse and adultery. Aunt Mary's observations did not come from a place of resentment that she had been treated dismissively, but regret that in failing to take seriously the female leaders and women within the congregation, male leaders who sincerely wanted to magnify their callings were unconsciously limiting their ability to serve and bless others.

I acknowledge that many Latter-day Saint family members and friends say they have never noticed or experienced sexism at church and that they feel fully valued and respected for the vital work they do in demanding callings. In my academic work, I have made the case that indeed, informal institutions and influence have tremendous gravity within the Church and that those who focus only on male-dominated formal institutions will miss the bigger picture. At the same time, formal institutions play a significant role in the life of the Church, and to the extent that they do not include women as full participants on par with men, the message they send is potentially very harmful.

In the same address from October 2018 about eliminating racism, sexism, and nationalism, Elder Ballard continued, "Let it be said that we truly believe the blessings of the restored gospel of Jesus Christ are for every child of God."[24] Elder Ballard's use of the phrase "let it be said" gestures toward the value of others viewing Latter-day Saints as people of fairness and integrity. We must do a better job of outwardly expressing our belief in the divine nature of every woman and man, created in the image of a Heavenly Mother and a Heavenly Father. And the people who most need to observe this faith in action, to see girls and women working alongside boys and men as spiritual equals, are not people "out in the mission field," but our daughters and sons who sit in church each Sunday.

The real investigators

Though we do not often see it in such terms, it is our children who are the real investigators at church. We can do our best to teach doctrine, to model our values, to show through our actions our love for the restored gospel and the powerful communities it creates. Ultimately, however, it is up to each Latter-day Saint girl, boy, young woman, and young man to choose to cultivate the seed of faith—to patiently nurture it and give it time to take root and become established. This is a long-term process that parents or church leaders cannot micromanage or coerce. It requires such dogged persistence (beyond baptism, beyond Primary, beyond a mission, beyond temple endowment and temple sealing, beyond a first and second and third crisis of faith) that unless individuals really, really *want* to believe, they will run out of steam.

In many places around the world, our daughters are growing up in a culture in which they expect to be treated as the full equals of men. If they go to university and find out that at this university, male professors are addressed as "Dr." and female professors are addressed as "Ma'am," many will switch universities. If they get a job at a law firm and discover that male associates write memos and go to court while female associates, equally prepared and intelligent, make copies and compile binders, many will switch law firms.

When they go to church, young women like Ana of the rising generation will be—and already are—much more sensitive to gendered asymmetries in language and duties than my own generation, or my mother's generation. Appeals to fulfillment in future wifehood and motherhood will not—and already do not—solve the problem for them because for their generation, being a sensitive spouse and nurturing parent are roles to which both men and women aspire. More than any generation heretofore, our daughters want to know whether there is a place for them in the institutions of the Church. They recognize that the Church is a special sort of organization (i.e., that it is led by divine revelation and is not a democratic republic or a gardening club), but they also see that it has a human institutional life, ranging from leadership to budgets to classes to social events to vacuuming. And if they perceive that the Church's institutions exclude women from decision-making authority and women's spiritual authority is always secondary to men's in church culture, they will switch churches. I'm no statistician, but among my own acquaintances I have seen this scenario frequently among moral, smart, Christlike young women from stalwart Latter-day Saint families.

Girls today are growing up with different expectations. An eight-year-old girl in my sister-in-law's Primary class in Austin, Texas, recently asked why women couldn't hold the priesthood. A four-year-old girl, my friend's daughter, recently observed the deacons passing the sacrament and asked if she could do that someday. Despite her parents' attempts to explain the facts of the matter gently, she was inconsolable to learn that according to existing policy, the answer was no, because she was a girl.

What are the messages we send, explicit and implicit, ritual and structural, in our words and in our deeds, that might dampen Ana's enthusiasm or create obstacles on our children's path to wholeheartedly embrace the work of building Zion? What are the asterisks that they might perceive as appended to the scriptural teaching, "all are alike unto God"? In other words, what are the ways in which we signal that God intends for women to receive the blessings and responsibilities of the restored gospel in a more limited, derivative, or less direct way than men? We need to ask ourselves how young people like Ana, with their fresh eyes and honest hearts, can help us see aspects of our institutions, liturgies, policies, and protocols that detract from the core project of accepting Christ's atonement and becoming more like our Heavenly Parents.

In the twenty-first-century Church, individual Latter-day Saints, women and men, participate in a broad range of activities that go far beyond the scope of performing priesthood ordinances such as baptizing and confirming. Latter-day Saints are called to give talks, direct meetings, teach lessons, allocate budgets, approve expenditures, listen to concerns, share counsel, give interviews, make decisions, show leadership, and exercise judgment. Being male or female has no bearing on an individual person's capacity to perform these activities in a way that guides and blesses the Church at large. Holding the priesthood does not automatically make someone a competent leader. At all levels within the Church, women do have opportunities to give spiritual counsel, participate in institutional decision-making, and receive formal expressions of respect. However, there is a great imbalance between the frequency, weight, and perceived necessity of these opportunities for women when compared to men. I hope we can do better at separating "higher authority" from being male.[25] If this "separation" sounds subversive and undesirable, please consider the "unseparated" reality, which is that the only people who are officially permitted to give authoritative spiritual counsel, make important decisions affecting both women and men, and receive formal public expressions of deference, are male. Women, by default, are always the "lower authority." To me, this seems just as subversive and undesirable.

All hands on deck

The responsibility for getting the powerful messages of the restored gospel to resonate in the hearts of young people today lies squarely with us, those who believe. Just as missionaries who grew up in Bountiful, Utah, cannot just march into a village in the mountains of eastern Taiwan, start preaching to the locals in English, and expect great results, we cannot convert the youth of today using the exact same language with which we were raised. Like Ammon with King Lamoni, we need to make the effort to carefully work out the imagery, terminology, and logic through which our audience will be able to understand the value of our message (Alma 18:24–35).

If our children—girls and boys—are unable to see the good fruits of the gospel because they also perceive the rotten fruits of sexism, then we will have failed them. Around the world, there are cultures in which female inferiority is explicitly proclaimed and in which girls' and women's opportunities for education, health, and the exercise of agency are drastically circumscribed compared to boys and men. If we cannot find ways to transform our global structures and culture to visibly demonstrate that women are full human beings on par with men, then we will have failed in our mission to be a light and a leaven in the world, a voice for truth.

Each of us would respond to Ana's outburst in different ways, but all of us must take her concerns seriously, for she is Ana times tens and hundreds of thousands of young women. Although not all of us, and perhaps not all of her peers, are currently raising these concerns, when a hand gets a wound, we don't ignore it because the feet are fine. Perhaps we can ask ourselves, as every generation must, how Ana may be seeing things we don't see, and how what she sees matters. She is raising concerns not because she is uninformed, unrighteous, or lazy, but because she has her eyes wide open and harbors a deep desire to serve as a full partner in God's kingdom.

I have been heartened to see that female and male leaders with the authority to direct the worldwide Church are taking positive steps. President Bonnie L. Oscarson's call to action in the April 2018 general conference was inspiring. She called on bishops, ward councils, and anyone holding a calling to "see the young women as valuable resources to help fill the many needs within our wards" and ask them to do jobs that would "help with their preparation to be missionaries, gospel scholars, leaders in the Church auxiliaries, temple workers, wives, mothers, mentors, examples, and friends." The welcome and more flexible language and structure of "ministering" likewise calls us to be creative and proactive in sharing the work of the Church with young women and stepping up to challenges wherever we find them.

While in the long run, adequately resolving Ana's concerns cannot occur without ongoing official, churchwide, institutional change, neither can it occur without a lot of hard work at the grassroots to reshape our culture. Instead of the "slothful" course of waiting to be commanded in all things, we rank-and-file members can be proactive and "anxiously engaged" in this worthy cause (Doctrine and Covenants 58:27). Women can step up by accepting requests to give talks, supporting sisters in their diverse situations, and sharing concerns or offering solutions when problems arise. Men, who hold the levers of institutional power, can conscientiously ensure that women are included in opportunities to speak, teach, give spiritual counsel, participate in collective decision-making, and receive visible respect. Both women and men can use respectful terms of address for female church leaders and invoke the love and divine parenthood of both Heavenly Father and Heavenly Mother. Both women and men can set examples of collegial and respectful behavior as we work together to build Zion.

Change in our Church is both a bottom-up and top-down process. It is unrealistic and unfair to demand that our leaders be telepathic and omnipresent. Indeed, good inspiration depends on good information, and we can do our part. We can sustain our leaders and minister to the rising generation by volunteering eyes, ears, voices, hearts, and helping hands.

THE PROBLEM WE
WANT TO HAVE

9 June 2018
Boise, Idaho

Sometimes at church we become uncomfortable when we note that our teachings, policies, procedures, and rhetoric have changed over time. The notion of "change" makes us feel icky. We might think: God's laws are eternal, and a church that is aligned with God's laws shouldn't change. But actually, we should very much hope that as a church, we will change a great deal. It's not an easy problem to deal with, but it's the problem we want to have, because it's the problem that religious movements have when they last a long time and become major players in shaping human events.

Most new religious movements do not last more than a decade or so. In 1833 in America a religious movement arose around the teachings of William Miller, who predicted that Christ would return by 22 October 1844. When Christ did not return on the appointed date, this was the end of the Millerite movement, though offshoots such as Seventh-day Adventism persist today. In 1850 there was a man in southern China named Hong Xiuquan, who claimed to have seen God the Father and Christ the Son in a vision. He believed that he had been given a divine mandate to establish a Christian kingdom in China. Hundreds of thousands of people flocked to the banner of the rebel movement eventually known as the Heavenly Kingdom of Great Peace, but in 1864 it all came crashing down. Hong and other top leaders became corrupt and distant; eventually, the troops of the Qing imperial army besieged the Heavenly Kingdom, breached its defensive walls, and slaughtered its inhabitants.

Some religious movements don't even last a year, and that's why no one ever hears about them. The other day in the Beijing city archives I stumbled across the records of a religious organization known as the Great Unity of the Religions of the World. It was founded in the spring. In the summer it attracted waves of followers throughout China when a leader named Tang Huanzhang prophesied five days of natural disasters and total darkness. By fall, it had fizzled out.

All of these short-lived religious movements had a number of problems, but they never had the problem of wrestling with significant change in moral common sense over a long period of time. They just didn't last long enough.

Moral common sense

As a professional historian and amateur student of the Bible, it is clear to me that what some people regard as moral differs depending on where and when they are. In the era of the book of Judges, it was apparently not a big deal for Samson to kill thirty people and steal their clothes because he had lost a bet and had to pay up. In the era of the Gospels, the "right" thing to do when a woman had a relationship outside of marriage was to stone her. Jesus's radical teachings upended some of these existing moral understandings. In late imperial China, if a mother did not tightly bind the feet of her daughter from a very young age, turning the toes under the sole of the foot and wrapping so tightly that sometimes circulation was cut off and the flesh died, she was considered a selfish, horrible mother. Small feet were a sign of beauty and morality. By neglecting to force her daughter to have small feet, even though her little girl might scream in pain, a mother would be condemning her daughter to poor marriage prospects and a rotten life. In the days of the early American republic, George Washington and many of the founding statesmen who penned words such as "we hold these truths to be self-evident, that all men are created equal, that they are endowed by their Creator with certain inalienable rights" were slaveowners who established a constitution in which a Black person was counted as three-fifths of a person. These statesmen were gifted and well-intended people whose moral vision was nonetheless constricted by their historical circumstances. Similarly, when the Latter-day Saints came across the plains, some of their covered wagons were driven by enslaved people forced to work without pay, whom they bought and sold like cows or sheep. For example, the first pioneer wagon to arrive in the Salt Lake Valley on 22 July 1847 (not 24 July) was driven by an enslaved man named Green Flake, accompanied by Orson Pratt.[1]

The fact that humans' moral common sense differs according to place and time does not mean there are no fixed moral laws. God's commandments do not change over time, and Joseph Smith taught that even God had to work according to eternal, unchanging laws. I believe that Jesus's radical message of love and grace in the case of the woman caught in adultery was better, and closer to the true way in which the children of God should relate to each other, than the traditional solution at that time. I believe, with all my heart, Christ's teaching that the first and great commandment is to love God, and the second is to love one's neighbor as oneself, and that everything else hangs on this.

However, anyone who takes a long look at human history can see that people's understanding—even Christians' understanding—of right and wrong, and the ways in which they interpret and prioritize the laws of God, are subject to shifts over time. In hindsight, we see that the beliefs of the day sometimes caused people to act in a way that we now see as clearly wrong, such as enslaving human beings.

Recalling President Dieter F. Uchtdorf's admonition, "Don't judge me because I sin differently from you," we can see that it is very easy to judge the people of the past for their sins.[2] And yet they were constrained by the conventions and culture of their particular past, just as we are constrained by the conventions and culture of our particular present. Until the past century or so, most human beings have not lived long enough to become moral aliens in their own life. Significant social, cultural, and even moral shifts have been problems left to the next generation. Now, however, as a rule people are living longer and culture is shifting more rapidly.

God willing, I will live long enough to become an old lady with views my great-grandchildren find completely wrongheaded and even immoral. As citizens of the early twenty-first century, there is something that you and I do or say now, without even thinking twice, that future generations will find morally reprehensible. This is inevitable.

Our church is an infant in the history of religious movements. At this point, we aren't even two hundred years old. We haven't yet lasted as long as the reigns of the first six emperors of the Qing dynasty in China, or as long as the sum of the tenures of the fourteen Catholic popes named Clement plus the first three popes named Innocent (there were thirteen Innocents, and over 260 popes, altogether). Catholicism is a good example of a mature religious movement in history that has learned to live with substantially different versions of itself over the course of two thousand years. With 1.1 billion adherents (half of all Christians and 16 percent of all people on the planet), it is a truly global force.[3] Over the course of its history it has supported world-class centers of learning and knowledge, sponsored bloody Crusades, burned Protestants at the stake, radically revamped its liturgy, protected priests who were known pedophiles, and produced popes acknowledged worldwide as spiritual leaders, even by non-Catholics.

Some Latter-day Saints might scoff and say, "Well, but those Catholics are just a 'great and abominable church,' and we are the one true church, so there's nothing we should admire about them." To this I would respond that our church is one of very many churches and belief systems in human history that have claimed to be the one true church or belief system. Most of those one-true somethings have come and gone. They weren't true enough to last more than a few decades, or a couple of centuries.

History demonstrates more than one way for a church or people to lose their way, their truth, and their authority. This may happen, for example, because of corruption or the death of a movement's leaders. But another path to falling away is stagnation: failure to remain what the Lord called a "true and *living* church"—a church that is organic, responsive to changing circumstances, hungering not only for what God has revealed, but for what

God now reveals and will yet reveal, line upon line (Doctrine and Covenants 1:30). Religions that are living are religions that grow and evolve.

The desirability of ongoing change, so that eternal truths can continue to shine out in a variety of different social and cultural contexts, should give Latter-day Saints some perspective as we look over our own short and therefore relatively uneventful church history. Over time, some Latter-day Saint policies and teachings have changed, leading to the policies and teachings of today. In the twenty-first century, we can still feel the Spirit witnessing the reality of Christ's atonement, the truths of the Restoration, and the inspired guidance of women and men called by God to lead us in this time.

Since ancient times, it has always been inadvisable to suppress evidence of change over time in an attempt to bolster faith in the status quo. In the twenty-first century, however, willful ignorance of the past is not only inadvisable, but impossible and strategically counterproductive. The narrative of "everything has always been this way, and nothing will ever change" produces a brittle, static faith that is vulnerable to shattering under just a little stress. Just as the miracle of a living human body (as opposed to a wooden doll or a china figurine) is its ability to grow and change, the power of the true and living church is its presence in the bodies, hearts, and minds of the Latter-day Saints. Mature faith cannot be rooted in a frozen artifact, but in the living body of Christ. Here I will list five such changes in our history.

1. *Abandoning plural marriage*

The most dramatic example of internal doctrinal change is the Church's turn away from plural marriage in 1890, which for half a century had been proclaimed from the pulpit as the crowning doctrine and practice of the restored gospel of Jesus Christ.[4] Those who entered into plural marriage often sacrificed a good deal, believing that they were thereby accessing the fullness of the gospel and achieving a greater degree of glory than those who did not.[5] Many believed that plural marriage held the key to solving society's problems, such as poverty, social isolation, and moral decay. In response to US legislation outlawing plural marriage, the Church's response was initially civil disobedience.[6]

Hence abandoning plural marriage was a decisive moment for the Church. As the Gospel Topics essay on lds.org puts it, "as federal pressure intensified, many essential aspects of church government were severely curtailed, and civil disobedience looked increasingly untenable as a long-term solution."[7] In this moment, hemmed in by the coercive power of the US government like the defiant Taiping Christians surrounded by the forces of the Qing dynasty, church leaders made the critical choice to de-escalate tensions and abandon the illegal practice.

"Inasmuch as laws have been enacted by Congress forbidding plural marriages," President Woodruff explained, "I hereby declare my intention to submit to those laws, and to use my influence with the members of the Church over which I preside to have them do likewise."[8] Latter-day Saints eventually became among the US government's most loyal supporters, and contemporary church policy specifically identifies advocating plural marriage as evidence of apostasy, even in societies where polygamy is accepted.[9] Late nineteenth-century Latter-day Saints who disagreed with this accommodation to prevailing American moral sentiment split from the Church and became small clusters of Fundamentalists living at the fringes of society. These Fundamentalists assert that they have not changed with the times, and they may be right. However, Fundamentalist movements are not able to build temples in Rome or claim thriving congregations in Ulaanbaatar. These projects require a certain amount of demonstrated respectability in accordance with widely accepted twenty-first-century standards for religious groups regarded as normal, respectable, and beneficial.

2. Allowing contraception

Another dramatic change in Latter-day Saint attitudes occurred on the matter of contraception.[10] In the nineteenth century, Latter-day Saints and Americans more generally tended to view contraception as immoral. This prevailing moral common sense is evident in the strong anticontraception stance of George Q. Cannon, First Counselor in the First Presidency, in 1894. Speaking of contraceptive practices, Cannon wrote,

There is one thing that I am told is practiced to some extent around us, and I say to you that where it is practiced and not thoroughly repented of the curse of God will follow it. I refer to the practice of preventing the birth of children. I say to you that the woman who practices such devilish arts . . . will be cursed in their bodies, cursed in their minds, cursed in their property, cursed in their offspring. God will wipe them out from the midst of this people and nation.[11]

Around the turn of the twentieth century, however, attitudes in society began to shift. Between 1910 and 1920, Latter-day Saints, like Americans more generally, had fierce debates over contraception. Debates within Relief Society meetings became so vigorous that in July 1916, the *Relief Society Magazine* published five statements from members of the Quorum of the Twelve Apostles in a volume-leading article on "Birth Control." These statements expressed the sentiment that contraception was immoral and offered prescriptions for family size. For instance, Elder Rudger Clawson wrote, "Woman is so constituted that, ordinarily, she is capable of bearing, during the years of her greatest vigor, from eight to ten children, and in exceptional cases a larger number than that. . . . [S]he should exercise the sacred power of procreation to the utmost limit."[12] Elder George F. Richards wrote that "the doctrine that [couples] should limit the number of their offspring to three or four children, and how this can be accomplished, is both pernicious and an abomination in the sight of the Lord. . . . My wife has borne to me fifteen children. Anything short of this would have been less than her duty and privilege."[13]

In the present day, however, the Church's official teachings on fertility state that "the decision of how many children to have and when to have them is a private matter for the husband and wife. . . . Decisions about birth control and the consequences of those decisions rest solely with each married couple."[14] This current teaching reflects not only awareness of economic and medical realities (children in modern society require greater economic resources, some women face serious health risks by becoming pregnant, and so on) but also shifts in thinking about the purpose of sexual relations in marriage, from a more strictly procreative ideology to understanding that healthy sexual intimacy can strengthen marriages.[15]

3. Administering the sacrament

A third example is a significant change in the policies governing preparing, blessing, and passing the sacrament.[16] Articles and Covenants, a founding set of rules and regulations revealed by Joseph Smith in 1830, specifically stated that priests could administer the sacrament but banned deacons and teachers: "neither the teacher nor the deacon have the authority to baptize nor administer the sacrament."[17] Furthermore, from 1851 to 1877, "priests," "teachers," and "deacons" were all adult men. For instance, the duties of a teacher during this time ranged from reporting families' poor parenting, to bringing charges against adulterers, to settling disputes over property. And yet, the problem with this policy was that local units had trouble filling "lesser" Aaronic Priesthood quorums because their members were always being recruited by Melchizedek Priesthood quorums. In 1877, this need spurred a change in policy whereby boys were permitted to serve alongside men in the Aaronic Priesthood quorums as apprentices.

These changes were implemented unevenly until a General Priesthood Committee was established in 1908 to reevaluate and reorganize priesthood operations. Within a few years, the committee had set formal Aaronic Priesthood age groupings at twelve, fifteen, and eighteen and drawn up a new list of duties "geared to the youthful capabilities of the Aaronic boys," including the following:

- assist in ward teaching
- assist with the sacrament
- be instructors for boy scouts
- collect ward funds
- speak and sing at meetings
- notify quorums of meetings
- help renovate meetinghouses
- care for meetinghouse grounds
- cut wood for the poor
- be auxiliary officers
- be clerks of branches
- be choir members[18]

When these new organizational structures and duties were introduced, they raised eyebrows because since the founding of the Church, teachers and deacons had been explicitly prohibited from administering the sacrament. Leaders spearheading the new policies responded that passing the bread and water was not "administering" and consequently was not technically a priesthood function, noting that women regularly passed the trays down the benches during the service.[19] The young boys simply needed a job to do at church. In some places, women continued to prepare the sacrament tables as recently as 1957. By the 1990s, however, church members had come to see preparing, blessing, and passing the emblems as "administering the sacrament" and to view these activities as exclusive male priesthood functions.[20]

4. Blessing the sick

A similar shift occurred with regard to the Latter-day Saint practice of laying on hands to bless the sick. For over a century, Latter-day Saint women regularly gave blessings, invoking not the power of the priesthood but the name of Jesus Christ. When Joseph Smith Sr., the prophet's father, gave patriarchal blessings, he blessed women and men alike with the gift of healing and specifically authorized women to perform healing rituals.[21] In April 1842, Sarah Cleveland and Elizabeth Whitney, members of the Relief Society presidency, administered to a woman for the restoration of health. Shortly thereafter Joseph Smith addressed the Relief Society and explicitly endorsed female ritual healing, declaring that those women who had been "ordained" to their offices had received spiritual authority, including the authority to heal the sick.[22] Joseph Smith's successors, including Brigham Young, John Taylor, and Wilford Woodruff, also encouraged women to use the gift of healing.[23] Zina D. H. Young and Eliza R. Snow were prolific, well-known healers who trained other women in the proper performance of the healing ritual.[24] Beyond administering to those who were sick, women also washed, anointed, and blessed women in the early stages of childbirth.[25]

In 1880, the Quorum of the Twelve Apostles drafted a circular letter for the entire Church acknowledging the practice of unordained women and men administering to the sick.

> It is the privilege of all faithful women and lay members of the Church, who believe in Christ, to administer to all the sick or afflicted in their respective families, either by the laying on of hands, or by the anointing with oil in the name of the Lord: but they should administer in these sacred ordinances, not by virtue and authority of the priesthood, but by virtue of their faith in Christ, and the promises made to believers: and thus they should do in all their ministrations.[26]

These healing ordinances and the spiritual authority they entailed set Latter-day Saint women apart from most other Christian women of their day. At that time, the churches of the mainstream Protestant establishment in America did not recognize women's authority to perform religious rites.

Drawing on extensive archival research, historian Jonathan Stapley argues that it is possible that at the turn of the twentieth century more healing rituals were performed in Utah by woman than by priesthood officers.[27] Joseph F. Smith regularly supported female participation in healing, joining with women in giving blessings and receiving blessings from at least one of his wives.[28] In 1914 he wrote in a circular letter to all church leaders and spoke in General Relief Society Conference, sustaining women's right to participate in healing rituals. Until 1968, the Relief Society handbook section on "Care for the Sick" included the text of a letter from Joseph F. Smith acknowledging that it was "permissible, under certain conditions," for women to perform healing rituals.[29] However, by the late twentieth century, through various processes of correlating and streamlining administrative structures, church policy shifted so that blessings of healing were identified as a Melchizedek Priesthood ordinance only.

5. Race, temple, and priesthood

In the early days of the Restoration, Zion was radically inclusive of all races. Elijah Able, a Black man, was ordained to the priesthood in March 1836, and Emma Smith welcomed Jane Manning, a free Black woman, into the Smith home in Nauvoo late in 1843.[30] Yet even during the Church's early years, attitudes toward race were shifting, including the views of the Prophet himself. Although in a letter of April 1836, Joseph Smith expressed views in support of Southern slavery and the notion that Blacks bore God's curse, later on the Prophet vocally opposed the enslavement of Blacks and included an antislavery plank in his presidential platform.[31] This significant change in the views of the founding prophet of the Restoration underscores the fact that everyone can learn profound moral lessons over time.

Following the death of Joseph Smith, Latter-day Saint views and teachings with regard to Black persons came to increasingly resemble the racist attitudes of the world outside Zion. Some early Latter-day Saints were slaveowners. Nineteenth-century church leaders, beginning with Brigham Young, taught that all people with Black ancestry were cursed and should be banned from participation in priesthood ordination and temple rites.[32] Church leaders and members advanced various theories to justify the priesthood and temple restrictions, none of which are accepted today.[33] This restriction was in line with prevailing morality in American society in the late nineteenth and early twentieth centuries and may have even served to burnish the Saints' good public reputation.

Finally, in 1978, President Spencer W. Kimball announced a revelation reversing these policies. Although many of these mistaken views and prejudices have persisted to this day, 2015 marked a milestone when the Church published an essay on lds.org titled "Race and the Priesthood." This essay reviews the Latter-day Saint history of racist teachings and policies and declares,

> Today, the Church disavows the theories advanced in the past that black skin is a sign of divine disfavor or curse, or that it reflects unrighteous actions in a premortal life; that mixed-race marriages are a sin; or that blacks or people of any other race or ethnicity are inferior in any

way to anyone else. Church leaders today unequivocally condemn all racism, past and present, in any form.

This dramatic change has occurred not only in official church policy, but in the hearts of most individual Latter-day Saints. Our consciousness shifted until it has seemed plain to many that past teachings of racial inferiority were wrong and sinful.

Throughout this span of time, the divine nature of Black Latter-day Saints never changed. Christ's commandment to love others as ourselves never changed. What changed was Latter-day Saints' awareness of how our actions did or did not reflect our stated beliefs. As President Dallin H. Oaks declared on 1 June 2018, racism is a sin for which we are all called to repent.[34] It was sinful in the 1850s, when Latter-day Saints like James and Agnes Flake claimed to own Black Latter-day Saints like Green and Martha Flake and their two children.[35] It was sinful in April 2017, when, in the temple, a fellow church member called my friend a n*gger. This reality of ongoing racism, both overt and veiled, is sobering. We must help bear this heavy burden by refuting racist words and actions whenever we see them.

The optimal tension

These examples of abandoning plural marriage, allowing contraception, administering the sacrament, changing policies for blessing the sick, and expanding access to the temple and the priesthood are not flukes or aberrations. They demonstrate a succession of shifts over time. They show that some things we now take for granted as the way things should be were once seen as edgy, and some things we now see as edgy were once taken for granted as the way things should be.

While God's commandments and moral standards never change, changing social or institutional circumstances mean that the ways in which people seek to apply God's commandments or live Christlike values do vary. George Q. Cannon, quoted above condemning birth control, was himself clear-eyed about what church leaders could and could not see. Speaking at general conference soon after the 1890 Manifesto ending plural marriage, Cannon, a member of the First Presidency, told the Latter-day Saints, "The Presidency of the Church have to walk just as you walk. They have to take steps just as you take steps. They have to depend upon the revelations of God as they come to them. They cannot see the end from the beginning, as the Lord does." Cannon's distinctions suggested that to expect church leaders to be omniscient like God was tantamount to idolatry. Speaking of the First Presidency, he said, "All that we can do is to seek the mind and will of God, and when that comes to us, though it may come in contact with every feeling that we have previously entertained, we have no option but to take the step that God points out, and to trust to Him."[36]

Indeed, our history shows that when leaders and ordinary members alike seek the mind and will of God, over time God often points them in new directions. Sometimes, it has been a case of Latter-day Saints responding sensibly to new situations or learning new facts, as in the examples of polygamy and birth control. Sometimes it has been a case of institutional restructuring, as in the examples of administering the sacrament and women's blessings. At other times it has been a case of church members allowing their understanding of divine truths to be gradually clouded by the sins of the world, as in the example of racial exclusions from priesthood ordination and temple access. Sometimes, change leads us to new places; at other times, change points us back to our roots.[37]

Accepting the possibility of change in our existing policies or understandings is healthy and realistic. As President Dieter F. Uchtdorf has reminded us, "to be perfectly frank, there have been times when members or leaders in the Church have simply made mistakes. There may have been things said or done that were not in harmony with our values, principles, or doctrine." Affirming that "God is perfect," President Uchtdorf explained that God must always work through us, God's "imperfect children—and imperfect people make mistakes."[38] In April 2018, President M. Russell Ballard reminded us that "stories in the scriptures detail incidents about men and women who were called of God to accomplish a great work . . . striving to do their best, but none of them yet perfect. The same is true of us."[39]

The thought that we Latter-day Saints have definitely been wrong in the past and will definitely be wrong in the future may not feel especially comforting. It may even feel paralyzing or off-putting. Some people, encountering this handful of historical examples, may feel threatened. They may feel that it is better to conceal, deny, or ignore how significantly some church policies and teachings have shifted, because (they believe) if people learn this history, they will lose faith in the whole project altogether.

I disagree with this defensive perspective. I think this impulse to avoid evidence of change might be valid if the Church were the Wizard of Oz and I were pulling aside the curtain.[40] But the Church is not the Wizard of Oz. We are the Church of Jesus Christ, who does not work in darkness. Our history is the history of God working through humble people, of flawed disciples steadfastly seeking Christ. Trust and faith in Christ's Atonement must be based on truth about the necessity of this atonement in Christ's work among the Saints. The truth is, in the past, Latter-day Saints did, said, and even believed some things differently. The current work of historians at the Church History Department and archivists at Brigham Young University to publish key early church documents, even documents that give evidence for significant change over time, supports this view that we need not hide or edit our history because it gives a different picture from today. Change over time is natural, and to be expected, in any living thing.

Thus, change naturally provokes discomfort. Yet discomfort—this ongoing stretching and recalibrating in our institutions and culture—is part of God's design. Just as we value learning to deal with hardship and rise to challenges in our individual spiritual progression, I believe we should value growth and adaptation in the life of the Church.

The Church of Jesus Christ of Latter-day Saints, with its teaching of human imperfection even in paramount spiritual leadership and its unique doctrine of ongoing revelation, is much better positioned than many other religious groups to deal with the coveted problem of change over time—of ongoing life. Our standard for change should never be "going along with surrounding society." For us, complete comfort with surrounding society—with its violence, injustice, apathy, crassness, selfishness, materialism, contentiousness, superficiality, racism, sexism, nationalism, lack of spiritual and moral curiosity, and craving for "quick and easy" solutions to complex challenges—is indeed the kiss of death.[41] If we allow ourselves to be in total harmony with the values of surrounding society, we have nothing to offer—no prophetic voice, no light to shine in darkness. In every age and place, we must continually find balance between the twin dilemmas of respectability and disrepute.[42]

Instead of digging in our heels and insisting that nothing will ever change, which is clearly not reality, we can eagerly seek ways to follow God's commandments that the cultural blinders of our time have partially obscured. Seeking to overcome the blinders of the present can mean looking both to the future *and* to the past, searching for wisdom from people in different places and situations, as the Prophet Joseph Smith instructed.[43] How do we live the gospel of Jesus Christ, according to the light and knowledge we have received, and are eager to yet receive, in our diverse circumstances today?

In response to this question, our faith's combination of prophetic revelation and personal revelation are mutually reinforcing. Neither can be disregarded or discounted. Prophetic revelation and the leadership of inspired women and men, are things that make the Church special. Church relationships, like intergenerational relationships, are hierarchical. Just as I value guidance from my parents, aunts and uncles, and senior members of the academic community in which I work, even though I know that they all have individual flaws, I value the humble and prayerful admonitions of leaders who have consecrated their time and care to building our worldwide fellowship. Hierarchical relationships, at their worst, enable abuse of power.[44] At their best, however, senior-to-junior relationships transmit experience, wisdom, perspective, and care. Without them, we lose our connections to our past and the value of the lives and experience in which our own lives are rooted.

What I have learned from Chinese culture is that it is always a blessing to have teachers—people whose substantial experience commands respect, masters who transmit knowledge and skill. Respect and idolatry, though sometimes conflated, are not the same thing. Centering our faith on church leaders instead of on Jesus Christ is clearly wrong, idolatrous, and unbecoming of members of the Church that bears His name alone. However, centering our faith on the self only is similarly impoverishing. In my life, I've learned many important things simply because I've listened to people I was supposed to listen to, such as my mother, my father, my Uncle Charles, my Auntie Annie, Gordon B. Hinckley, Chieko Okazaki, Bonnie L. Oscarson, and so on. I have found many wonderful teachers within the Church, with its rich and regularly reordered patterns of teaching relationships.

With regard to personal revelation, this is the lifeblood of the Restoration. The story of Joseph Smith bypassing the church authority structures into which he was born and seeking wisdom directly from God has inspired people for nearly two centuries. The dignity and authority by which every child of God may exercise agency and access spiritual guidance through the witness of the Holy Ghost are divinely given. In April 2018 general conference, President Russell M. Nelson said, "You do not have to wonder whom you can safely trust. . . . Regardless of what others may say or do, no one can ever take away a witness borne to your heart and mind about what is true."[45] Over time, the witness of the Holy Ghost can work on a larger scale within the body of Christ. In April 2012 general conference, Elder D. Todd Christofferson quoted an anecdote from J. Reuben Clark to explain the essential role of the Holy Ghost in confirming leaders' teachings to the members of the Church: "The Church will know by the testimony of the Holy Ghost in the body of the members, whether the brethren in voicing their views are 'moved upon by the Holy Ghost'; and in due time that knowledge will be made manifest."[46] Anyone who has felt the witness of the Spirit knows the power and joy of such an experience.

The weight of revelation at the individual level creates a grassroots reality that is strong, durable, sprawling, and intertwined—more "roots" than "grass." The lay quorums, women's society, presidencies, councils, and temple priesthood rituals of the early Church created horizontal as well as vertical dimensions within which to be a Latter-day Saint. In the Book of Mormon, the baptismal covenants made by those at the waters of Mormon were not simply vertical obligations to follow Christ but horizontal obligations to each other: to be one people, to mourn with those who mourn, to comfort those in need of comfort (Mosiah 18:8–10).

Like the crosshairs of a scope, the vertical obligations that support the order of the Church and the horizontal obligations through which we learn from one another and fulfill sacred covenants on an equal footing as children of God will help us stay centered on Christ, though probably never right on the mark. But if we keep trying, we'll keep getting close. As President M. Russell Ballard said in his April 2018 talk acknowledging "the reality of our human weaknesses and shortcomings," the way forward is through mutual support and faith in Christ.[47] Because of our mutual weaknesses, we will frequently fail to live up to the sacred name we bear. But if we are humble, and diligent, we will be blessed with a struggle that is unceasing.

Annual Newsletter

December 2015
Auckland, New Zealand

Dear Friends:

Long time, no write! The big news this year is that after being semi-nomadic for our entire marriage we are now committed to staying in New Zealand for at least a few years. The obvious explanation is that as of November, Joseph has a new lawyer job and Melissa's professor job is permanent. But this is not the whole story. The main reason is that after a year of anticipation, Joseph's passionfruit vine in the front of the house just barely made its first baby passionfruit (extremely cute—possibly even cuter than cucumber sprouts). So as you see, we can't possibly move. Please, come visit!

After a year and a half as a full-time, stay-at-home dad, Joseph just started working at a law firm that serves the Chinese community in Auckland. The kids like going to the Auckland Table Tennis Stadium every Tuesday for the firm's weekly ping pong night. For Joseph, landing the job has been bittersweet, since it means the end of long hikes with Han through the Waitākere Ranges, his Monday and Tuesday Chicken Soup Night(s) and Thursday Pizza Night, and dislocation from various parenting innovations that he introduced during his tenure. Melissa now goes to work early and comes home at 3:00 p.m. to pick the kids up from school.

Melissa got a job too, but barely. She almost missed her permanent-position job interview. The interview was in the

Ice skin
mooncake
RECIPE

afternoon, and so that morning she and Joseph decided to go on a nice long run at Te Henga, one of the beautiful black sand beaches in West Auckland. It took about forty minutes to drive there. The tide was unusually high as we headed north along the beach at the beginning of the run, and an hour and a half later it was higher still, the waves licking at the base of the dunes. As we made a dash around a rocky headland, a rogue wave hit us, sweeping us off our feet. Soaking wet, we returned to the car and found that the car key had slipped out through a hole in Melissa's pocket. Luckily, the one other person in sight was a really nice lady with two kids who gave us a ride all the way back to our house. But because the house keys were in the car (left at the beach), we were locked out. Joseph had to boost Melissa up high so she could climb in through the open bathroom window. This was difficult to do because it was a small window, right above the toilet, and it is hard to be flexible when you are shivering uncontrollably. It was a great relief to even arrive at the interview, and it could only get better from there.

In the meantime, Joseph had to get the car to pick the kids up from school. So he rode his bike all the way along the winding, hilly road to the beach and was nearly there when he came to a place where the road was blocked by a truck that had collapsed a bridge. He then had to double back and take a long detour through the town of Waitākere (35 kilometers in all), finally reaching the car and rushing back just in time. The moral of the whole story: Always check for holes in your pocket, and always give rides to people in need.

Bean (nine years) has enjoyed playing keyboard in the school rock band. Because New Zealand primary schools almost never give homework, he has plenty of time for his various interests like watching science videos on Youtube and learning about beekeeping. He is enterprising

PAPA'S KITCHEN

MON: Chicken soup (simmer chicken frames for hours so that broth will be solid when cold)

TUE: chicken soup

WED: Some sort of curry or butter chicken

THU: pizza

FRI: Something special, like fried chicken or sweet potato fries

161

and adventurous, the only member of the family willing to get up before dawn to go hiking with Joseph on the Omanawanui Track overlooking Manukau Harbour. He and Joseph bring blankets and Mint Slices (half chocolate wafer, half mint patty, enrobed in chocolate) and watch the sun rise.

Mint Slice Exterior → *chocolate* *mint* *Mint Slice aftermath*
Chocolate wafer cookie

Sprout (seven years) loves machines and mechanisms like cameras, lighters, jumper cables, and things powered by batteries. He is the only one in the household who uses our landline phone. He likes science experiments. The other Sunday afternoon, he and Joseph tried to make a hydrogen bomb. They ended up just making hydrogen bubbles, but this was plenty exciting for Sprout. He has started to learn piano in addition to cello. He is cheery and loquacious, especially at bedtime, and is known for his random conversation-starters that often begin with "Did you know . . ."

Leaf (five years) started primary school and is thriving in the social and structured environment. She is often found up a tree somewhere. She loves to garden. This January, the Leaf accompanied Melissa on a month-long trip to Shanghai, where she went to a Chinese kindergarten and refreshed her Chinese. She is independent and busy. Recently she has been collecting snails as pets in terrariums made of upside-down plastic containers and stocked with bok choy. Unfortunately, on one particularly hot day, the snails cooked. Escargots!

pet snails!

Shoot (three years) goes to "kindy" at the farm. He has become much more talkative, with a vocabulary up to the tasks of arguing with parents and telling long stories. Joseph burned about twenty Chinese fairy tales to CD and Shoot has them all memorized. He is punky during the day but sweet at night. Nearly every

escargots

night this year, he has requested that Melissa sing him the same song at bedtime, with this final verse:

> *Will you leave me now, as I sit beside you in the lamplight?*
> *Softly I sing; more softly are my eyes upon you*
> *Close they hold you now, and only let you go*
> *When some strange thing cries in the dark.*

At the end of the song, the Shoot always pipes up: "What thing cries?" Melissa always answers: "Maybe a baby cat who lost his mama." Shoot always says: "Oh." Then he curls up into his blankets and is out like a light.

All in all, we have had a wonderful year—punctuated by meltdowns, quarrels, missed appointments, and late nights, but steadied by familiar rhythms. At this time, we are acutely aware of the fact that our relatively tranquil year of breakfasts and bedtimes stands in stark contrast to the experience of violence, want, or sudden tragedy that is the reality of so many. We've tried to do what we can, but even if we could do much more it would not be enough. What is to be done? Is there balm in Gilead? Such questions bring us to Jesus Christ, whose atonement gives us the opportunity to keep trying despite our mistakes as we struggle to live up to the full measure of our belief that every human being is the beloved son or daughter of Heavenly Parents, with infinite worth and potential. Thank you for your friendship and good examples. May you have a joyous and happy new year!

Love,
Joseph, Melissa, Bean, Sprout, Leaf, and Shoot

SNIPPING AND UNSNIPPING

24 October 2014
Modern China

At the beginning of the semester, a noticeable divide separates university teachers and university students. Although higher education is an expensive, highly sought-after commodity, it often seems that once the "customers" acquire access to it, they are surprisingly passive about claiming it. Often students don't show up to class, don't do assigned readings, or don't ask questions. Part of this reticence is because of the distance students perceive between themselves and the instructor. Part of it is because many of them have never encountered Chinese history before and struggle to take it all in. Over the course of the semester, I work to bridge both divides—to show the students that a teacher is also a student, just with slightly more experience, and that the experiences and concerns of people who lived in China were not so different from their own.

At the end of every semester of my "Modern China" and "Late Imperial China" history classes, I always give a final lecture that ventures beyond the subject matter of Chinese history and on to life in general. I speak to them as I would have liked someone to speak to me when I was a university student eager to find my place in the world. In these final lectures, I don't hesitate to share personal stories or engage in direct exhortation. I feel that by the end of the semester, the students and I have established a rapport and are able to relate to each other candidly and authentically. Knowing them, I love them and want them to flourish.

Let's take a moment to think about the purpose of learning, which is directly related to the purpose of life.

I want to tell you about one of my life's great regrets, a time when I feel that I clearly made the wrong decision and that this decision reflected poorly on my values. I was a first-year university student in Boston, Massachusetts. Like most first-year students at this particular university, my identity was strongly linked to getting good marks. It was my second semester; it was spring. The Boston winter is long and gray—just as damp and gray as Auckland, but also snowy and icy for several months. On Easter weekend, instead of basking in the sun with my friends, I was holed up in my dorm room, wrestling with an essay due on Monday. I wanted to earn an A. I was working hard.

I felt stressed about this essay because I had only about thirty hours until the deadline, and yet only a few pages were written. That evening I was supposed to go to my uncle's house to have Easter dinner with him, my aunt, and my two cousins. One of these cousins was Mie, around twelve or thirteen at the time. Ordinarily I felt a special connection with Mie and enjoyed spending time with her. But on this day, I decided I couldn't spare the four hours. In my mind I thought it might make the difference between a B and an A. I called my uncle and told him I was very sorry, but I just couldn't get away. He offered to drive to my dorm room and pick me up, then take me back directly after dinner. He said, "Mie is really looking forward to seeing you. She's prepared a gift." I insisted I had no choice but to keep working. I stayed home and kept staring into my laptop screen, proud of myself for my hard-core work ethic.

On Monday I handed my essay in on time. It wasn't a great essay. I can't remember whether it got a B or an A. It certainly wasn't that much "greater" because of the additional four hours I'd gained. The mark from the essay was absorbed inconsequentially into my final mark, which was likewise absorbed into my transcript, which was eventually bundled up with other irrelevant data in my graduate school applications. In the end, the extra four hours that I spent on that essay left no visible trace. But I had missed out on a precious opportunity to renew my ties with my family.

As trivial as missing a dinner may seem, this is one of my life's great

regrets. My choice betrayed insecurity and a narrow preoccupation with a few marks. When we don't make time to be with people, we can't learn from them, nor they from us. This mutual learning and growth is the whole purpose of life.

You might say, "Well, you were learning because you were working on your paper," and to a certain extent that's true. But some kinds of learning are limited in that they will fill the space that we allot to them, and no more. An essay is like this. An exam is like this. It's like a receptacle that will expand or shrink to fit a given allotment of time and brainpower. After your efforts fill this set shape, you've got something you didn't have before, but that's it. The kind of learning that you get from people, learning in the context of relationships, is unlimited. It grows in the living, breathing parts of the self and in this sense it is much more valuable.

The point of this story: All learning is good. Some kinds of learning are better than others. Set aside ample resources of time and talent to fill buckets and buckets of learning from lectures, readings, courses, books. But always make time for learning from people, which is the best kind of learning of all.

Finally, I want to show you two pictures and tell one last story.

This is a suspicious hole that appeared in the duvet cover of one of our blankets. "No one" knew how it came to be, even though it was clearly snipped with scissors. My daughter the Leaf (four years) and my son the Shoot (two years) are both really good at snipping things apart.

The skills of critical thinking and analysis you learn in the university will be an asset to you for the rest of your life. In this course, I hope you have learned to not just swallow any information or idea set before you, but to pick it apart, know where it comes from, accept what's sound, but set any rotten bits aside.

With this sort of intellectual independence comes real power. You have the power to poke holes in harmful narratives that oversimplify and divide people as either friends or enemies. Like Superman's X-ray vision, critical thinking gives you the power to see what is unseen—the historical burdens of a current event, the subtle cross-references within a text, the face of untrammeled political power behind the mask of harmony and the rule of law.

That last bit about "untrammeled political power" behind a mask sounded rather negative. Yes, I do think that it is rather negative when state institutions use ill-defined categories and labels to shore up control, destroying people's lives in the process. On this issue I'm a universalist, not a particularist. However, I want to issue a general caution.

For some reason, just as two-year-olds are great at snipping things to shreds but are unable to put them back together, it is much easier to use intellectual power for negative purposes (to poke holes in a theory, to bust popular myths, to tear someone down) than for positive purposes. Perhaps this is also why in an overview of China, which is a complex and diverse society full of complex and diverse people, there have been times when I have adopted a critical tone. It is easy to spot gaps between state propaganda  and people's everyday realities, or to show how Mao Zedong did not always act like a great, benevolent sage.

It is less common to apply intellectual power to positive projects. I'm not really sure why this is. I think positive narratives may be inherently less interesting. Classes on "Why China is the greatest nation in the world and why the ruling party is the best thing that ever happened to China and her people" do indeed exist (mostly in China). And yet in such a project there are no problems, and problems are in many ways what makes something worth learning about.

One certain thing is that the world desperately needs people who use their intellectual powers to stitch things together instead of just snip things apart.

These are quilts my mother made. In sharp contrast to the narrow deconstructionist skills of two-year-olds, my mother had the skill and the artistry to cut things up and then stitch them back together in a way that was both beautiful and useful.

There are both serious differences and compelling commonalities between "China" (the land, the people, the party-state, the civilization) and the democratic societies we currently inhabit. These differences have the potential to wreck the world (maybe not *everything*—I'm not talking about Armageddon here—but a great deal). These commonalities have the potential to repair it (not *everything*, but a great deal). Neither these differences nor these commonalities are going away any time soon.

As educated people, you have learned to *both* take things apart *and* put them together. How will China and China's people continue to emerge from the tumult of the twentieth century and engage with the world in the twenty-first century? It's a puzzle with many pieces. It is not all positive. It is not all negative.

Very few things are all good and not bad, or the other way around. Everything is mixed up together. Human endeavors, including human communities, are by nature full of contradictions, because contradiction is the nature of reality itself. Being able to take complexity in stride is a prerequisite for becoming a person who is really useful in today's world.

Polarizing, demonizing characterizations are bad for the world. Therefore, amidst the world's contradictions, amidst wheat and chaff, be cultivators and builders. Use the ideas, skills, and understanding that you've acquired to constantly rethink assumptions, recognize truth, pursue things of real value, build bridges, and in so doing open yourself and your generation up to the vastness of human inheritance.

Thank you for your hard work, and thank you for being my students.

THE TROUBLE WITH
REVOLUTIONS

22 October 2015
Modern China

Chairman Mao said we should "seek truth from facts."

A great range of interpretations exists for the events and processes that unfolded in China during the nineteenth and twentieth centuries. The most controversial of these events may be the numerous revolutions that have taken place—events during which large numbers of people have risen up, organized, and used their bodies, voices, and lives to transform the world.

Recall the words of the young student, Zou Rong, executed by Qing imperial officials in 1905 because of his 1903 pamphlet, "The Revolutionary Army." He said: "Revolution is a universal principle of the world. . . . Revolution follows nature and corresponds to the nature of man. Revolution eliminates what is corrupt and holds on to what is good."[1]

The Chinese Revolution of 1911 was trying to overthrow the whole imperial system, including not only the rule of the Qing emperor, but also the dominance of a tiny elite class. The 1911 revolutionaries wanted to replace the old system with a parliamentary democracy that would give all people a voice. They succeeded in overthrowing the old system. But these victors killed each other and faded from significance as they quarreled over the shape their new world should take.

The 1927–1928 Nationalist revolution was an attempt to once again save China by defeating regional warlord governments and reuniting its vast territories and peoples. The program they put forward once they were in power was the New Life Movement, which sought to revive Confucian values in a modern context and on a mass national scale. This New Life Movement of the Nationalist government preached the virtues of courtesy, duty, honesty, and honor to the masses. At the same time, Nationalist soldiers hunted down Communists and in the process of "draining the pond to catch the fish" carried out terrible atrocities against local populations.

The 1949 revolution sought to wrest control of China from corrupt militarists, officials, and powerful foreign interests and to place it in the hands of the working classes. Inspired by Mao Zedong's admonition to "serve the people," Red Army soldiers and Communist party cadres won popular respect and support as they endured terrible privations, exercised moral discipline, and set about righting long-standing socioeconomic inequalities. They expelled foreign businesses and missionary institutions. They reformed patriarchal legal structures. They removed from power those whom they found responsible for everything that had been wrong with the world, such as urban capitalists, rural landowners, men and women of learning, and foreigners and those who had associated closely with them.

During the Cultural Revolution of 1966–1976, people tore down ancient symbols of privilege, corruption, hypocrisy, and superstition and replaced them with bold slogans and the fresh, unformed enthusiasm of youth. In other words, during the Cultural Revolution, groups of teenage punks were authorized to destroy thousands of years of cultural heritage and rend the carefully woven fabric of local community and family ties.

What do all of these revolutionary stories have in common? They simultaneously exemplify the best and the worst of human nature. In the name of a better world, China's revolutionaries have done admirable and despicable things.

The freshness and ambiguity of this revolutionary legacy continue to affect how other countries relate to China. Is it ideal for the United Kingdom to welcome Xi Jinping, China's supreme leader, without speaking up on behalf of the thousands of people who under his rule have been harassed, imprisoned, tortured, and even killed for holding political or religious views that do not conform to the Party line? No. But on the other hand, is it productive for the nations of the world to shun China and its 1.3 billion citizens, to demonize an entire group of people on account of the political system that holds them together? No. Can we forget the century of imperialism during which Western nations and Japan roamed with impunity over Chinese soil, stealing valuable resources, disregarding Chinese laws, and allowing their soldiers to rape and kill innocent civilians? To what extent have other nations and peoples helped create the sort of authoritarian, nationalist system that has united the "new China" for over sixty years?

Similarly messy questions surround nearly any modern nation-state, of course. My own homeland, the United States of America, comes to mind. The nature of modern mass movements is that charismatic, inspiring ideals are hitched to large, cumbersome organizational structures in which the nuts and bolts are flawed human beings. This awesome synergy between powerful ideas and powerful organization brought us the Spitfire and the computer, world war and the nuclear bomb.

As participants in a globally integrated world, what role should we play?

On the one hand, how can we accept evil? Who will answer for the sufferings of prisoners of conscience? How can we allow tyrants and bullies to prosper while the innocent come to harm?

On the other hand, how can we decisively silence those who perpetuate harm without doing harm ourselves? Can we fail to acknowledge the way in which we or our own histories have played a role in creating the problem? How should we decide at whom to cast our stones? If we do not agree with the views of a person, or a party, or a nation, is the best course of action to treat our opponent as an enemy, someone whose welfare we seek to erode? I don't think so.

These are complex questions that continue to matter today, especially where China is concerned. China is not a monolith. It is not simply the party-state. There are many Chinas, and they are enormously important. The world will be much better off with people who can help others understand its history, culture, and people. One-fifth of all of human beings are Chinese. To understand China is to understand humanity.

To study human history is to learn that everything is mixed together: good and bad, the pure and the despicable, that which refines and that which corrupts. Yes, it is true, as Zou Rong says, that revolution follows nature and corresponds to the nature of humankind. But there has never been a revolution that wholly succeeded in "eliminating what is corrupt and holding on to what is good"—not in China, not anywhere. Whenever revolutionaries have set out to make all things right, they have always ended up doing things that are terribly wrong.

In a world where so many things are devastatingly wrong at the same time that strawberries are sweet and the summer sun shines on cool green grass, how are we to make sense of the tension between purity and pragmatism? Taken to extremes, ideological purity unleashes the horrors of the Cultural Revolution, in which even thirteen-year-olds could find something wrong with everyone, in which no extenuating circumstances could justify political incorrectness. On the other side of the coin, extremely pragmatic thinking leads to a place where we have neither integrity nor anything original to contribute to the human project of defining life's meaning.

"Seek truth from facts." Actually, Mao Zedong did not invent this phrase. It is an ancient expression dating back to the Han dynasty, over two thousand years ago. Mao probably remembered it from his schoolboy days. Another way of reading it is to say, "From actual evidence, seek truth." What does the evidence of history teach us?

Our own lives and our own experiences look so miniscule and insignificant compared to the sweeping range of human experience in Chinese history. And yet, as we each know, one's own life can feel plenty long. Perhaps it's not the Great Leap Forward, but we all have our struggles.

The conflict I posed earlier between purity and pragmatism is not an impossible dilemma or a zero-sum game, but rather a necessary tension that helps us to sort out our priorities. As you go through life, struggling to balance your values and your actions, to reconcile what is ideal with what is productive, your priorities will become clearer to you. In fact, your priorities will become who you are. They will shape your impact on other people and the legacy that you leave behind.

I wish you the best as you continue to pursue your studies and careers. Life is messy, terrible, wonderful, and hard. Understanding history gives us this perspective from the lives of others. The longer you live, the more you'll gain this perspective from your own experience until your life, too, is someone else's history.

Thank you for your hard work, and thank you for being my students.

HUMAN INFRASTRUCTURE

29 May 2015
Late Imperial China

A couple of months ago I got an email from a student asking for "mercy" in footnote errors in a submitted essay. This student reminded me: As Confucius once said, "He who refuses to forgive breaks the bridge over which he, too, must cross."

I appreciated this email because I've been thinking about this quotation ever since. It's true. Forgiveness is something each of us needs. In some ways, forgiveness is a public work, a structure of civil engineering upon which we all rely, just like bridges and roads.

As a professor, I have asked students to maintain a professional, not casual tone in their email communications because I am not a peer, but a teacher. Confucius said, "Let the ruler be a ruler, a subject a subject." The University version of this is "Let the teacher be the teacher, a student a student." It's a hierarchical relationship, so it's not egalitarian. But it is a mutual relationship, a relationship with responsibility on both sides. I try to live up to my responsibility, but at times I may have failed to *be* a teacher. For these times, I apologize and ask my students' forgiveness.

Lecturers are not very different from students. We are students too, but just a little further down the road than those we teach. We're not smarter, but we have more experience. We have developed systems for collecting and sorting information, systems for doing things on time. (They don't always work like clockwork, just as the well-ordered Chinese bureaucracy often became dysfunctional because of exceptional population pressures or natural disasters.)

Being able to learn at a university level involves developing a good judgment for limits. In many ways it's like learning to drive a car. For example, learning how to research and write a major essay—and submit it on time, without panic and begging for a last-minute extension—is like developing a sense of safe "following distance" and "stopping distance" when driving a car. Essays have a "finishing distance." Over time, and perhaps after a few wrecks, you develop a sense of finishing distance (how much time you need to get things done) and how to order your other pursuits so you have enough time.

When you set out to produce a major piece of work, like a research essay, it is necessary to put in several times as much work as what is eventually displayed in the final product. I know this is hard to quantify or break down into numbers of words or hours, etc., but hopefully you get the general idea.

Writing a mediocre paper is like being a one-person moving company. You pick up several boxes of ideas. You load them into the truck until the bed is filled. You drive them to the professor's online depot and dump the load. Quality academic work is more time-consuming, but also more creative. It's like making wild-caught salmon with sorrel and mushroom sauce: fishing, harvesting, cleaning, chopping, searing, seasoning, plating, and serving. All of those processes are distilled into something original, shaped by your own sense of proportion and style. This is the work of advanced scholarship. It doesn't require brilliance—just practice, and time.

So one of the ways in which to characterize the relationship between lecturers and students is to see them as walking at different points along the same path of learning. If you look at things from the perspective of all human history, however, our relationship as lecturer and student changes. The distance between us radically collapses. You and I are basically at the same point on the path in terms of our relationship to people in the past.

What is our relationship to people in the past? Here I'm not just talking about the history of people in this place, but the people we came from, our parents and grandparents and those before them. They have created our world. This includes things that have made the world a less hospitable place, like nuclear weapons, the hole in the ozone layer, greenhouse gases in the atmosphere, interethnic hatred, and systems of structural inequality.

The people of our past have also created things that have made the world more joyful, like early-ripening rice, airplanes, golden kiwifruit, Honeycrisp apples, an awareness of the workings of the universe, and our very lives.

What are the works, words, and values you are going to leave the world?

One thing is certain: your life will be short. Against the backdrop of everyone who has ever lived, our lives scarcely cover any ground at all. And yet all of us are contributing, actively or passively, to shape the reality of billions of people who will walk the roads and cross over the bridges after us.

It's not for you to decide whether or not you're going to make a contribution to the world. That you will is a given. The question is, *which* works, words, and values will your life make more permanent in the world?

There are two different approaches to morality—the universalistic approach (one set of moral values should apply to all humanity) and the particularistic approach (within regions, cultures, and groups of people, there are many distinctive and valid sets of moral values). People are split in their views on this. I would like to point out that it is possible to acknowledge diverse particularities while still espousing a single set of values. Indeed, many value systems overlap and this overlap is the beginning of wisdom. Last week I was in New York for the Council on Foreign Affairs' Workshop on Religion, with religious leaders and scholars who were Muslims, Jews, Baptists, Mennonites, Zoroastrians, and so on. (I was the token "Mormon.") These colleagues' views were extremely different, and there was nothing close to a universal moral consensus. But these differences were very meaningful, not divisive, because they were articulated with integrity and good will. You can get pretty far on integrity and goodwill. The human world is enriched, not diminished, by a multiplicity of traditions daring to define what is real and true.

The fact that human situations throughout history have proven to be complex and multivalent does not mean there is never a right answer or that all moral values are relative. However, you should remember this: Moral claims and judgments are most compelling when they develop out of a broad awareness of human experience and a sense of perspective regarding one's relationship to all other people. This is why studying Chinese history is a worthwhile investment. There are a lot of people, there have been a lot of people, and many of them have lived in China as they've gone about their daily lives and passed their works, words, and values on to the next generation.

What are the works, words, and values you are currently passing on to the next generation? You might think, *well, I don't even know what I want to do, or say, or believe at this point in my life,* and you might be right. But the point is, even though you will be constantly evolving as an acting, thinking, moral individual, who you are at any given point has a real influence on the lives of others. The sooner you realize your life will be measured not in terms of "accomplishments" but in the quality of your relationships with others, the more deliberately you can apply yourself to inhabiting these relationships in a way that lives up to your ideals.

History, after all, is about trends and master narratives, but life is about relationships. This is the real influence we will have on the world— not in the final mass of recognition and material we will have accumulated by the end, but in the steady dissolution of our works, words, and values into the lives of others.

Let the student be a student; a daughter a daughter; a son a son; a friend a friend.

Thank you for your hard work, and thank you for being my students.

CIVILIZATION = ORGANIZATION?

2 June 2016
Late Imperial China

What is civilization? Is it inherently good or bad? Is it what human beings build is or is it who we are? Is it an end to be achieved, or the means by which to achieve an end?

Studying the governmental bureaucracies and infrastructure of late imperial China gives a sense of how organization makes new things possible. It was the Yongle[1] emperor's control of human and material resources that brought together shipwrights, the captains, and engineers to construct a treasure fleet of over three hundred ships and send them over the seas to Africa. It was the Qianlong[2] emperor's position at the head of the vast Chinese scholarly bureaucratic machine that allowed for the production in nine short years of the Siku Quanshu (the Complete Library of the Four Treasuries).

The Complete Library of the Four Treasuries aspired to put China's entire literary heritage in order. It was like an anthology of Chinese literature on steroids. The empire's top scholars collected rare books, reassembled fragments of lost ancient works using passages quoted from later writings. Three hundred sixty scholars from the Hanlin Academy[3] produced new critical editions of all works, including abstracts giving information on the author, work, and the transmission of each text—10,230 in all. Expert scholar-calligraphers transcribed manuscript copies in uniform format. The Complete Library of the Four Treasuries took up 79,932 chapters, or more than 360 million words.[4]

Wow, Qianlong! Organization is amazing!

And yet: getting all of China's literature organized necessarily meant subjecting large chunks of it to censorship. Words, phrases, and entire sections were discarded or altered, and many works were destroyed completely. As a matter of fact, the Four Treasuries are far from "complete." More works were suppressed than are included—perhaps 10,000 in all. All copies of the banned books were found and burned, and their carved wooden printing blocks, stored for reuse over centuries, were burned as well.

The compilation of the Complete Library of the Four Treasuries precipitated a literary inquisition of scholars whose work was deemed to be anti-Manchu or to contain negative attitudes toward peoples of conquest dynasties, such as the Mongols. Like the Manchus, these foreign dynasties had been China's powerful enemies and unsurprisingly bore the brunt of Chinese disdain and hatred. The Qianlong emperor at first brushed these examples aside, ordering simply that unflattering words (e.g., "malodorous savages") be replaced with harmless ones (e.g., "northern peoples"), but no more. Soon, however, he took a stronger stance. Writings that could be seen as pro-Ming,[5] antiforeign, salacious, or military in nature could be seen as forming pieces of a conspiratorial puzzle. These authors were in league with those who sought to destroy the Qing dynasty. One scholar has tabulated eighty-four major cases of censorship involving criminal indictments, of which seventy were prosecuted under the Qianlong emperor. In all but five of the eighty-four cases, one or more authors' works were found to contain treasonable content; the works were ordered destroyed and the authors, their families, and associates were subjected to punishments ranging from beatings and banishment to death and enslavement. In many cases, dead authors' bodies were exhumed and cut to pieces, while their living male descendants were executed and these men's wives enslaved.

How did the officials find all those people—the living authors and their families and associates, the dead authors' graves and descendants—and systematically destroy their lives? They found them by consulting the records and family registers that had been meticulously archived in capital, provincial, and prefectural offices, through published genealogies, and through living networks of informants that served the state.

Yikes, Qianlong—organization is fearsome.

If organization equals civilization, then I'm afraid I have to take a rather dim view of civilization. When we human beings combine our resources, time, and ingenuity to create something together, sometimes the result is brilliant. Vietnamese beef noodle soup, for instance, comes to mind. So often, however, we get it terribly wrong.

When I say this, I am thinking not only of the Qianlong emperor and his vast bureaucracy, but also of the trans-Atlantic slave trade, American systems of racial discrimination, large-scale industrial operations that despoil the natural environment, and the methodical, efficient horrors of the Nazi concentration camps.

Every day through the choices that we make, through the goods, energy, and media that we consume, and the political causes we support or ignore, we potentially strengthen complex, organized processes that, somewhere in the world, prevent our fellow beings from reaching their full potential.

Who will answer for the sufferings of those who are systematically excluded, whose lives are destroyed to serve the interests of those who hold political and economic power?

Who is not guilty in some way for failing to make our actions consistent with our words, or for failing to protect the vulnerable because we want to maintain our own comfort and convenience?

These are not new dilemmas, but old. Confucian philosophy had many things to say about a person's responsibility to behave like a human being among other human beings, regardless of convenience, expedience, or the vagaries of scale. In Book XV:24 of the *Analects*, Confucius's disciple Tzu Kung asked, "Is there a single word which can be a guide to conduct throughout one's life?" The Master said, "It is perhaps the word 'shu'— reciprocity. Do not impose on others what you yourself do not desire."[6]

In Book XII:19, when Confucius's disciple asked Confucius about government, he posed the situation of using the vast organizational resources of government to accomplish a moral outcome. The disciple said:

"What would you think if, in order to move closer to those who possess the Way, I were to kill those who do not follow the Way?"

Confucius's answer was that no project of government coercion can get human beings closer to where they need to be. A human project must unfold on a human scale—in the heart of each individual. He answered: "In administering your government, what need is there for you to kill? Just desire the good yourself and the common people will be good. The virtue of the gentleman is like wind; the virtue of the small man is like grass. Let the wind blow over the grass and it is sure to bend."[7] In his view, those who desired to do what was right and who were actively trying to cultivate themselves to be better would have a powerful, irresistible influence on those around them.

For Confucius, civilization lay not in the seamlessly turning cogs and gears of a vast bureaucratic organization, but in each individual's careful self-cultivation. This could not be accomplished in a steady progression, like the clunky computers of the 1940s that became smaller and faster with every passing year. In contrast to this ratchet of better-and-better, our desires to be good, kind, and honest are, as Confucius observed, both tantalizingly close to hand and disappointingly fleeting. "No sooner do I desire benevolence than it is here"[8]—but how often do I desire it? How often am I distracted?

From a Confucian point of view, civilization is not what people do or what they build. Civilization is what people *are*. It is the daily work of humans at being humans. It is something we both find within ourselves and borrow from each other. It is something we glean from ordinary encounters with frustration, disappointment, and love. From this perspective, projects requiring massive organization like the Complete Library of the Four Treasuries, the jet engine, and solar energy are impressive, but not coextensive with human civilization. Civilization is humans being civil—being ren, or benevolent, and acting in accordance with li, the rituals that have emerged over centuries to acknowledge our shared humanity.

You might think: Big deal. "'Being moral'—that's a great ideal, but in real life I have to do what works to make it."

The lessons of Ming and Qing history show that regardless of the high status or impressive political achievements of a given individual, from Zhu

Yuanzhang[9] to Qianlong, people will also always remember *what kind of a person* you were. Our career successes will never erase or obscure our personal failings.

On the one hand, this is comforting. Everyone has personal failings, so instead of letting our weaknesses weigh us down, let's work to turn them into strengths. On the other hand, the reality that people *will remember us* as we are today, and six years ago, and tomorrow, is sobering. Probably none of us will ever be emperors, or prime ministers, or even mildly famous. The main historical legacy that each of us will leave this world will be in the form of our influence in the lives of others. *Precisely because of us*, the lives of our parents, siblings, children, friends, and fellow students will be distinctly better or worse.

And so we see that who we are—including our facility for patience, compassion, and generosity—is inseparable from what we do, whether it be participating in a tutorial, or interviewing for a job, or managing employees.

If there's one sweeping generalization we can make about Chinese people in the late imperial period, in all of their diverse gender, class, regional, and dialectic situations, it's that they worked hard. Even the emperor worked hard, with his dawn audiences, piles of memorials, endless changes of ceremonial clothing, and the constant need to respond to crises across the vast domain. The emperor's subjects worked hard at memorizing texts, pulling grain barges, binding and bending the bones in dainty feminine feet.

Probably not all, but many of these people also worked hard to be good. Because of the Confucian philosophy permeating daily life, they believed human character can be cultivated and improved. They believed goodness is not an innate ability, nor a gift externally bestowed, but something you can and should work at, just like weeding crops or catching errant apostrophes.

As soon as we desire benevolence, then it is here. The more we work at being good, relying on rituals like "please" and "thank you" and "would you like to join us," the more we will succeed until someday, like Confucius in his advanced years, we will follow what our hearts desire, and what we desire will be right.[10] Then our lives, too, will be something worth remembering.

Thank you for your hard work, and thank you for being my students.

grapefruit tree

this way to the eel stream

Miko's favorite tree

View from the front of the house

Annual Newsletter

December 2016
Auckland, New Zealand

Dear Friends:

Greetings from the house with the table saw in the living room! We bought a house in April and have been in the throes of renovation ever since. The house is a disaster zone. No single room is in a finished state. There are no cabinet doors in the kitchen. There is no trim on the windows. The bedrooms are full of tools, cans of paint, and rolls of insulation.

It's bad now, but it used to be worse. When we first took possession, we immediately gutted the kitchen and the bathroom. This meant that for about a week and a half, when we crossed from the back kitchen door to the living room, we had to hop from beam to beam, about a meter (three feet) above the bare earth. We cooked on the table saw with a butane burner. We brushed our teeth at the laundry room sink. Atop the washing machine, toothbrushes were strewn around next to paintbrushes, tubes of toothpaste next to tubes of Alabaster silicone. Since the house is under construction, we have been living in the garage, which the previous owner finished—after a fashion—as two bedrooms. We hope to move into the house bedrooms in time for Christmas.

We are doing all of the building work ourselves, except for the plumbing and electricity. This has been very educational. We have

old box of laundry powder being used as toothbrush holder

actual laundry powder

spooky space

floor-leveling compound

porcelain tile

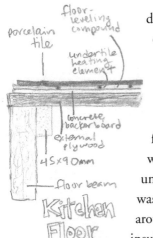

porcelain tile

floor-leveling compound

undertile heating element

concrete backer board

external plywood

45×90mm

floor beam

Kitchen Floor

discovered that tiling a floor is like parenting. At the end of the job you've finally figured out how to do it properly, but by this time the floor is already set, a permanent monument to your mistakes. The building process has ushered in numerous Mageddons. First there was Floormageddon, which involved ripping out the kitchen floor and then installing successive layers of external plywood, concrete backer board, floor leveling compound, undertile heating, tile, grout, and grout sealer. Then there was Rat-poop-mageddon, which involved climbing around in the rafters tearing out all the old ceiling insulation that had provided a nest for rats and vacuuming up the droppings and debris. We did this between the hours of 9:00 p.m. and 4:00 a.m. on a Tuesday night. It was kind of like a cross between rock climbing and yoga for seven hours straight, and by the end we were dead tired. Since then we have also experienced Plastermageddon, Wood-chip-mageddon, and Fruit-tree-mageddon.

Needless to say, this has taken a toll on our organizational life (which was never stellar to begin with). Things go missing frequently. Sometimes they fall down the two holes in the floor in the rear entryway, but at other times they simply disappear: keys, wallets, pillowcases, library books. Desperate times lead to desperate measures: Joseph has a secret stash of socks and won't tell anyone where it is. The Bean discovered it, but his lips are sealed. Despite the mess and inconvenience, we are basically happy to have a house. It's one hundred meters from the Sunnyvale Train Station, right on the bike path that connects to the city, and across the street from a big open field where the kids like to play. On the far side of the field is a stream where the kids have caught a number of tasty freshwa- ter eels. Gutting

Chicken fat

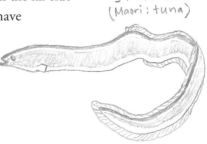

Happy 1st Birthday Bob and Angel!

Bob — fuzzy, nice, curious

Angel — fuzzy, grumpy

shortfin eel (Maori: tuna)

and skinning an eel is a messy job, however, and recently they have preferred fishing in the ocean, off a wharf.

Shoot (four years) is one of the big kids at kindy now. He does a lot of talking with his eyes, which are most often full of mischief. However, Joseph has a theory that the Shoot is a fundamentally polite person. The other day he was waking the kids up for school. He shook the Shoot, who said, "Can you wake somebody else up, please?" then fell right back asleep. The Shoot has gone through a number of alternately amusing and exasperating phases this year. For instance, he insisted on wearing a cape every day from late June to mid-September—first his blue windbreaker, then a blanket with brightly colored stripes. He seems to have taken the renovation in stride. You haven't seen joy until you've handed a four-year-old a hammer and told him to smash the bedroom wall.

Leaf (six years) is a gardener extraordinaire. She has her own little garden planted with strawberries and bok choy and is in the gardening group at school. Every morning she takes Joseph by the hand and leads him around the yard, commenting on the baby pumpkin that grew a third leaf or the apple tree that made two blossoms overnight, etc. She never met a worm she didn't find delightful. She has started learning the cello in earnest this year, after a long "soft start" at the suggestion of her wonderfully patient and experienced cello teacher, Ms. Margaret. She is always up a tree. She had a nasty fall from a tree at school earlier this year. It was essentially a face plant onto concrete, but luckily she was completely fine except for some scrapes.

Sprout (eight years) has become a fishing maniac. He is a regular at the local store, Norcross Fishing World, where the staff give him special discounts. He is also a regular at losing things in mysterious or dramatic circumstances. To name two separate instances, he lost half of his surfcasting rod and a new package of softbaits to sudden gusts of wind that blew them off Cornwallis Wharf. Each time Joseph had to jump into the water in his underwear to retrieve them. To pay Joseph back for

Recipe for homemade chocolate

~~~~~~

⅓ c. Samoan koko, chopped fine

⅔ c. shredded coconut

zest of 2 lemons

½ c. dried cherries, cranberries, or raisins

⅛ c. coconut oil, melted

1) Blend dry ingredients

2) add coconut oil + stir

3) press into chocolate molds and chill. Makes 12

185

this second wetting, the Sprout is now in charge of weeding the strip of pea plants along the side of the house forever.

Sprout and Bean have started busking. Their favorite spot is on Queen Street in downtown Auckland, where people passing in a constant stream exclaim at their cuteness, take videos on their phones, and drop money into Sprout's cello case. In one hour the boys can make a killing. They even have a municipal busking license and, most recently, a Youtube channel.

Bean (ten years) is finishing his last year at Henderson Valley School and his last year in the HVS rock band. He was very proud of his role in the school production, a very eclectic mix of songs like "One Little Fantail" (sung by native New Zealand birds) and Michael Jackson's "Thriller" (sung by zombies) tangled together in a plot about two aliens dressed up as Justin Bieber and Taylor Swift who learn about caring for the Earth. His role? He opened and closed the curtains. His most recent obsession is Pokemon, which has come roaring back into style.

Joseph is still working for the Chinese law firm. He has proven himself super handy. After finding store-made modular cabinets flimsy, he built the cabinets for the new kitchen himself out of three-quarter-inch plywood and bamboo panels. They were so solid the countertop installer proclaimed they would last forever. Melissa is still at the University of Auckland. She is getting close to finishing her book, provisionally titled *China and the True Jesus.* If you read this book, you will not only learn about China's very own restorationist Christian church, but will also effortlessly absorb the basic things everyone needs to know about modern Chinese history. Stay tuned!

Generally speaking, we feel very grateful for our lives, our jobs, and our health. We are also aware of the ways in which the world is becoming a more unfriendly and

Number of cockroaches that Melissa killed while illustrating this letter all alone in a two-star hotel in San Antonio, TX

(running across the desk) Number of times kids have gotten lice in 2016

at least 3 (Melissa has never been so smug!)

18 19

21

186

Cornwallis Wharf/
Huia Wharf

dangerous place. In the coming year we resolve to do what we can to promote human decency and civility, to adjust our lifestyle to fight climate change, and to be part of the glue that holds families and communities together. At the root of these resolutions is our faith in Jesus Christ, whose birth we celebrate this season, and whose daunting commandment to love our neighbors as ourselves we take seriously, even though we fall short. Thank you for your friendship. Best wishes for a happy New Year!

Love,
Melissa, Joseph, Bean, Sprout, Leaf, and Shoot

RICH ENTANGLEMENTS

7 June 2017
Late Imperial China

I would like to ask you a question about the meaning of life. The question is: Whose life is more significant—your life or the life of someone who lived in China during the Ming (1368–1644) or the Qing (1644–1911) dynasty? Further questions: To determine whose life was more significant, does it matter whether that person was famous, like Zhu Yuanzhang[1] or the Qianlong emperor?[2] Does it matter whether that person was the same gender or social class as you? Is the life of a privileged scholar who leaves behind a legacy of government service and published poetry of more consequence than the life of a poor rice farmer who leaves behind nothing more than chromosomes and the hardness of the dirt paths between the fields? Are all lives of equal value, or does this value vary? How would a Confucian answer that question?

Regardless of how you answered, studying history helps us understand all the other lives we could have lived, the chores, know-how, particular sufferings, and peculiar joys that would be ours if we had been born in another place and time. This perspective helps us to appreciate the current privileges and problems in our own lives. Because of modern conveniences and health-care advances, we ordinary folks now live a more comfortable, safe, and varied life than the Qianlong emperor in the seventeenth century or the American billionaire John D. Rockefeller at the beginning of the twentieth century.

This robe worn by a Daoist priest in 1800 is embroidered with silk and gold thread. None of us has anything this opulent and amazing—unless you count a centrally heated room, or a personal computer, or access to networks of buses, trains, and planes that take us wherever we want to go. At the same time, we now live with the possibility that all humanity and living things on earth could be destroyed with the touch of a few buttons, or that we could foul our own nest—our planet—beyond the bounds of habitability.

Daoist priest's robe, 1800

As in the case of the scholar who lamented the fall of the Ming state but felt twice as devastated at the death of his little daughter, these global problems sometimes pale in comparison to our individual challenges. Sometimes we're just trying to keep on moving forward in some sort of direction. Sometimes we're just trying to stay alive. This is currently my problem, actually. I'm currently fighting to whack back a major health issue. Please don't worry about me—I feel strong and I'm well-supported. But I am telling you because I want to let you know that I understand what it's like to feel vulnerable, or uncertain, or as if everyone else is rushing ahead in Life while you are just trying to keep your head above water.

What we learn from studying the *Analects* of Confucius, sixteenth-century Ming bureaucratic memos, and eighteenth-century poems about being bored or putting on makeup is that human experience doesn't really change that much. Within our various situations in time and space, we all face the same challenges: How do we live a good life? When power comes to us, can we exercise it in a way that empowers others? How can we show integrity in the face of injustice, courage in the face of danger?

We learn that the answer to a big question can depend on the role you inhabit and the relationships binding you to a given situation. As your teacher, I have tried to teach you not only about famous emperors and tax reform, but how to present yourself as a smart, educated person in professional communications.[3] I have tried to teach how cultural forms reinforce beliefs and values (for instance, the way in which the format of an email can signal respect and teachability). I've enjoyed getting to know you. You are all going on to do great and important things, except for the six of you who go on to be lawyers. Just kidding. (My husband is a lawyer.)

What you probably realize by now is that Confucian relationships have a very long shelf life. In 1402, the upright minister Fang Xiaoru stood up to Zhu Di, the Yongle emperor, after he killed his nephew and usurped the throne. Fang refused to draft (and thus legitimize) Zhu Di's accession proclamation.[4] Fang Xiaoru was killed, his family was killed, and all the people who had passed the civil service examination in years during which Fang Xiaoru had overseen the exams were killed, because they counted as his students. Luckily, I will never be important enough to get myself killed by a head of state, so none of my students has to worry about this particular outcome. But, remember, a Confucian teacher is always a teacher. I will always be available as a resource.

In the end, the question about the meaning or the significance of one's life comes down not to how it compares with a stranger's life in the distant past or future, but how it connects with the lives of others in the present. Every person, from a peasant in Ming China to a university student in the early twenty-first century, lives amidst a tangle of face-to-face relation-

With my teacher, Henrietta Harrison, at Oxford

ships: parent, child, brother, sister, teacher, student, partner, friend. Kindly influence within these reciprocal relationships is something not even historians, with their quick judgments and critical eyes, can take away. An economic policy can be a disaster, and a set of governing priorities can be deeply misguided. But no one can undo or discount what it meant to someone when you were a sympathetic friend, a loyal sibling, or a generous colleague.

Therefore: in the face of growing impersonality, amidst the tendency to digitally multiply "friendship" until you have nothing more than an audience of beeps and

With Popo (grandmother) in California

pings, remember to deliberately cultivate the relationships you have that are truly reciprocal.

Think of one person today to whom you owe a debt—your mother or father or grandparent might be a great place to start—and send them a cheerful note, or email, or phone call. Think of a relationship in which you occupy the senior position, and do something to reach out and be supportive.

As you live among these rich entanglements, day by day, year by year, you will both transmit your values to others and be changed beyond recognition. Having become acquainted with the struggles of people long dead, you will remember them as you wrestle with your own difficulties and anticipate your own triumphs—until your life, too, is someone else's history.

Thank you for your hard work, and thank you for being my students.

PART FOUR

*getting
disemboweled*

Performing with the kids and the other members at the Casa Do Engenho capoeira group at a Brazilian cultural event, October 2017

About a week after my colectomy (surgery to remove about a third of my colon), I suddenly realized, with delight: Hey! I've been disemboweled!

This section contains selections from the series of emails I wrote to my friends and family members from the time I was first diagnosed with colon cancer to the day I finished my twelve fortnightly chemotherapy treatments. Tanya Samu, the ward Relief Society president and also a lecturer at the University of Auckland, accompanied me to the first nine out of the twelve treatments. (For the last three treatments, Tanya was out of the country, and my family was around.) As Tanya and I sat together in the padded blue chemo chairs, we chatted about family, the university promotions process, Māori and Pacific student education, and church. Deep associations have been made. Sometimes when I see her at church, or even visualize her face, I get the metallic "chemo" taste in my mouth. Tanya and other members of our ward have been so kind to us. I really don't know how to repay them, though I will try.

We especially needed this kindness because all our family members live far away. However, our family did find many meaningful ways to connect with us. In August 2017, having completed the first chemo treatment, I traveled to Utah for my youngest brother's wedding. On my birthday, two days before the wedding, I asked the women in my extended family (cousins, aunts, great-aunts) to come with me into the mountains and pray for me. In the early evening, we hiked into a beautiful canyon near Spanish Fork. In a quiet place under some trees at the side of the trail, we gathered in a circle. Those closest to me placed their hands on my body and those around them placed their hands on each other's shoulders. *In turns they prayed aloud for me, praying over every cell and molecule in my body, invoking God's blessings upon my family and my spirit, exhorting me to remember that those who had gone on before, including my mother, were at my side. On the next day, I asked my father and four brothers to give me a priesthood blessing. I sat in my aunt's front room, along with my grandmother, my aunt, and my cousin. Like my cousins and aunts, my father called on me to remember my mother—someone who intimately understood what I was going through, someone who could help. He reminded me that I had important work to do and blessed me with resilience and capability.*

Words cannot describe how much it meant to be surrounded by the people I loved most in the world, who most loved me, knit into unity not just through ties of kinship but through ties of faith, prayer, and the laying on of hands. I returned to New Zealand and resumed my treatments with a sense of peace.

FYI

25 May 2017
Sunnyvale, Auckland, New Zealand

Dear All:

I hope this message finds you well. I'd like to give you a little update on my life, which is that I have cancer. I found out last week. It's colon cancer, and it has possibly spread through lymph nodes, though possibly not. Worst-case scenario: chemotherapy to whack it down periodically until it outruns the chemo and becomes uncontrollable. Best-case scenario: "keyhole surgery" that takes it out completely. Scheduled colectomy operation on June 19. I definitely won't be able to travel to the States this summer; Joseph and the kids will go without me. As you know, I like to be prepared, so I try to hold both scenarios in my hands at the same time.

To be candid, it's a difficult time for me emotionally. As you may know, my mom died of cancer about eight years ago, so I have been through all this before (operation this, lymph nodes that, a scan here and a scan there), with a not-very-encouraging conclusion. As I walk the same path, I can scarcely tell where grief for her ends and fear for myself begins. From my personal experience I see that my mother, who was far more righteous and faithful and deserving than I, was not granted any special medical miracles. Furthermore, the closest ancestral examples of bravery in the face of life-threatening conditions that I have at hand are my samurai ancestors, who believed that life was beautiful but short, like the cherry blossoms in spring. So on the one hand, as an individual all by myself I feel that the best approach is to remember, as an appreciator-of-Buddhism, that attachment is a source of suffering, including attachment to life, plans, visions of the self, and so on. On the other hand, I am deeply attached to my children—that's my native religious paradigm—and even the mere possibility of leaving them by themselves when they're young fills me with pain. And there are stories in human history of people wrangling, wheedling, and dealing with God to buy themselves a bit more time. Of course I can't help but do this as well.

197

I am preparing for the worst while hoping for the best. As the daughter of someone who once buried a ton of coal in the backyard and who has numerous devices and weapons stored up in eager anticipation of the Zombie Apocalypse, it feels much better to be prepared. I'm not depressed. As a matter of fact, my past few days with the kids have been very full and happy. I made bagels yesterday to commemorate my CT scan (the scanner looks like a big donut or bagel). I don't think I have yelled at anyone once, though I did haul the Leaf out of the bathtub tonight after she peed in it (with two other siblings in it). I told her she had violated the Fundamental Law of the Bathtub. She refused to budge, etc. I don't think I'm giving up. I am simply trying to look the worst-case scenario in the face and come to terms with it. Life is sweet when it's possibly shorter than you thought it would be.

I apologize for breaking this news over a mass email because it is an extremely rotten way to receive distressing news. However, just in the past few days I have found that there really isn't any good way to *give* distressing news, either. It's easier for me to tell everyone at once than to have to repeatedly go through the shock and horror of people's initial reactions.

I was instructed by the cancer psychologist to ignore people's advice for how to cure cancer through diet, miracle drugs, or other health practices. I was also instructed to not feel obligated to respond to people's well-meaning emails or letters or Facebook whatevers. Both of these pieces of advice make sense—though I will certainly try to respond—so please don't depend on prompt replies from me. If you feel like getting in touch, I think it would be especially helpful for me if you could recount some sort of memory in which I might have taught you something about something, or was clearly proven to be awesome. :) It is helpful to feel awesome when preparing for war.

To sum up, I am completely functional and I feel fine, but I would like to give you a little heads up because cancer, like a marathon, demands respect, and it may compromise my ability to function as usual for at least a short period of time. Thanks so much for your love and support. I'm writing because I know that you care about me, and that means a great deal.

Love,
Melissa

Hello from Post-Op

20 June 2017
North Shore Hospital, Auckland, New Zealand

Dear All:

The senile lady across the room is rattling her bed rails again. She did this all last night to try to get attention. I spent last night lying flat on my back, trying to move as little as possible, and so I couldn't see who it was who was making those noises and shouting things like: "It's all a racket, I tell you; you can't fool me anymore!" "Counting members of Parliament! Winston Peters!" "What do I have to do to get something to eat or drink around here!" "I'm calling my daughter in the middle of the night, at 2:00 a.m., so *she* has to wake up and *suffer* the way I've suffered!" The nursing staff have quietly promised to move her somewhere else before the evening. I certainly hope they do because now there is a new girl in the room who looks tired and in pain.

One minute I was there in the operating theater, holding an oxygen mask over my face, and the next minute I was waking up in post-op. I felt like a slacker for sleeping through the whole thing. I took a shower today and found that I have been shaved and painted bright pink. I had horrible back pain yesterday, which apparently came from lying on the operating table in an unnatural position. I didn't understand how this worked at first, because I have always prided myself in my ability to sleep on hard surfaces. However, the surgeon explained that even when you are sleeping, your postural muscles are engaged, but when you are under general anesthetic, everything is completely floppy.

In the pre-op waiting room before the surgery, I sat cross-legged on my bed, quiet and naked under a too-large hospital gown. I thought the Buddhist thoughts: Be free of attachment. I thought the Daoist thoughts: Go with the flow; don't resist. I thought the collective ascetic thoughts: People who love you are fasting and praying. I made the personal appeals: Father! Mother! Mom! please be with me. I looked around me and saw

199

several other people, quiet and naked under their hospital gowns, waiting for surgery. Truly, the world is full of suffering. Truly, all is vanity. Truly, our fellow beings are holy.

The hospital staff are unfailingly kind. I walked into the operating theater in my thin hospital socks, and they welcomed me into the room like hosts at a dinner party. They spoke with warmth and humor as they swabbed my back with red-paint-antiseptic. They laid me down on my bed in the night like a child and covered me, layer by layer, with warm blankets. They speak patiently to the senile lady across the room as she refuses to take her medication and as they change her soiled linens. They stand by her bedside and listen to her incoherent rants.

This morning, I sat up for the first time in several hours and finally beheld the person who had been rattling the bed rails and cursing the world all night. Her voice had been quite deep and gruff, but she looked surprisingly small and frail. She stared straight at me and said, "When did they shave your head, mate?" I explained that I'd always had no hair. She said: "Are you going out to walk today?" I said I was going to try. She said, "I haven't been able to walk for days, so I've got no sympathy for you." At this, the third woman (in our room of four beds) met my eyes. It was a marvelously eloquent communication. In that simple look, she said: I am sorry for her, and I hope you are fine. I smiled back.

The surgeon said that the surgery went well. On Monday we will find out whether the lymph nodes surrounding the tumor were cancerous (i.e., whether I will need chemo). If I need chemo, I believe it will start in about a month, though hopefully I can time it so it doesn't interfere with my travel to Peter and Megan's wedding. I kind of feel that I should demand chemo in any event, just to get my money's worth out of the free New Zealand healthcare system. Thank you for your thoughts, fasting, and prayers. It means a lot to me. It is emotionally taxing, and also frightening, to feel the weight of others' sorrow and fear on my behalf. But it is also powerful, and humbling, to feel the force of that love. I am very thankful.

Rattle rattle, rattle rattle. Tap tap, tap tap. Clink, clink, clink.

With gratitude,
Melissa

Chemo

22 June 2017
Sunnyvale, Auckland, New Zealand

Dear All:

The post-surgery histology report came back, and seven of the twenty-four lymph nodes were cancerous. The good news is that not all of them were cancerous, so the big chunks of cancer are officially removed from my body. However, the fact that the cancer was aggressive enough to spread beyond the intestine into the lymph nodes means there could be little microscopic cancers zooming around my body. At this point, you bring in the chemo. It will be a six-month course—something like one week on, two weeks off. Sounds like a running workout! I would of course have been pleased to be told that there were absolutely no lymph nodes affected and I can now end my "month-long battle with cancer," but that does feel like a cop-out. Now I'm getting the full-blown cancer experience!

The University is being incredibly kind and giving me paid sick leave, so at this point I'm going to forgive it for going through a corporatizing process that cuts humanities classes and saddles academics with time-consuming administrative duties. Thank you, University of Auckland! I'll just try to get as much done as I can when I'm feeling well. I should be able to work the chemo schedule around Peter and Megan's wedding in August and my conference trip to Taiwan in October.

I came home from the hospital today. Just before going home, I had a meeting with my surgeon in which we discussed the histology report and I presented him with a haiku. He read it aloud, to the amusement of the junior doctors on his team. I can't share the haiku with this wide, dignified audience, because it was scatological (an answer to the question that doctors and nurses are always asking patients who have had bowel resections), but I feel it was really funny. Every time I think about it, I start to laugh.

My mother had a similar surgical result. It appeared that the cancer was entirely contained within the tissue that was removed, but eventually she had to have chemo. After chemo, it was apparently gone, until it came back. I can't quite remember the timeline, but I believe that she died within about a year and a half of the surgery. I recall this to define my horizons. I feel reasonably sure that I will be around until at least the end of 2017, and this is a long time to be sure about (unless I'm killed in a car accident, or in a US shopping mall shooting, or by a jellyfish sting). Sure, every cancer is different, and I will hopefully not follow in these same footsteps, but what I'm saying is that even in the absolute worst-case scenario I feel that I've got quite a lot to work with. So I'm not stressed out—not on that score, at least.

As I sat there in the hospital, surrounded by many people in pain, lying in bed hooked up to undignified tubes, most of them older, I realized I was seeing my future. Death comes to all of us, but when we're young we don't worry about when it will come because we are sure it is many decades down the road. I feel that is a gift to see it now, so clearly and so close at hand. No one wants to learn wisdom through suffering, but the truth is, this is how it works. I hope that God will try to get their money's worth out of me and keep me in circulation for a long time—and indeed I have made many silent vows with this in mind—but ultimately, the point of life is not to have it but to do things with it.

So, in sum: Definitely not the worst-case scenario. Mostly what was expected. Still a possibility, though not a guarantee, of a cure. Life has no guarantees.

Thanks for your love and support.

Love,
Melissa

FOLFOX[1]

27 July 2017
Sunnyvale, Auckland, New Zealand

Dear All:

You ask: How was your first day of chemo? I am in a hurry because I want to get to bed for my new strict bedtime of 10:00 p.m., but here are three observations.

Music

I was all hooked up to my IV tree, the oxaliplatin dripping down through the plastic tubing, typing on my computer. All of a sudden, I realized I really needed to go to the toilet. This was strange because I hadn't drunk anything but one cup of water. Then I realized: if you are going to give someone toxic chemicals, of course you are going to majorly dilute them in huge bags of glucose solution. And yes, as I glanced up, there were big fat bladderfuls of liquid, hanging from the top of the tree. When the childish word for what comes out of the bladder popped into my head, I was suddenly gleeful. You see, I have twelve sessions of chemo. So, I thought, to help the kids mark time and count down the days, why not make a song, modeled on "The Twelve Days of Christmas":

> *On the first day I went for my chemotherapy*
> *I really, really had to pee.*

I imagine that the song will not improve in presentability or dignity, so probably I won't share more than this. Be assured, however, that the verse for round five will be very carefully crafted, because you sing it slowly (sometimes with harmony), in just four notes.

Manifestations

I came home to the empty house and washed my hands. All of a sudden I could feel a cold, icy feeling running through my nerves. This is a common side effect, but I didn't realize it would manifest itself so soon. I also felt the famous tingling in the hands and feet. (*Now I know how you felt, Mom!*) In the evening, around 8:00 p.m., I started to feel nauseated and popped an additional antinausea pill. Its name is something like Doxymethodone or Dextroparaben or Dystotrumpadrone or something like this. When I washed my face, all of a sudden my lips froze. It was so weird. It was like I had been sitting on a very long ski-lift ride for a very long time with no face mask or scarf.

When I feel the symptoms, I feel humble (this is no joke!). At the same time, it reminds me of the time when I was in labor with the Leaf. Usually women are conditioned to want to avoid the pain of labor, but because the Leaf took so long to get going, and I had to be induced, I welcomed the pain, even as the contractions grew more and more intense. Every time I feel the tingling, I think: Ha ha! Die, little cancers!

Things

Feeling a bit nauseated, and also suitably tired, and somewhat freaked out by my frozen face, I retired to the bedroom. Walking through the dark hallway alone, I noticed things around me, the physical manifestations of people I love: the walls Sharyn washed when she came to keep me company two weeks ago, the jacket Auntie Annie gave me, the mismatched socks I stole from Joseph's sacred sock drawer, my college-era sweatpants. I opened my dresser, took out the silk scarf given to me by the mother of Hui, my PhD student, and wrapped it around my nose, mouth, and face to prevent the frozen-face syndrome from escalating into the (apparently dreadful) frozen throat, in which you feel like you can't breathe for a few minutes.

I went to the closet and fetched the lip balm and "skin-conditioning oil" Amy gave me during her visit last week. I have never been into "beauty things" or even

Vacutainer needle

Varieties of needles

portacath needle

butterfly needle

lip balm. My nightstand is a pair of cardboard boxes and my usual beauty regimen amounts to smearing and washing off soap. But tonight, alone on the verge of a new frontier, the things made me thoughtful. I rubbed the balm on my frozen lips. I put the oil on my cheeks, but there was more of it than I expected. So I touched my head, my lips, my neck, my hands. My body remembered this as the feeling of a blessing—of receiving a blessing, and of performing such blessings myself during my time as a worker in the Boston temple. I don't believe applying skincare oil is the same thing as a sacred temple ritual, but the familiar sensation brought back the memory of what it means to connect with people in a way that acknowledges your mutual, most fervent hope—that God is real, and manifest in the world, in people, and even things.

Love,
Melissa

400 Meters; 6 Miles

8 September 2017
Sunnyvale, Auckland, New Zealand

Dear All:

Here I sit at the picnic table in Parrs Park, hooked up to my cute little cytotoxic chemical balloon pump. As I type, the spring wind gusts over my hands, setting off little oxaliplatin-induced chills at the base of my fingernails and sharp tingles as I strike the keys (A and F in particular) with my fingertips. The Sprout is in the pool at swimming lessons, and as they wait for their turn, the Bean, the Leaf, and the Shoot are passing the time by running up and down the skateboard ramp. Now they are running across the green grass, the Bean holding the Shoot's hand and the Leaf bounding ahead, her hair and blue dress blowing in the wind.

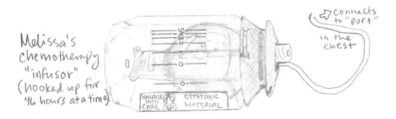

Melissa's chemotherapy "infusor" (hooked up for 46 hours at a time)

connects to "port" in the chest

HANDLE WITH CARE   CYTOTOXIC MATERIAL

Dear All:

Now it's Friday, not Thursday. I had to stop typing because the cold wind gave me pins and needles in my fingertips (like little electric shocks, each time a finger struck a key) and froze my hands into immobile shards. I wrapped my head and mouth and throat in the kids' swimming towels and sat on the ground in a sheltered corner of the playground. I peered out through a gap in the towels and watched the kids tearing around the playground, swinging on the giant swing, climbing the tower, running and shouting in the wind. When it was time to go in for swimming lessons, my hands were still frozen and useless, so I had to ask the Bean to open my backpack for me and get out my wallet. "You should be tucked up in bed with a bowl of hot soup," chided the usually forbidding Swimming Lessons Front Desk Lady.

Yesterday (Thursday) was my third chemo (out of twelve). I'm thinking of the whole chemotherapy thing in terms of long races, so it would be the equivalent of the 400 meters in the mile or the 6-mile-mark in the marathon. At this stage in a race, you're not yet tired, but the jitters are gone and you are running strongly, at a steady pace.

Like the cytotoxic chemicals seeping into my system and abiding for the long term, we are developing some regular routines. On Thursdays and Fridays, which are Day One and Two of chemo and I am alone with the kids when they come home from school, I give them the Chemo Special. This means that when they practice their instruments, they just have to do all of their songs twice (with some sort of focused improvement the second time). When my hands freeze up I ask them to open my backpack, or get something out of my wallet, or take cold things out of the freezer. Every few days there is some sort of blood test, or hospital procedure (like getting unhooked from the pump). I usually leave the big kids at home, but take the Shoot to keep him out of trouble. He watches with intense interest as they swab my port with disinfectant, pierce my veins, collect blood in tubes. On Days Twelve and Thirteen (just before the next chemo) I feel up to eating junk food. On Days Two and Three I feel like eating protein and fruit. I think I am starting to lose some of my taste buds. Fruit is starting to taste funny, which is too bad.

Although some things become normal, they do not cease to arouse fear, or pathos, or pain. Yesterday, I settled into the blue padded chemo chair with a book, chatting with Tanya Samu, who sat next to me. We were talking about something interesting and engaging. Nevertheless, as I saw the chemo needle on the nurse's tray, I could not help but notice how it looked matte black and curved, like barbed wire, instead of shining and straight like most other medical needles that one associates with healing medicine. The nurse told me to inhale as he pushed this needle through my skin into the port. I flinched. "Are you okay?" he asked. "You just stabbed me!" I replied, looking down as the dark blood bubbled out of my chest into his tube. I hope I didn't say it in an accusing tone of voice. But stabbing is stabbing.

Later, as I sat in the chemo chair, typing on my laptop, I looked at the man in the chair across the room. A woman was sitting next to him, leaning her head on his shoulder, weeping as she read from a Cancer Society booklet. I noticed that she was reading from the part toward the end. Perhaps she was reading the section at the end titled, "When your cancer is in an advanced stage," where the booklet admonishes you that while it is good to have hope, it is also good to be realistic. It gives scripts of things you can say to your kids, like, "So-and-so will still take you to soccer practice." I remember walking down Symonds Street toward the bus stop sometime in June, reading this section and weeping. I saw the woman across the room and felt she was right to weep, whatever it was that she was reading, as she sat next to her loved one in the blue padded chemo chair.

It was so good to travel back to the States for Peter's wedding in August. It felt like I was gathering strength for a long fight—like the psychospiritual equivalent of carb-loading before a race. I absorbed the blessings, prayers, and admonitions of my girl cousins and aunties and the blessings, prayers, and admonitions of my father and brothers. Some powerful promises were made to me, which have given me peace as I run this race.

For some reason, sometimes we voluntarily sign up to experience physical and psychological pain. I remember that one of the last marathons I ran was the San Diego Rock 'n' Roll marathon. It was in June 2011, about a year after the Leaf was born. I pumped a lot of breastmilk and left her with Joseph, then drove down to San Diego with some rice and a rice cooker. I crashed on the hospitable couch of Amy and Chris O'Keefe, UCSD grad students. I ate rice for dinner and rice for breakfast. I kept waking up throughout the night for fear I would sleep through my alarm. In the predawn dark, I drove to a parking lot, boarded a shuttle bus, and arrived at the starting line. The first couple of miles wound through Balboa Park and the San Diego Zoo. Then you run through the Old Town (downtown) area of San Diego city. At this point, around miles four and five, my energy levels were still high. I checked my watch and was right on pace.

This is where I am now, in my chemo. I am sure things will get more challenging, but this is par for the course. I remember the final few miles of the San Diego Rock 'n'Roll marathon. The course looped around an island, out by SeaWorld. From the island, you couldn't see the finish line. I was tired and my legs had lost their spring. I struggled to stay ahead of the pacer, who wore a flag and a band around his chest with the time "3:40." I had to come in ahead of this pacer or I wouldn't have a Boston marathon qualifying time, which was my goal for the marathon. The sun was well overhead and hot. When I finally came around the island and got onto the straightaway leading to the finish line, I was in so much pain. The pacer came up right behind me. I could hear his feet on the pavement and see his flag flapping out of the corner of my eye. I cried out in despair and stumbled on. I crossed the line at 3:38.59. On the other side, I collapsed onto the blacktop, happy to have a Boston qualifying time. I sat there for a minute or so. And then I got up, popped open a bottle of cold water, climbed back onto the shuttle, got into my car, took a shower, changed my clothes, and met Amy and Chris at church. The formal clothes felt strange over my sore muscles, but besides this, everything was back to normal.

I remember that particular race as a time in which I felt both pride and strength along with despair and weakness. It didn't take long to traverse the distance between the two extremes—just 26.2 two miles and under four hours. I have run many long races, which begin and end in the same way. Sometimes the ending is so painful, I go for months or years before signing up for another one. And yet—kind of like childbirth—I have signed up, repeatedly. A long race is kind of like living, and dying, and being reborn. It is a draining, exhilarating process which brings a deep sense of satisfaction.

I didn't sign up for this particular race, but at mile six, I feel reasonably strong. This morning I went to the Uni, put some books in my office, scanned some readings for a guest lecture in a secondary school next week, sent my electric bike off for repairs, delivered Popo's[1] printed fabrics to the soft materials teacher at the Bean's school, and went shopping for fruit. One of the nashi (Japanese pears) and an entire carton of strawberries turned out to be rotten. I am debating whether to go back and demand replacements. Probably I won't get to it, which is a shame, because a rotten nashi is the worst. The kids are about to come home from school. (The Shoot started at Sunnyvale just a couple of weeks ago, and he has taken to it really well.) Mile six is still part of the beginning, but beginnings are also worthwhile.

The kids have come home from school, whooping and exclaiming. Bertie the puppy is wagging his tail. The house is noisy again.

Love from the One with the Frozen Everything,
Melissa

Looking Ahead

11 January 2018
Auckland City Hospital, Auckland, New Zealand

Dear All:

I write to you from the padded blue chemo chair itself. Outside the window, the sky is blue and fluffy white clouds are trundling northward. I am hooked up to the IV, but still waiting for my oxaliplatin to arrive. Today is the Last Chemo. I am very pleased about this. The dawn of a new era is at hand. It includes a colonoscopy, a CT scan, the deinstallation of my port, and thrice-yearly CEA (tumor marker) blood tests. It includes summer vacation with the kids. It includes a research trip to Shanghai, two conferences, and another wait in line in a PRC visa office. It includes trying to find someone to dog-sit Bertie for six weeks while we are away. It includes gearing up to teach two courses in Semester Two, including a new course ("Asia and New Zealand").

The oxaliplatin (the first chemo drug) has just arrived in a plastic pouch. Following the usual protocols, I rattle off my name, date of birth, and hospital number. They hook me up. Drip, drip, drip. Hooray for you, therapeutic poison! Mop up!

I surprised myself yesterday during my meeting with the head oncologist. Tears came into my eyes as she talked about the road ahead. I suppose this is because I still feel fear. I suppose I still feel sorry for myself. I suppose this is okay. Cancer is big and scary. Fear and sorrow are real. I don't think it is possible for me to conquer them by making them go away forever. I think the way to overcome fear is to outrun it. Not a helter-skelter "running away," but a purposeful "running past."

In my life I have run many races, starting with Estancia High School cross-country, to the Harvard team, to running marathons after pregnancies to prove to myself that I was still an athlete. In Auckland, when I had to commute for the first time, I started biking instead of running. I rode 20 kilometers (12.5 miles) between the Central Business District and our home in West Auckland. It took a little over an hour every day. Sometimes rain fell in torrents. Sometimes strong headwinds blew. Sometimes the buses came too close for comfort, or drivers pulled out without looking for me. I enjoyed riding my bike. It saved money and reminded me I was strong and tough.

After my surgery in June, I stopped biking. If I had to go into the city, I took the train and then the bus. First it was because of my incisions, and then it was because the weather was cold and the wind blowing across my hands set off chemo-induced tingling in my hands and face. About a month ago, I started riding again. My quads were out of shape, but it was so fun. I gleefully zoomed down Symonds Street on the way to the University, swerving around buses. The route back home was mostly on bike trails, but there was one segment of the journey in which I had to ride on the road with cars, down and up a big hill. As I sped down this hill, I glanced back over my shoulder. Usually this makes the car behind more careful so it follows at a safe distance or gives a wide berth when passing. I gathered speed, traveling as fast as the cars, feeling bold and brash. I wondered: Young, strong, healthy bike commuters die in car accidents every day. Why don't I feel fear when I take this risk?

I pondered this as I cruised down the hill and concluded I was long accustomed to the risk of riding a bicycle, but a life with cancer in it was a new kind of risk and also a risk I had not purposefully chosen. I thought I could become accustomed to this new risk as well. I thought: *I'm strong. I'm tough. I can do hard things. I can do new things. I'm tough, I'm strong.*

This has been my mantra for the past few weeks as I begin to look ahead. I am grateful for the powerful promises of time that have been made to me, but even more grateful for the positive convictions and prayers of people who have faith in these promises. For some reason it is easier to have faith in other people's faith than in my own. (This doesn't mean that I am trying to slack off, but just that I really, really appreciate you!)

I am grateful to be a runner and a biker because this gives me a context for being brave. I think about the races I've run, particularly in high school. I remember the mental work of feeling tired and a bit desperate but making myself drive arms and lengthen stride as I neared the top of

"Puke Hill" (the steep final hill on the Estancia High School cross-country course). I remember the panic-inducing sound of pounding feet just behind me. When you hear this sound, you don't look back. Looking back is demoralizing, and it wastes energy. You just *go*. I remember the sound of pursuing footsteps fading away, and recall the satisfaction of knowing I had yet more to give in that race.

At the beginning of this long encounter, I believed nothing I could do would have any effect on whether my body was able to conquer cancer. After all, I had been young, strong, and healthy, and still the cancer formed within my body. But after a conversation with Sahar, Emily's friend who is a GI cancer researcher at Harvard, I began to feel that what I do can indeed make some sort of a difference. Being young, strong, and (recently) healthy does not immunize a person from major difficulties, but it does mean that one can address these difficulties with considerable energy and a good will. With the grace of God, I'll run hard, and I'll run to win.

Thanks for your faith—in me, in medicine, in God, in time.

Yours from the IV tree (really, really have to pee),
Melissa

PART FIVE

looking
to the
future

Dawn breaks over the Manukau Harbour

Hiking in the Waitakere Ranges

The last four pieces in this book are letters to young people. Three are letters to my children—Bean, Sprout, Leaf, and Shoot—even though they aren't quite old enough to absorb them now. One letter was written for a seventeen-year-old Latter-day Saint young woman who is the daughter of a friend, in response to an earlier conversation.

Young people are this book's most important audience. I originally wrote it for my children. I wanted to write to them in a format that would endure long enough to intercept them as teenagers and young adults, and in a format that was easy to find. Joseph and I are forgetful people, and our children have inherited some degree of this forgetfulness. A stack full of manuscript pages is bound to get lost. I thought: If it's a book, if they lose it, they ought to be able to find another copy somewhere.

A few months ago, I realized with shock that I am now the same age my mother was when I left home and went to university. I almost don't know how this is possible, but I've double-checked the math. I always thought my mother was so old! But she was just me! I wish I could tell her about this realization in person. I would plant myself in front of her, fling my arms open wide, and say, "Ta-dah! I've officially become you!" I would wrap my arms around her slight frame and give her a big hug—my little Mama.

I have also written this book for my children's friends, and my friends' children. Very-Slightly-Younger Friends, I hope that something in this book is useful for you and your big adventures. If all else fails, learn Chinese. It's the language of one-fifth of humanity. You can't go wrong.

A LETTER TO MY NOT-YET-TEENAGE CHILDREN

3 July 2017
Auckland, New Zealand

This is a letter about why I'm a Latter-day Saint for my not-yet-teenage children. I wrote it on a Sunday night, sitting at a kitchen table in a cold and empty house. I was recovering from surgery for my tumor, and my husband and kids were away on our annual trip to the United States to visit family. I doubt my kids would get through a letter of this length now, but I hope someday they will find it thought-provoking. I've changed most people's names, except the names of those who already operate in public spaces.

Dear Buddies:

Since I've been diagnosed with cancer, I've been writing letters to you. The prognosis is pretty good, but I believe in backup plans. I don't think that you will really be interested in these letters for at least another few years, but if the can of wheat will keep, so will words. I have been thinking about reasons why people decide to leave the Church or stay. Being at church today reminded me why I choose to live as a Latter-day Saint.

There are many reasons people stop coming to church. Demographically speaking, most people experience being a Latter-day Saint as a phase, but not as a lifelong identity. Sometimes new members find that this churchy life is a bit much. All of a sudden they must adjust to a new schedule, new vocabulary, new social circles. Sometimes they have already strained relationships with family or friends in deciding to get baptized, which is a difficult situation to continue. Sometimes they feel that they joined the Church during one particular phase of their life, but now this phase has passed and they now want different things.

Primary children grow up to be young adults. As they're developing their own ideas and their own priorities, they start to think the Church isn't as awesome as it used to be. Teachings at church seem full of contradictions and dilemmas. Some—or many—church members, including

218

leaders, turn out to be capable of sexism, racism, unkindness, or unbecoming ignorance. Sometimes young Latter-day Saints find that the scriptures, people's records of their dealings with God, sometimes tell troubling stories. You wonder: *What crazy person put that story in there!?* They begin to see inequality and imperfection within the institutional structures of the Church, historically and also in the present. When you thought something was perfect, but then discover that it has flaws, it is natural to feel discouraged.[1]

Finally, sometimes people just get tired. They have already gone through a painful process of living with disillusionment—discovering the Church isn't perfect, but trying to keep contributing just the same—but going to church and being a Latter-day Saint still feels like endlessly treading water in a choppy sea, just trying to keep one's head above water. Or it feels like having to carry a large, heavy sheet of plywood everywhere, making it hard to go through doors and turn around in the kitchen. I could go on and on with the similes. As a university student, I once mused to a friend, "Being Mormon is like trying to fly with an elephant on your back. Some people do it so beautifully. But can I?"

This Sunday, I had a full experience at church that reminded me of why I love being a Latter-day Saint. Below, I'll tell you about four particular moments that stuck with me.

1. Music in sacrament meeting

It started with sacrament meeting. I came late, on purpose. Because of my surgery and my upcoming chemotherapy, about three weeks ago I told the bishopric I was going to have to stop playing the organ in church and it was time for the youth to step up. In a coaching session, I told the youth who played the piano that I needed to take a break while I dealt with cancer. I told them I was merely doing to them what my piano teacher, who had also been the ward organist, had done to me when I was around sixteen.

So last week, four youth, including the Bean, covered all the hymns in sacrament meeting. Afterwards people remarked that they had felt the Spirit in the meeting because the young people's musical contributions invited it. There were some mistakes and hesitations. But it was this very imperfection, and the fact that the youth in the ward were contributing what was needed, that was transformative. The Spirit, after all, often comes (for me) as a feeling of transcendent empathy in response to someone's vulnerability. Through their willingness to perform imperfectly, the four young pianists invited care and reciprocity from the congregation. This mutual reaching out brought the Spirit. Yesterday was the second week of this new arrangement. I showed up late because I didn't want to be a reliable backup. I wanted the youth to feel that now it's their time to carry the meeting, and if they don't do it, nobody will. As I walked into the chapel, I heard the final strains of "I Am a Child of God" and was happy.

Throughout the rest of the meeting, as we sang the hymns, I felt that this culture of amateurism—of lay participation—is one of the great strengths of our church. No one here is perfect, from the youth pianist to the President of the Church. We're all just trying to do a job we've been asked to do, as best we can. Sometimes this is a bit constraining, but growth is always ongoing. I have faith in this.

2. Testimony meeting

This Sunday was fast and testimony meeting. I almost didn't go, actually, because I was worried about ongoing pain at the site of my incisions. I thought: I have a perfectly good excuse not to go to church. But I was fasting, so I decided to go and renew my covenants. The first person to get up in testimony meeting was Brother Hamilton. He and Sister Hamilton are a senior missionary couple from America. They've been here for two years, and now they're going home. Brother Hamilton teaches Sunday School. Sister Hamilton used to coteach Sunday School until she assigned herself to be the Primary chorister. She is also the sacrament meeting chorister.

In Primary, Sister Hamilton is a real professional. She gets through six or seven songs in a singing time, including the perfect mix of old and new songs. This takes confidence, experience, and much preparation. Now, Brother Hamilton and Sister Hamilton, like us, are Americans. Because of the Church's origins in the United States, American culture seeps into church culture abroad. As a missionary in Taiwan, for instance, I remember a visiting American General Authority telling the emotionally reserved Taiwanese Latter-day Saints that loving their spouses meant engaging in more physical displays of affection. He summoned his wife to the stand and kissed her in front of the entire congregation. You could have cut the discomfort in the air with a knife. At times like this, I want to shriek: Jesus was not an American! American culture does not equal "gospel culture"! Lay off the Americanism!

However, following Brother Hamilton's and later Sister Hamilton's testimony, many women and men got up to thank them, quite emotionally, for their contributions to the ward. It became clear that their major influence on the ward was not that they embodied American styles of being Latter-day Saints—which they had—but that they were two generous, loving individuals with much life experience who had come to serve in our community. They are just wonderful people. This is why in the middle of sacrament meeting the Leaf often jumped up from our pew and went to sit next to Sister Hamilton. I think Sister Hamilton reminded the Leaf of Grandma. Your friend Moroni always sat next to Brother Hamilton, who in a similar manner was like another father figure for him.

This is what we get at church: other mothers, fathers, brothers, sisters, teachers. From different family, cultural, and national backgrounds, we come together. These relationships have a different quality from those established within a charitable group or a sports club. The ties that bind our community arise out of sacred covenants. At baptism, we covenant to be one people (Christ's people), to bear one another's burdens, to mourn with those who mourn (Mosiah 18:8–10). In the temple we covenant to consecrate all we are to build the kingdom of God, which consists not of bricks and mortar but of people joined together eternally. I have walked into many a meetinghouse in places foreign to me like Mongolia, Hungary, and the Democratic Republic of the Congo and felt instantly at home—not because of the decor, or the pictures on the wall, but because I knew I was among my people. In today's world, this sort of belonging is both rare and empowering.

Currently in the Church—particularly within administrative structures—there is a huge need for many more relationships that bridge cultures and other fundamental human differences. As these kinds of interpersonal crossings increasingly penetrate the entire Church, we will receive the empathy and strength we need to overcome sins such as sexism, racism, and pride.[2] And yet we should also give credit where credit is due. Joseph Smith's prophetic genius was to receive from God a way of organizing people that would germinate and cultivate these kinds of relationships. Such relationships are like money in the bank, like tangerine trees and pea sprouts. They make life fresher and full of nutritious variety.

3. Primary sharing time

After fast and testimony meeting was Primary. There were only seven kids present. Sister Aupouri taught a lesson on the law of the fast.

I think of how Papa and you three older kids fasted for me on the day of my surgery. At the same time that you were fasting, members of our family far away, on the other side of the world, were also fasting. We all theoretically want to "pray always," as the scriptures tell us, but it is easy to get distracted and forget. But when we fast, every time we get hungry, we remember: *Hey! Something is important! Time to ask God for a special blessing.* I thought of all of you as I sat cross-legged on the hospital bed, naked under a flimsy gown, waiting to be wheeled in for surgery. I thought how you were hoping for me, not just with your brains, but also with your bodies.

Does fasting "work"? If you mean "work" in terms of, "if no one fasts for me then I will definitely not get better, but if one hundred people fast for me then I will definitely get better," then I don't think so. God's grace is not a popularity contest. However, though it is not easily quantifiable, fasting does have power. It is a form of sacrifice (of time, attention, and comfort) that invites the Spirit by putting sacred things first, even though it is hard. In April 2016, Second Counselor in the Young Women General Presidency Neill F. Marriott spoke about the relationship between hardship and power. Quoting Elder Orson F. Whitney, she taught that following God's plan and becoming a builder required sacrifice. "'All that we suffer and all that we endure, especially when we endure it patiently, . . . purifies our hearts . . . and makes us more tender and charitable, . . . and it is through . . . toil and tribulation, that we gain the education . . . which will make us more like our Father and Mother in heaven.'"[3] The hard work of fasting (emptying the self, becoming hungry, focusing the mind) demonstrates to God that we are open to revelation and eager to receive guidance. It signals our openness and receptivity. If we aren't ready to catch, even if God is constantly slinging blessings our way, they will fall into the grass.

For an eight-year-old (this is the age at which we start fasting in our family) to forego two meals shows a lot of discipline. I am grateful to have been taught this discipline as a child. When we exercise control over our body's hungers, we gain power to see the world outside of ourselves. We also come to appreciate the extent and degrees of our agency. Negotiating our faith's particular matrix of commandments, both the positive imperatives and thou-shalt-nots, forces us to practice being sensitive, sensible, and accountable.

As Sister Aupouri taught, there are different ways to respond to commandments, depending on your situation and your understanding. Jesus said that the Sabbath was for people, not people for the Sabbath. This means commandments like keeping the Sabbath are designed to help us, not control us. When we were living in Hong Kong and Papa was in an urban jungle six days of the week, the thing he most wanted to do on Sunday was to get outside and be around green, living things. We started going on hikes in the mountains on Sundays, after church. For our family at this time, this was the ultimate rest. Other families do things differently. The point is, when we obey commandments, we protect spaces for the sacred in our lives. Within these spaces, we find freedom to follow Jesus and, more generally, to realize our divine nature.

4. Relief Society

Relief Society began with President Samu introducing the new Relief Society secretary, Stephanie, and the special assistant to the Relief Society presidency, Karen. Both Stephanie and Karen are young women in their early twenties. They looked a bit bemused as President Samu called on them to stand in front of a group of mostly older women and be recognized as the newest members of the Relief Society leadership. President Samu is a natural leader. She recently finished a post as associate dean in the Faculty of Education at the University of Auckland, and she knows how to run a meeting. You have to have the right combination of enthusiasm, realism, and confidence that what you are trying to get the group to do is what they actually want to do, deep down. President Samu said, brightly, looking out at the two young women: "Now our Relief Society leadership can be dynamite! A model of efficiency!" Everyone laughed, but the fact that she said it this way went a long way toward making it true.

Everything I learned about being a leader, I learned at church. Whether it is in Primary (the most challenging place of all to lead), or at the organ, or in Sunday School discussions, I have been learning all along how to hold a group of people together. It isn't easy. One set of criteria is found in Doctrine and Covenants 50:17–22. Amid competing desires to lead and competing interpretations of how the Church should be led, the Lord asks: How can you know whether a person is preaching by the Spirit, delivering the message God wants people to hear? The answer is that both those who preach and those who receive "understand one another, and both are edified and rejoice together." So, while worldly leadership often involves arrogance, intimidation, and even coercion, spiritual leadership (leading people to be more like Christ) has to be mutual and reciprocal. You can't just lay down the law and tell people to get in line because you're more important and you say so. Instead, you have to get people to want to follow you because they feel, through the Holy Spirit, you are helping them follow Jesus.

Common sense and culture

This was my Sunday. You may be thinking that a few good experiences on one Sunday afternoon cannot counterbalance a systematic accumulation of serious problems over time. In different times and places, people have had ideas that we now see as clearly wrong, but which they felt were clearly right. There was a time in American history in which the majority of American citizens believed that Black people were inferior to people with lighter skin. There was a time in Chinese history in which nearly everyone believed that girl children were absolutely inferior to boy children. These ideas, and others that contradict our current teaching that each person is a beloved child of Heavenly Parents, with infinite divine worth and potential, still circulate today. There are certainly ideas we have and things we do now, that in one hundred years will be regarded as clearly morally wrong—the sure sign of a horrible person. What will it be, I wonder? Eating meat? Driving cars powered by fossil fuels? We must have empathy for those whom the passage of time turns into moral strangers, because someday, surely, those people will be us.

As we look back at our past history, it seems clear that at times our formal and informal institutions have had serious problems. For instance, explains the Church's official essay "Race and the Priesthood," "for much of its history—from the mid-1800s until 1978—the Church did not ordain men of Black African descent to its priesthood or allow Black men or women to participate in temple endowment or sealing ordinances." This essay explains that Latter-day Saint leaders cited "the curse of Cain" and a teaching that Blacks had been "less than fully valiant in the premortal battle against Lucifer."[4] One example of the "curse of Cain" theory can be seen in the 1859 speech in which Brigham Young described African Americans as "black, uncouth, uncomely, disagreeable and low in their habits, wild, and seemingly deprived of nearly all the blessings of the intelligence that is generally bestowed upon mankind" and argued that the mark of Cain was "the flat nose and black skin," a "dreadful curse."[5]

One example of the "less than fully valiant" theory includes a popular book, *Mormon Doctrine*, first published in the mid-1960s and still present on many Latter-day Saint family bookshelves, though no longer in print, in which apostle Bruce R. McConkie argued,

> *Negroes* in this life are denied the Priesthood; under no circumstances can they hold this delegation of authority from the Almighty. (Abra. 1:20–27.) *The gospel message of salvation is not carried affirmatively to them. . . . negroes are not equal with other races where the receipt of certain spiritual blessings are concerned*, particularly the priesthood and the temple blessings that flow there from, but this inequality is not of man's origin. It is the Lord's

doing, is based on his eternal laws of justice, and grows out of the lack of Spiritual valiance of those concerned in their first estate.[6]

Today, explains the official essay on lds.org, the Church disavows these and all other theories, along with related theories that mixed-race marriages are sinful or "that blacks or people of any other race or ethnicity are inferior in any way to anyone else." The essay declares, "Church leaders today unequivocally condemn all racism, past and present, in any form."[7]

Indeed, when I type and read these words of church leaders from the 1850s and the 1960s, proclaimed and received within a Latter-day Saint context, I feel ashamed. I feel sorrowful. I do feel, unequivocally, that these teachings were racist and wrong and sinful. These kinds of false and hurtful things were said by many Latter-day Saint leaders and members, in public and in private, until 1978, and in many cases well beyond 1978. Some people left the Church because of our racial exclusion policies, and I don't blame them. Many people I love and respect, including your grandparents, and including many Black Latter-day Saints, stayed within the Church despite this policy.

Today, we're in a much better place, but racism is still endemic to our global fellowship. As President Dallin H. Oaks said in his address at the celebration commemorating the history of Black Latter-day Saint pioneers, we all need to repent of the sin of racism.[8] Racism (rude comments, bad jokes, name-calling, treating someone based on how they look as opposed to who they are inside, ignoring and suppressing the voices of whole groups of people) is not like a cucumber sprout or tangerine sapling. It is like a weed. It's growing in our church garden, stealing the nutrients from the crops we actually want to grow. Will you please pull it out wherever you see it?

How can a church that struggled and continues to struggle with racism, sexism, abuse, and other problems, be led by Jesus? This is a thoughtful question. I think the basic answer is related to what I said about kids playing the piano in sacrament meeting (we will never be perfect, but we should always try to be better) and about the Primary lesson on fasting and prayer (ultimately the burden is on us to prepare ourselves to receive light, knowledge, and blessings from God). God speaks, but we can only hear if we are receptive to the Holy Spirit. If we keep trying to do what's right, despite our sinfulness, God can lead us in the right direction. Now is the time for recognizing the sin, asking for forgiveness, and trying to make amends. The saying that the Church is not a country club for Saints but a hospital for the sick is true. Having recently come out of a hospital, the image sticks with me: frail people in nonslip socks walking unsteadily round and round, carrying their catheters and IV lines.

Amid the historical churn of shifting values and mores, remember what Jesus said: The first great commandment is to love God, and the second is to love your neighbor as yourself. Even throughout confusing historical and cultural shifts in our understanding of who our neighbors are, we can follow the charge of Moroni (7:48): "Wherefore, my beloved brethren, pray unto the Father with all the energy of heart, that ye may be filled with this love, which he hath bestowed upon all who are true followers of his Son, Jesus Christ." If this charity, the pure love of Christ, is truly the desire of our people's hearts, we will get closer to Zion. Christians have been trying to follow Jesus for thousands of years now, and I have to say our track record is spotty, but that doesn't mean we should stop trying.

Thankfully, Latter-day Saints believe in ongoing revelation. According to the ninth article of faith, we believe that there are *many* "great and important things" about the kingdom of God which have *yet to be revealed*. Christ's atonement for our sins never changes, but the ways in which church members get together to live the gospel, deal with the world's problems, and build institutions definitely change. Sometimes we don't change fast enough. Sometimes we change too fast. The core of our worldwide community is our collective attempt—fumbling and stumbling though it is—to receive Christ and be his disciples in our times and places.

I have felt the sacredness of this project, and it's enough for me to stay. Alice Faulkner Burch, a fellow Latter-day Saint woman who is Black, was baptized in 1984, and has endured innumerable instances of ugly discrimination at church, once said, "I am often asked why I've stayed in the Church and how I was able to. I always reply: I know the ordinances that this church offers are true and of God and that the priesthood power that administers them is a direct line from God. I stay for the ordinances and the blessings they are to my life."⁹ I felt the Spirit powerfully as she spoke these words. To me it is a transformative, soaring, solemn feeling. I hope you have occasion to feel and recognize the Spirit many times throughout your lives, but just a few times is enough to make a lasting impression that God is real and God's power is among us. Such an experience is, as Eugene England has said, a pearl without price.¹⁰

So if church leaders, even apostles and prophets and General Relief Society Presidents, sometimes say things or make rules that are mistakes, can we still trust them? If we go back to the example of President Samu in Relief Society on Sunday, I think we can. President Samu has been called of God to lead our ward's Relief Society. This doesn't mean she has become a mindless, mechanized, God-puppet. She is who she was before her calling—funny, chatty, warm, very busy—but she is now trying to do her bit, just like the kids who played the piano in sacrament meeting. Not every word that she speaks before our ward Relief Society is straight dictation from God, especially since everyone in her Relief Society audience is in a different situation and needs to hear different things. But she is willing, and trying, to hold our community together by protecting what we have in common: scriptures, history, time spent together. I trust her because I know she is trying to be a disciple of Christ and because I have felt the Holy Spirit in her work.

I don't have the same face-to-face relationship with senior leaders, such as the President of the Church, or the General Relief Society President, or the General Primary President, as I do with President Samu, but the same standard applies. The Spirit testifies of truth. When a church leader speaks through inspiration and tells us something God wants us to hear, the Spirit will confirm it. On numerous occasions I have felt the Spirit testify that what I am hearing in a lesson or talk is counsel I personally need to receive. Our leaders interpret the gospel according to their individual backgrounds, in a way that may sometimes seem inconsistent. Taken as a whole, however, they combine their various gifts and perspectives to hold the Church together, just as President Samu holds Relief

Society together. Keeping a large group of people together is not a tidy business. Nevertheless, the leaders who bear the burden of togetherness must work through God's grace, confirmed by the witness of the Spirit, or else they work in vain. Everyone is entitled to this witness.[11]

Togetherness takes organization and structure. It's not spontaneous, but it's solid. At the end of today's Relief Society lesson, President Samu asked people to let her know if they were willing to be called upon to bring a family a meal, or provide transportation, or be generally available for service—"so we can start building an infrastructure for service and support," she said. "Infrastructure" means real, solid things that make a larger system work. For instance, motorways and tunnels and the airport are part of the Auckland City infrastructure. In the Church, infrastructure includes not only physical things like church buildings, but meeting schedules and the kinds of callings that exist and, most importantly, members who serve in callings. These kinds of structures, built out of people instead of concrete, are very sturdy. Some people nowadays say they're fed up with "organized religion." I think organization is one of the best things that religion has to offer, fraught though it is. I'm an Organization Woman. I just love how people, working together, can do so much.

Breaking the fast

I returned from church and broke my fast with a handful of macadamias from our own backyard tree, along with some banana bread muffins made out of the massive stack of blackening bananas in the fruit bowl. As I felt once again the pleasure of food and felt the energy moving into my bloodstream, I reflected on the day's fast. All day, today, I have wrestled with the desperate uncertainty that comes with having cancer. While singing the alto line in hymns and reading scriptures on charity, I have struggled to make sense of the gap between God's omniscience and omnipotence on the one hand, and our own human understanding and petty, sometimes futile actions on the other. I have silently carried this struggle through the meetings of our little congregation.

I have at times remarked on the fragility of the Church's balancing act between charisma and organization, but today, in the midst of my own fragility, I felt our community's strength. In Primary, a parent who happened to be there because she was coaching her son through a short talk in opening exercises asked about my prognosis and told me, confidently, "You'll be fine. We'll all pray for you." In the midst of my uncertainty, I received a jolt of comfort. Having cancer, and recovering from surgery, creates all sorts of opportunities to fear one is not as awesome as one had originally supposed. Her confidence bound up my raggedness.

When you have come face to face with the potential extinction of everything that you hold dear and were used to seeing as permanent, you realize that you need help—help with life, help with death, help with everything. In the Gospel of Mark, the father of a child possessed with a spirit cried out to Jesus: "Lord, I believe; help thou mine unbelief" (Mark 9:24). Sometimes, the burden of faith feels like too much to bear alone— not just faith in the Latter-day Saints' particular set of truth claims, but faith in Christ's gift of redemption, in God's care, in life after death, in goodness, in the endurance of things of value. These are unseen things that I desperately want to be true, in good times and bad. But I can't do the work of faith all by myself.

I write all of this to you, my kids-who-are-too-young-to-make-it-through-this-letter, to explain my commitment to the village within which your father and I have chosen to raise you. As your Uncle Charles has said, it's not the only game in town. There are many other communities, religious and areligious, working to take care of people and make the world a better place. I admire and appreciate the work that my friends do in these communities, and the various worldviews that hold them together. I acknowledge, with pain and regret, that for some people, The Church of Jesus Christ of Latter-day Saints is not the same safe haven it has regularly been for me. Right now, it's difficult to be a gay or lesbian Latter-day Saint. It's difficult to be a Black Latter-day Saint. In church communities all over the world that do not recognize their own ethnic and cultural particularity or their history as refugees and immigrants, it's hard to be an ethnic minority or an immigrant. Now that I think about it, sometimes it's actually quite difficult to be a Latter-day Saint woman. I think we're getting better, but we still have a long way to go. To loosely paraphrase the

Chinese revolutionary Sun Yat-sen on his deathbed: "The Restoration is not yet complete; Sisters and Brothers must still work hard!"[12]

In sum, Latter-day Saints probably aren't the best people, or the most correct people, or even the nicest people in the world. (I have no idea who the best, most correct, or nicest people may be, or whether such people even exist.) But they are my people. Our shared project of building Zion has given me so many gifts—not just as a religionist, but as an individual, a woman, an athlete, a scholar, and a member of a global society. I value them enough to stay. I value them enough to hope that when you are old enough to form your own worldview, you will find that what the Church has become—or where the Church is heading—is still home for you, for the divine, and for others whom you have learned to love.

With love,
Mama

SAMURAI COME OUT SWINGING
AND GET SCARS

25 July 2017
Auckland City Hospital Cafeteria

Dear Buddies:

I am sitting in the Auckland Hospital Cafeteria after my meeting with the oncologist. Sunlight streams in through the window. In the background, something is playing on the television. Out the window I see the brightly colored pillars outside Starship Children's Hospital, where the Sprout went for surgery to remove the phoenix palm spine that lodged in his leg when he tried to jump over a fallen frond. Poor Sprout! However, I know he is really proud to have that scar.

I now have a couple scars to be proud of myself. I have:

- A medium one across my belly button
- Three little clumps around my tummy where the scope went in
- A notch on my neck
- A line across my chest, on the right side where the port-a-cath went in

The other day I was hanging out with one of my friends who had dealt with many challenges in life. This person had been diagnosed with diabetes as a baby and had not been expected to live to the age of one, and after that, to the end of primary school, and after that, to the end of high school, and so on. She had difficulty using her hands for fiddly little tasks like using chopsticks because of previous surgeries. She was on various medications. As a young single woman she had felt like no one would ever love her (until she met her husband, who is wonderful). In the course of her husband's career, she had frequently moved around, never able to get settled, which is why although she started her PhD about ten years ago, she hasn't finished it yet. All of these things take a toll.

In the past, I think I might have felt sorry for this friend of mine, because her life had been so full of really difficult challenges. I might have thought: She had never been "at 100 percent." I think at a certain point in my life—perhaps when I was running on the university cross-country team, still inwardly insecure but outwardly at the top of life's physical game—I would have even felt a sense of superiority because she was "damaged" and I was "whole." Now, however, I feel wholehearted respect as I realize how very awesome she is to have come through so many trials with such grace and resilience. She has, in fact, lived life at 300 percent. Far more than those who have sailed through life without a hitch, people who have kept going amid setbacks, delays, and crushing defeats are people who are worthy of respect. They are the people who have gained the ability to see clearly, to heal others, to warn with authority. I realize that a truly valuable life involves being battered, scarred, and frightened in generous proportion to feeling happiness and enjoyment.

The physical toll of a life of farming was evident in Great-Grandpa Charles Ichirō Inouye, who had lost his ring finger in a vegetable-crating machine, and Great-Grandma Bessie Murakami Inouye, who had lost her thumb to the unloading device on a potato truck. I remember her trying to entertain me with paper crafts on a long car ride when I was a little kid. She couldn't fit the stump of her thumb into the holes of my little plastic scissors, and she thought it was hilarious. Until recently, I have never felt real cause to be frightened, except at the thought that my smoothly humming life might run off the rails. There have been many small hiccups, but I have always felt in control. Of course, this control was an illusion. Now I finally understand how arbitrary and insecure life can be.

I have tried to teach you that attachment is a source of suffering (the insight of the Buddha Sakyamuni). I get it. I think it's a true principle. But in truth, this principle is hard to live. It is the nature of human existence to be attached to things, people, ideas, and so forth. Even when we think we are at peace with our fragility and transience, we find we are very deeply attached. This is why I suddenly began to weep last Sunday when I ran into Jenna Clyde at church and mentioned, offhandedly, that I was moving the kids to another school within walking distance of our house because I was going to have chemo and it would make our lives easier. You think you have it all under control, and then suddenly you realize you are still sad and afraid. The candor of other people's reactions when they first hear (i.e., their expressions of shock and horror) revives the shock and horror you have tried so hard to suppress.

The hardest thing for me has been trying to not connect my life to the life of your grandmother, Popo. It is hard not to think: If God didn't want to save Mom, there is no reason God would want to save me. She was no less beloved, no less needed. She was no less righteous. Indeed, she was probably much more righteous. The oncologists say: *Every cancer is different. What will happen to you has nothing to do with what happened to your mother.* And yet it is difficult to see around someone who looms as large as your mother. I am sorry to be doing this to you, either now or in the distant future. I suppose the best way to deal with this is to concentrate on one's own body. That's the body that is sick. That's the body that needs healing. That's the body in which one's spirit resides.

At the beginning of my encounter with cancer, I focused on the possibility of death. I wanted to be ready. (Hence, these letters to you kids.) I wanted to be at peace with it. I wanted to look it in the face without flinching. Sometimes I joke about it. (I just made a joke about it to my colleagues in an email about upcoming PhD supervisions, which I now gather was an awkward and unprofessional thing to do because it was met with awkward silence. Cancer: there's a learning curve!)

One of the reasons I felt death was such an important thing to consider was because I realized how entitled and prideful I had been. I had thought: *I'm young, strong, healthy! I'm (bald but) attractive! I'm smart! I cook from scratch! I'm a helper, a fixer, a healer of the breach!* I never imagined that I would be vulnerable in a way that was outside my control (besides being bald, which was actually a significant way to be vulnerable). In facing death, I felt suddenly humble. I realized that I am not entitled to health and longevity because I am awesome. Even if I were awesome, I would not be entitled. I began to drive more slowly.

Now, I think, I am ready to be proactive about receiving every good thing I can receive from God, from others, and from myself. I think it's the way of the samurai—be brave by accepting the possibility (and indeed the likelihood) of death, and then go out and fight. A couple years ago, an exhibit on samurai armor came to the BYU library. I stood there, looking at the swords and daggers in the glass case. They were beautiful, long, heavy, and lethal. I saw how the thick metal blade came down into an incredibly fine, sharp edge. It was both a work of fine art and an instrument of brutality. I wondered at the courage it would take to wield that blade against others with similar blades, to swing and lunge knowing what those shining edges could do. Our ancestors, who were samurai in southern Japan, lived and died by those edges. Now, I too have finally been given an opportunity to show real courage in the face of death as a young, vital person. Opportunities like this are rarer in the twenty-first century than they were in the thirteenth, perhaps.

In sum: I've learned a lot in the few short months of being cancerous. Courage is not about being impervious to danger, but being alive to it. Scars—and the damage we incur throughout the knocks and cuts and struggles of life—are not signs of devaluation, but symbols of hard-won strength. People in whom these physical, emotional, or spiritual scars are apparent, are people who have many things to teach you, because they have had many things to learn.

Love,
Mama

ROTTEN THINGS ROTTEN, GOOD THINGS GOOD

19 March 2018
Shanghai, China

I had a conversation with a young Latter-day Saint woman, "E." She was seventeen years old and was waiting to hear back on her university applications. She was smart, compassionate, and engaged. An exciting future lay ahead of her, but she was not sure whether that future included ongoing practice within The Church of Jesus Christ of Latter-day Saints. During her teenage years she had seen many of her peers walk away from the Church, troubled by various tough questions, including questions having to do with history, exclusivist theology, gender and sexuality, and ecclesiastical abuse. In our conversation, she laid out her feelings of deep frustration with the current status quo and her sense that the Church, currently constituted, didn't have a place for her. The following is a letter I eventually sent in response.

Dear E.:

I've been thinking about our recent conversation. I've thought about it while doing dishes, painting doors, walking down hallways, riding my bike into Auckland. I've thought about it while waiting in line to board a plane, pulling luggage along the streets of Shanghai, watching steam pour from stacks of bamboo steamers.

I've been thinking about you because of the burden of your questions. Your concerns are thoughtful and valid. When I was your age, I was at a similar crossroads. To be candid, this in-between place is where I still sometimes find myself, muttering savagely and tearing my metaphorical hair.

Take, for instance, the matter of abuse of women and children in a church context. Yes, there are a few bad apples in every community, and we probably have about the same number of domestic abusers and sexual predators as any other religious group. Yet we in our church institutions have been so obsessed with presenting picture-perfect appearances that we have long discounted, ignored, or hushed reports of abuse. This betrays a

lack of faith in the divine durability of our project and prideful unwilling-
ness to be accountable and repent. The problem is more than "a few bad
apples." The problem includes an institutional culture that systematically
fails to catch the whiff of rottenness. Thus, accounts of Latter-day Saint
men who use their patriarchal privilege to abuse women and children continue to come to light. It is sickening. I won't accept it! We have to fix it!

Yet here I am. Still! *Why!?* (I can't tell who's shouting, you or me.)
Because I believe in the strength of our covenants, and I believe in Christ.
I believe that, flawed as we are, we can repent and become better. I know
my sisters and brothers, and I know our power for good.

A tree may bring forth both good and rotten fruit. I refuse to let my
faith and my people and my church be defined by our rottenness. This
does not mean I will ignore our rottenness. It means I will call rotten
things rotten. And I will also call good things good.

Once, my ward went on an apple-picking excursion in rural Massachusetts. We plucked McIntosh, Pippin, and Golden Delicious apples. The
orchard air was cold and clean. I bit into a crisp, gorgeous red apple. The
white inner flesh sheared away. Then—ugh! Inside was a soft, rotten bit, and
in that soft bit there was a worm. I told this tale to Mimmu Hartiala-Sloan,
a Finnish sister and family friend who had passed her European family tradition of celebrating Advent on to the entire ward. In her classic deadpan
manner, she replied, "Well, the only way you know a fruit hasn't been sprayed
with poison is if someone is living in it."

With our volunteer-intensive structure, we are closer to a state of nature—so to speak—than many religious organizations. We are a living
church because who we are in any given time or place depends less on
what is written in a sacred text or handbook and more on who shows up
and puts their warm bum into a seat. This is both a strength and a weakness. Because we are an "organic" church, our institutions are comprised of
natural, family-farm, somewhat haphazardly selected human beings.[1] We
are bound to encounter the human equivalent of wormy, rotten apples,
especially when we lack rigorous processes for sorting apples and keeping
the bad ones out of the kitchen. But! The cold, sweet cider! The warm, tart
pies! The polyphenols and anthocyanins!

Here are six of our global community's "good fruits" I hope you will consider.

Good fruits

1. Consider your good self

Not only do I personally sympathize with your concerns—as a feminist, a person of color, and a historian of religion—I also sympathize with your parents, who are old friends. I don't know you well, but it's clear from your questions that you are a caring, intelligent person with a deep sense of integrity. Your parents have poured blood, sweat, tears, and hours of prayer into helping you become this person. They have taught you to believe in God, to scorn evil, to use your talents to serve others. Of course, you also get credit for being an awesome person from the beginning, but your parents have been with you every step of the way. In doing so, they have made deep, persistent sacrifices. I needn't list them here. You know.

One major reason your parents have worked so hard to help you develop your talents and instill in you the values of compassion and critical thinking and integrity is because they're Latter-day Saints. Of course, many wonderful families of other faiths are also capable of producing compassionate, critically thinking children who have integrity, but you wouldn't discount the beauty of a masterful work of art simply because it hangs on the wall next to other beautiful works. In your parents' case, their Latter-day Saint faith helped to inspire the diligent artistry through which you were raised. It is possible that, had you been raised by crime bosses or wolves, you would not have grown up singing "Give, said the little stream," or "If you don't walk as most people do, some people walk away from you, but I won't, I won't!" Teachers in Primary, Sunday School, and Young Women also played a role. The little church village within which you were raised has helped form you into a sensitive, engaged, and morally fearless person.

A Māori proverb my kids recently learned at school:

Ehara taku toa i te	I come not with my own
toa takitahi engari	strengths but bring with me
he toa takitini	the gifts, talents and strengths
	of my family, tribe and ancestors

2. We are a living tradition

It's hard to be patient when urgently needed changes trickle down slowly. I'm terrible at waiting, myself. Do remember, however, that the Church's culture, policies, rituals, and even doctrinal teachings have evolved steadily over time. History shows we have come a long way on issues of race, gender, global worldview, and so on, though we still have far to go (and, if we're lucky, we'll always be "going"). In order to flourish in the twenty-first century, we must tackle issues such as racism, sexism, America-centrism, and bureaucratic paranoia (to name a few). Nevertheless, a long view reveals that we are moving forward on all of these fronts.

Indeed, we believe in being "anxiously engaged in a good cause," in doing many things of our own free will, and in bringing to pass much righteousness (Doctrine and Covenants 58:27–28). For instance, Latter-day Saint women have always backed ideas with organized action. It is a reflex. Indeed, Latter-day Saint women's confidence in their ability to collectively transform the world for good is what makes some unconcerned by the issue of structural inequality within church administration, just as it moves others to advocate for women's ordination. The late-nineteenth-century plural wives who agitated for women's suffrage come to mind, as do twenty-first-century women who lead delegations to the United Nations Commission on the Status of Women, or who have become a national voice for ethics and integrity in US government.[2] If you choose to lead a Latter-day Saint life, you will find many sisters and brothers pulling alongside you, eager to uplift both our church community and the world.

Some religious studies scholars speak of a "religious marketplace" in which religions are vendors and believers are consumers. As a Latter-day Saint scholar, I think this model has a blind spot. As we know from our religious practice, believers are not merely consumers of religion, but also producers of it. We don't just attend church. We do church, prepare church, teach church, interpret church, create church, *are* the Church. It's *your* church too. What will you do with it?

3. Cultures and languages are valuable

What you have is not just a church, but a culture. Every culture is its own distinctive kind of inheritance. This becomes clear to me, here in Shanghai, as I scarf down street food (roasted sweet potatoes, sticky purple rice balls with crushed peanuts and pickled vegetables, crispy scallion-egg crepes, tapioca pearls in coconut milk, fresh Xinjiang walnuts) and gingerly walk in and out of public toilets (no supplied paper, wet seats on sit-toilets, urine on the floors of squat toilets, no supplied soap). Impossibly generous hospitality to friends, rock-solid intergenerational family ties, and commitment to education abound, but so do widespread bureaucratic corruption and disregard for public resources. Chinese culture is not "pure," but it is *rich*, and its value in my life and within the family of humanity is inestimable. Along with my Chinese, Japanese, and American heritage, I value my rich cultural inheritance as a Latter-day Saint and seek to bequeath it to my children. You may not be able to see it very well now because, as a young person in your parents' house, it is the water in which you swim. Before you walk away, find ways to immerse yourself in other cultures, including the Church in other places, so you will have a better sense of what you may leave behind.

Church culture is not monolithic but is a conglomeration of many local traditions, ideologies, languages, and, most of all, experiences. Between 2003 and 2004 I conducted oral history interviews with Asian Latter-day Saint women and men living in the United States and Canada. They lived in ordinary subdivisions outside of Atlanta, Sacramento, Toronto, and so on. But their stories were extraordinary. Some had grown up in poverty in places such as Hong Kong or the Philippines, had worked two or three jobs to support their education, and were now accomplished professionals. Some had come from Cambodia, fleeing the Khmer Rouge, walking for days through thick jungles, carrying their young children and foraging for plants. Most of these Latter-day Saints would have been horrified if you called them "feminists," and if you told them you were worried about "structural inequality," they would think you were talking about buildings.[3] But they were (and still are) amazing people with awesome spiritual power.

All of us tend to believe that our individual worldviews, abilities, experiences, and problems are more valid than others'. Indeed, we must follow our individual convictions and conscience. At the same time, Latter-day

Saint faith in all human beings' divine dignity cautions against self-centeredness. Keep in mind the fact that most of the world's 3.3 billion women do not speak your dialect of feminism. For instance, they might not define power in terms of the ability to hold a position in a bureaucratic hierarchy. Of course, use the languages in which you're fluent to do the work you're capable of doing. But don't forget that others' languages and discourses are valid. For instance, to discount women's "unenlightened" voices and viewpoints simply because you don't understand them is the opposite of feminist. At church, through frequent interaction with many beloved Others, we learn to be polyglots. We learn that people can be wise and good in different ways. Someone with little formal education can offer an eloquent and moving prayer. Someone with "ignorant" and "wrongheaded" political views can teach us how to meet life's challenges with grace and compassion.

In today's world, it is possible to take one's doses of diversity in a rather shallow, selective way, like the interpersonal equivalent of going out for sushi one night and tacos the next. But our culture of communitarianism and consecration means that the Latter-day Saints are stuck with each other, in the same chaotic global kitchen, forever. This is a very confronting way to experience diversity, but it does provide regular opportunities to take the Savior up on his challenges to be meek, show mercy, make peace, give to those in need, seek reconciliation and forgiveness, and look for the beams in our own eyes. Encountering deep, multifaceted differences at church has helped make me a more versatile and useful person in the wider world, with all its fragmentation and complexity. On this score, the Latter-day Saints really have something unique to offer. We are small and weird enough to be serious about all working together in the same world kitchen. It's highly problematic, but also super cool.

4. Organization helps

Organization in the service of a lofty ideal is always a fraught endeavor. When people get together (in a social club, corporation, city government, university, nation-state, or international humanitarian organization), things become messier still. In each category of the institutions named above,

I can instantly think of numerous examples of how people have abused power, promulgated racist or sexist views, or conspicuously failed to live up to stated institutional ideals. People, organized together, can be the absolute worst. Yet, if people don't organize together, often nothing gets done. It's one thing to adopt "correct" ideological positions or use elite manners in spoken and written word. To actually get out into the world and *do* things is another matter altogether. Our church supplies both the ethos and organizational tools for *doing*.

In March 2018 I attended an academic conference on Global Mormon Studies in Claremont, California, organized by Dr. Patrick Mason, a respected scholar and also a practicing Latter-day Saint.[4] The conference's keynote speaker, Elder Patrick Kearon, discussed Latter-day Saint humanitarian responses to the Syrian refugee crisis in Europe, where he had served in the area presidency. He told the story of a Syrian family with four children, including a daughter named Lilia.[5] While the family was trying to find a border crossing into Jordan, Lilia was shot in the back by a sniper and paralyzed from the waist down. When the family reached the Zaatari refugee camp in Jordan, Lilia received a wheelchair but felt ashamed of her condition and deeply depressed about how her life had changed. A Latter-day Saint senior missionary serving in Jordan visited Lilia regularly and helped lift her spirits. Elder Kearon concluded his story with his most recent photo of Lilia, a confident young woman, sitting comfortably in her wheelchair and smiling in her new role as a counselor to other girls who had endured trauma. People have a deep spiritual need to marshal their unique talents and life experiences in the service of others, he pointed out.

At the end of Elder Kearon's talk, Melissa Mason, Dr. Mason's wife, went unexpectedly to the podium. She recounted how in November 2016, she, another Latter-day Saint woman, and six other women from the local community of Claremont formed a resettlement group to help refugees start their lives anew. Six months later, these efforts led her, the other Latter-day Saint sister, and two others to form Claremont Canopy, an organization to help refugees flourish over the long term through language training, internships, educational opportunities, and so on. On 19 April 2017, Melissa went to the airport to meet an incoming refugee family.

The family was originally from Syria, with four children, including a seventeen-year-old daughter named Lilia. She was, Melissa said, the same Lilia as the Lilia in Elder Kearon's story.

The odds are very, very low that a Syrian family that had connected with Latter-day Saints at a refugee camp in Jordan would get off the plane in their new home in Los Angeles and also be received by a Latter-day Saint, and that the Kearons and the Masons would both happen to be in the same auditorium on the same night to tell the two sides of this story. And yet this is what happened. It only happened because the Church, more than any religion I know, works to build human infrastructure for service and connection. In Lilia's case, institutional efforts such as Latter-day Saint Humanitarian Services projects and the Relief Society's "I Was a Stranger" program combined with the independent initiatives of individual Latter-day Saints like Melissa and her friends. Although our formal and informal institutions are sometimes deeply flawed, sometimes they work miracles. Our organized endeavors form webs of support extensive enough to catch people when they are torn from their homes and flung across the world.

5. It's not a spectator sport[6]

Latter-day Saint faith is not a spectator sport. Like practicing football or a musical instrument, it becomes worthwhile only after a significant investment of time, boredom, and even pain. And yet, like these other forms of discipline that release endorphins and help us to understand beauty, the hard work of living a Latter-day Saint life has intrinsic rewards.

In 2013, during our time in Hong Kong, I signed up to run a 50K race on Lantau Island. Lantau is a rugged, mountainous island in Hong Kong's New Territories. Up until that point I'd run multiple marathons, but a trail race on Lantau was serious business. The race connected five peaks for a cumulative elevation gain of 2,300 meters. I trained for about four months, running in the mountains just south of our apartment on Hong Kong island. On the day of the race, I woke well before dawn and took the subway to the ferry piers in Central. Around 5:45 a.m. I boarded a ferry to Mui Wo, the race's start and finish point. Many other racers were also on the boat. The atmosphere was festive. I thought: *All these people are excited to get up in the dark and run fifty kilometers on Lantau? They are crazy!*

All day, I ran. I enjoyed the spectacular scenery as the course wound along azure beaches, through green foothills, and across windy ridges. At first, I felt strong and well-trained as I tackled steep ascents like Sunset Peak via stone steps rising nearly as high as my knees. About three-quarters of the way through the race, my quads tightened up. All elasticity left my legs. The muscles slapped against each other with each painful stride. Every curve of the coastline led to another. Altogether, it took eight hours and forty-eight minutes to finish the race. I arrived back at our apartment after sunset. Walking hurt. Standing hurt. Everything hurt. I creaked through the door and slung my bag to the floor. "How was it?" my husband asked. I groaned, "Besides childbirth, that was the worst thing I've ever done to my body!"

Perhaps it was, but I was also glad to have done it. Through the process of training and racing, both my body and spirit became stronger. Distance running, which some might see as a destructive habit of self-inflicted torture, has given me strength to wrangle my kids, recover quickly from surgery, and work through the discomfort and pain of cancer treatment. Similarly, a strenuous life as a Latter-day Saint builds our capacity to be strong, useful, and kind. In the accounts in the scriptures, the Savior himself seems to have always chosen the path of greatest resistance. He ministered to the poor, the Others, the ugly, the foul, and those whose commitment to follow him wavered because they were full of fear.

6. Christ's pattern exists in more than one dimension

When I was your age, I raised questions about gender and race in the Church with my Uncle Charles. I laid out my frustrations as we drove along the 5 Freeway, through the foothills north of Los Angeles, on the way to a family reunion. Clearly, I told Uncle Charles, the Church was fundamentally flawed. There was no way an organization or group of people that had made such harmful, unkind missteps could possibly be led by God.

Uncle Charles said that when he was a graduate student he, too, had once decided he had no choice but to walk away. But here he was, still a Latter-day Saint.

His advice was provocative: "So walk away. Or look for the pattern."

When I asked what he meant by a "pattern," he answered that throughout the scriptures there was a pattern in what Jesus did, how he interacted with people, and what he taught. Truth wasn't a right or wrong answer to a litmus-test question. Truth was in a pattern. His Latter-day Saint faith helped him find that pattern and live by it.

My life hasn't been very long, but by now I'm more than twice as old as I was when I was seventeen. I think what I understand now, in contrast to what I understood then, is that we live life in multiple dimensions. Truth and goodness exist in multiple dimensions. "Structural inequality" is a valid concern in its own dimension. But there are others. When I think about the meaning of life and people who live the life I want to live, I see that they are not just "correct," or "right," but good. I think it is more challenging to be good than it is to be correct, or right, or even righteous. All those things (correctness, rightness, righteousness) can be cultivated within a single self-contained ideological system. But to be good, I believe, one must grapple with realities and problems that thrust themselves upon us, that intrude into our native spheres of thinking and being. Our vertical and horizontal church structures are engineered to force this kind of negotiation upon us.

In the company of my sisters and brothers, I feel the power of the pattern Christ left for us to follow. To be clear, I don't mean to imply that people who leave the Church have simply "failed to find the pattern"—that is, failed to find Jesus or come up with "the right answer." If you do choose to walk away, or take a sabbatical, you can still find Christ's pattern, follow the Holy Spirit, and live a beautiful and meaningful life that reflects the divine nature within you. You will still have my love and deep respect for having the courage to live with integrity. You won't suddenly become "someone else" in my eyes. What I mean when I recall my uncle's words and echo, "look for the pattern *here*," is that when I spot-check my religious tradition, I get wildly differing results (number of volunteers mustered for disaster relief: yippee!; number of female speakers in general sessions of conference:

long sigh . . .). But when I look for the larger pattern in both the scriptures and our Church community, I see a complex, multidimensional picture. This Church is not the only place where you could go to find God. *But, you can find God here.*

Some might feel that this is a sort of tepid endorsement, as if I am saying that the Church is just one of many plausible religious options you could choose. Actually, it is. Around sixteen million Latter-day Saints of record constitute .02 percent of the world's population, so there's a lot out there in the religious worlds of the other 99.98 percent.[7] Depending on how much work you put into it, you could be a great Buddhist, or a great Muslim, or a great Catholic. I think God would rejoice in your faith and service. You could be a great atheist and refocus all the considerable energy you currently spend on deism into service of your fellow beings (which, as you learned by studying Mosiah 2:17 in seminary, Latter-day Saints believe is the same as service to God). If you go this way, applying your parents' good teaching and what the light of Christ teaches every person about right and wrong, your life will not automatically sink into degradation. You will probably be fine.

Some people would prefer for me to respond to a faith crisis with an exhortation like, "Don't leave, or else you'll never be truly happy!" or "Don't leave, or else your life will always have a gaping void!" I understand why we sometimes invoke fear when arguing that people should choose to be Latter-day Saints ("or else"). As a parent who yanks her six-year-old well back from the edge of the train platform, I know this sentiment well. However, life is densely crisscrossed with many train tracks, busy thoroughfares, and high-voltage wires. The planet is crowded with rich and meaningful religious cultures. At a certain point, people have to learn to navigate sensibly and explore new territories, all by themselves. We're not in Primary anymore. And so to you I say: The world is large. Where do you hope to go?

This might sound like a trite, "Sunday School" answer, but it's true: Ultimately, finding answers to your questions is up to you. There is no good way to frighten, flatter, or reason a person into living a Latter-day Saint life. The only truly satisfying responses to your urgent and valid concerns must come through the witness of the Spirit as you move thoughtfully through the wide world. In this letter, I have merely listed some reasons why I believe you may find it worthwhile to continue to spend time and effort seeking such sacred interceptions within our global community. If you want to find God and every good thing that comes from God here, among the Latter-day Saints, I believe you can. If you want to practice loving others as yourself, and bearing the burdens God has given you strength to bear, I believe you can. Christ, our guide, said, "Seek and you shall find."

At church, I see the love of our Heavenly Parents reflected in all kinds of people, including those with no feminist consciousness or no skill in irrigating a field or no desire to hold babies, who consecrate their unique talents to bless others. I discover I owe deep, unrepayable debts of gratitude to people whose ideological positions are nearly completely opposite my own but who dropped what they were doing and came to me when I needed help. I belong to a diverse but distinctive global community of many languages, cultures, and socioeconomic and political situations. I feel the Spirit start to grow within my heart; I feel my Savior's love. Many aspects of this big, multidimensional picture are of immense value—particularly to people like you who are compassionate critical thinkers with integrity, who want to make the world a better place.

Two songs

I'll leave you with two more stories, both having to do with Primary. First, I recall a Sunday in which the Primary chorister asked me, the pianist, to play one of my least favorite songs, "The Family Is of God." I love families, and I love God, and I believe God loves families, but this song annoyed me for a number of reasons. The lyrics, I felt, strung clumsy rhymes and abstract phrases together without a natural flow. This was one reason the Primary kids had only managed to learn the first verse. I thought the second and third verses prescribed family and gender roles much too narrowly. In our Primary, for instance, kids lived in diverse family configurations. Mothers (not just fathers) were providers, fathers (not just mothers) were nurturers of children, extended family such as grandparents, aunties, or uncles (not necessarily mothers and fathers) were often the members bringing kids to church and teaching them the gospel, and so forth.

As I spread out the music, I cast my eyes over the page and noticed the songwriter was a man. I rolled my eyes. "Of *course* it would be a man," muttered the critical voice in my head. I played the first verse. As we began the chorus, a deep feeling of joy that I associate with the Spirit came suddenly into my heart. I can't fully describe it, but it filled my whole soul. It was so powerful I began to weep. I blinked hard to clear the tears from my eyes as I played, my heart full of awe and tenderness.

I've wondered about this experience many times since. What was God trying to tell me? "Don't be so critical of Primary songs, because songwriting is hard"? "Actually, narrowly prescribed gender roles are awesome"? As I think about it in the context of your questions, I think the message was a sort of "Carry on!," a reminder of the bigger picture. The Primary chorister, the Primary children, the songwriter, me—all of us were wandering in the wilderness, hoping to be found. And God was saying, "Here I Am."

The second story comes from a district conference I attended in Shanghai this morning. The Primary children had to arrive half an hour early to practice for the all-district combined Primary musical number. This was only our third Sunday in Shanghai, and the kids' third time in this building, but the kids scampered down the hall to practice like they owned the place. When it was time to perform, about ninety children stood in front, girls on the left and boys on the right, with one chorister leading each group. I couldn't see the choristers' faces, but I could feel their energy. The children's voices swelled, clear and confident. Again, I was powerfully moved. I felt in my heart a bright, wondrous hope.

Now, parents are reliably moved to tears by performing children. Children's innocent voices are often deployed for propagandistic purposes. The specific examples of righteousness in the song all referred to males. In an instant, all these caveats flashed across my mind. But what kind of hope also became real in this moment? In this moment, my children's divine potential to know God, to love and serve others, and to live a life of integrity, came fully into my heart—perhaps, even, into the hearts of the children themselves. I felt God's love for me and within me. This is the fruit of the Spirit, which binds people in empathy, which justifies our faith in things not seen, which testifies of truth.

Perhaps you have felt this Spirit yourself. Don't second-guess its significance. Miracles are always as amazing as they first seem. It's only later that we begin to lose the motivation to interpret them as such. A life touched by the Spirit of God, in addition to professional expertise and critical awareness and bicycles and cherries and Bach, is a life worth hanging on to. Such a life is the good fruit of my practice amid the Latter-day Saints.

You meet so many different people at church: scholars, homeschoolers, feminists, survivalists, professional street performers, elite runners, appliance delivery people, chicken sexers, lightning-strike survivors, the guy who runs Disneyland, big jerks, lifelong friends, musicians, and, just today, husband-and-wife intercontinental ballistic missile operators.[8] Among my sisters and brothers, I have lived not one life, but many.

Because it is rooted in history, institutions, and human beings, all too often in the Church we find apples that are rotten. When you encounter rotten fruit, follow the example of the lord of the vineyard in Jacob 5 and refuse to accept it. When you encounter institutional processes that systematically let rotten fruit into the kitchen, or chuck good fruit into the rubbish, please help us find a better way. It's true that being a Latter-day Saint can be a lot of work. Please consider your tremendous power to lead us where we need to go. You are the future of our Church. You are who we may become. You may find that God will consecrate these struggles for your good, and for ours. As a people, where would we be without fearless questions and a fierce will to press on toward Zion, over bogs and rivers and mountains?

At church I have encountered rottenness, to be sure, but also an abundance of good fruits. Here I've found things which are true, by which I mean spiritually vital, connected to Christ's pattern, and embodying all the gifts our Heavenly Parents can bestow. There are real hazards to undertaking a spiritual journey in the company of so many others, as Latter-day Saints do. But for me it is a rich life, a consequential life, a life worth living.

Good luck!

Love,
Melissa

ON FEAR

18 June 2018
Auckland, New Zealand

Dear Bean, Sprout, Leaf, and Shoot,

On the days you first came into my life (among the happiest days of my life) there came something else. It was fear. I remember holding the Bean. They toweled off the gooey stuff and fluffed up his fuzzy hair. I held him in my arms and looked down at his face. I felt a tremendous surge of love within me. At the same time, I felt a wave of fear. I loved this baby so much. What would I ever do if something happened to him? What if I couldn't protect him from everything? What if I messed him up?

When you have a baby, you suddenly learn that your capacity to love has exponentially increased. I felt such sudden love for each of you. You came from my very large belly, but this love seemed to come from nowhere.

I remember the first night in the postpartum ward after the Sprout was born. During the delivery, I had hemorrhaged and lost a lot of blood, so I was humble and quiet, feeling a hearty respect for childbirth. I lay there in the dark, recalling the long hours of labor. All of a sudden the Sprout woke up and began to cry. He was all swaddled up like a sausage, with just his head sticking out. "Waaah!!" said Sprout. I put my hand on his little head. "It's okay, Pink Sausage," I said.[1] He quieted down right away. I marveled at how human he already was—able to be soothed by a warm touch and reassuring voice, even though he had only been "in society" for a few hours.

I remember the Leaf throwing up all over me. She spat up cupfuls of milk at a time. She would be looking so cute, peering over your shoulder with her big eyes and shock of black hair, and then all of a sudden she would make a noise like "glopp" and the entire contents of her tummy would be soaking through your shirt. Her eyes would kind of widen, like, "Oh, did I do that?" But she was so cute! How could I get mad!? Bak Po[2] helped me sew wide terrycloth bibs with Velcro fasteners to go around her neck and absorb the spit-up.

250

I remember holding the sleeping Shoot in the hospital. I was still getting used to how he looked, like how I have to get used to every new baby. I always expect them to look just like my beloved existing children; I always get a horrible shock when they come out looking like themselves. I remember holding him on my lap, inspecting his nose. I bent down so my nose was just above his and smelled his sweet baby breath. I turned my head so that my ear could hear those soft, faint breaths, and feel the air going in and out, in and out.

To come to love another person is to feel fear on a whole new scale. The world becomes brighter and darker at the same time. The colors pop and zing, but the shadows are deeper. Every problem is longer-term. Every mistake has more ramifications. Every horrible possibility multiplies many times.

To face the fear of cancer, for me, has been about facing not only the memory of my mother's death, and the possibility of my own, but also the fear of leaving you without a mother for a long time. This is a real and present fear. I can feel my body becoming sober as I type it out. Of course, we all have to lose our parents at one point or another. It's painful. You'll be okay.

Above I've talked about the fear of losing someone you love, or seeing someone you love suffer pain. In a sense, this kind of fear is self-centered—you love them, and suffer on their behalf, simply because they are yours. There's another kind of fear, which is the fear of empathy. This is when someone else is in pain, or suffering, or facing terrible danger, and you are afraid that this pain, or suffering, or danger is terribly close to home. In other words, this pain is *not* yours, and you badly want it to stay not-yours.

The other day I was chatting with a friend when another mutual friend of ours, survivor of multiple bouts of breast cancer, now facing a terminal diagnosis, walked over to join the conversation. She is fiercely resilient and often comes across as intimidatingly self-assured, but on this day she looked tired and drawn. We made our quiet inquiries; she gave her quiet reply. Tears filled my eyes as she walked away—tears for her, tears for me, tears for everyone who has ever faced the specter of involuntary separation from those they love. A sentence sprang into my mind, which

I barely had strength to suppress before it reached my tongue. It was a cry of despair: "I am full of fear and sorrow."

In the silent space she left behind, I struggled with two competing responses: empathizing with her deep grief on the one hand, and, on the other hand, separating myself from her and her situation. Part of me wanted to weep aloud, to sit in that moment of suffocating terror, so I could share her burden. But part of me was fleeing from the spot as fast as I could, waving my arms and shrieking, "Remember, she's not you! You are different! You are going to be okay! Let this roll right off your back!"

I feel that, while the second response is certainly understandable, and not wrong, the first response is what Christ would have done. We believe that Christ lovingly took upon himself all of our sins and all of our sorrows, suffering alone while others slept in the Garden of Gethsemane. We believe that the weight of these burdens, and the emotional and physical suffering that resulted from Jesus's redemptive actions, caused him to cry out in despair, "My God, my God, why hast thou forsaken me?" (Matthew 27:46). In that terrible, silent space, Christ was alone with the crushing burden of human fear, suffering, injustice, and uncertainty.

You and I are not called to suffer for the sins of the world. Yet, we are called to follow Christ, to the best of our abilities, for the purpose of finding our heavy burdens made light. How does this work? Can we learn to hold both things in our hands—our love and care for others, and our love and care for ourselves? To what extent should we try to bear another's burden when we ourselves are already stumbling under a similar load? How can we open ourselves up to others' fear when we know that we are particularly susceptible to this very kind of fear? It's not that we're healthy and we worry about being infected. It is because we're sick, and we fear that when we stop to help someone struggling with the same disease, we will lose the strength we need to win our own fight.

This problem—the problem of empathy in times and places of fear— is not limited to life-threatening illnesses. It applies to all fears. This may be why siblings in loving homes sometimes pick on each other and refuse to laugh at each other's jokes. This may be why kids at school so cruelly label others as "dumb" or "ugly" or "losers." This may be why some devoted, staunchly faithful Christians are so harsh in their judgments of those whom they deem morally flawed or afflicted with doubt. It is easier to empathize with people when all we know about them is how their accomplishments and strengths are similar to our own. It is harder to empathize with people when we know we share their very same vulnerabilities and weaknesses. I am hardest on you kids when I see you acting like me at my worst. This is ironic.

I don't have a solution or method to offer in terms of solving the problem of empathy and self-protection. Both values have a place in a righteous and abundant life. I suppose one thing I would say is that in the worst-case scenario, working out the tension between empathy and self-protection is a zero-sum game. But I don't think that a zero-sum game is our situation as eternal children of God, and as people who have chosen to rely on the infinite atonement of Jesus Christ. As I have learned from the (really literally awesome but also frequently extremely tiring) privilege of being your mother, love does not have to operate according to zero-sum rules. *When you reach for it*, there is always more.

On inexhaustible things, there is the scripture in 1 Corinthians 13, echoed in the Book of Mormon's Moroni 7, extolling the pure love of Christ as something that can bear all things, something that never fails though prophecies, spiritual gifts, and knowledge will all eventually run dry. On things that come from God, there is the scripture in 2 Timothy 1 about how God does not give us the spirit of fear, but of power, and of love, and of a sound mind.

While I agree that God does not give us "a spirit of fear," I do believe that God has made us susceptible to fear for a good reason—namely, to help us experience vulnerability and thereby become humble, sensible, and compassionate. Just as new love opens the door to new fear, new fear opens the door to new love. It's a two-way street. Feeling our vulnerability, we call on God for strength.

Living with my fears has made me stronger. I realize that any life full of value is also a life full of fear. I am worried about messing you all up. I am "like a volcano"; when I get mad, I "explode" (this is what one of you wrote at school in a line for a poem in a Mothers' Day card). I worry about pushing you too hard. I worry about not pushing you hard enough. I worry that you are privileged. I worry that you are deprived. I worry that I will die and leave you motherless. I realize that everyone dies and everyone is eventually motherless. I worry that you will forget my teachings and reject my values. I feel, personally, that I have remembered my parents' teachings and absorbed my parents' values. However, I'm aware that I express these teachings and values in ways my parents sometimes don't recognize. The same thing will probably happen to you and me. I suppose it's okay, as long as you feel like you know what you're about and work hard to do all the good you can, in your own way.

Living with other people's fears has also made me stronger. Sometimes, it's wearing to answer people's questions about the latest scan or test. Sometimes it's hard to hear what people say when they say what they think. Once, as Papa and I stood together outside the chapel bidding farewell to a departing senior missionary couple, the husband said goodbye to me. Then he said, to Papa, "Good luck raising those children on your own." (There was an awkward silence, after which he mumbled, "I don't know why I said that . . .") Of course, everyone thinks these kinds of things, including me sometimes. But they can be hard to hear.

The fact is, however, that human life is full of fear. Historically many everyday fears have been mortal fears. Most of God's children who have ever inhabited this earth have lived short lives. Many of them died as infants or children. Many were killed and eaten by something or someone. Many got a cut or broke a leg and got an infection that did them in. Many died terrible deaths on battlefields or in raids or religious purges. Today, even in the twenty-first century, many face acute fears such as war, violence, disease, and abuse. To feel fear is to be in abundant human company. Most of us of are here.

This doesn't make me less afraid of truly scary things, but it *has* made me less afraid of many other things. For instance, I used to worry about wrinkles and receding gums, but now I don't care. As far as I'm concerned, wrinkles and receding gums will be trophies that I will accumulate the longer I live. I will be really, really happy to develop a completely wrinkly face. I am really, really happy to have the trouble and expense of having to find someone to look after Bertie, the dog, for two and a half weeks while we are in the United States to see family. A year ago, I wasn't sure whether I was going to be alive to deal with this problem. I don't care about head hair or leg hair or eyebrow hair. I don't care about being a famous professor or being seen as "the best." I don't care about whether my yellow gumboots are appropriate for a professional workplace. I don't care about people thinking I'm not righteous enough. At the end of each day, I check in with God. I say, "Thank you for this wonderful day. I hope you like what I did with it."

In sum, I acknowledge that fear is real. Fear is legitimate when life is wonderful and when it is terrible. This seems to be not only a mortal human condition, but also an eternal divine condition. If the God who weeps, who pours out tears like the rain upon the mountains, can feel sorrow, and anger, then surely this God can feel pain and fear—not as human insecurity, but as divinely chosen vulnerability.[3] Perhaps, just as Christ, though whole, opened himself up to anguish and despair in order to be able to heal others, when we who are definitely lacking wholeness open ourselves up to both our own fear and the fear of others, we become more able to access grace. Grace is not only "salvation," but love in time of need.

Fear provides opportunities to be brave, and it provides opportunities to be kind. It is perfectly reasonable to fear wild tigers, or invading armies, or serious health challenges, or being teased or bullied, or making a bad choice that damages your relationship with someone you love. But don't suffer pointlessly. Since fear is inevitable, use it as an opportunity to strengthen your spear skills, or your diplomatic strategy, or your ability to empathize with others, or your courage to stand up for people being teased or bullied, or your ability to apologize and learn from your mistakes.

Fear can be paralyzing, but it can also be a useful stimulus to something worthwhile. As you know all too well from observing me, life can be a long chain of missed opportunities to do the best thing in a given moment. But, life is full of moments. Something new will always come up. As in capoeira, train hard, learn to respond to others, and your ability to improvise gracefully under pressure will get better and better.

Love,
Mama

CONCLUSION

DEAR READER,

One way to understand Latter-day Saint faith is to analyze published doctrines, such as concepts of the Godhead, claims to restore Christ's primitive church, original books of scripture, and the pronouncements of ecclesiastical leaders. Another way is to study history, such as the founding claims of an uneducated but charismatic farm boy in upstate New York, a period of persecutions by the Protestant and civic establishments, westward migration to the Great Basin, assimilation to American society, and, in recent decades, a momentous new process of globalization. These approaches have their advantages and disadvantages. On the one hand, they are systematic and comprehensive in scope. They identify key actors, dominant trends, central concepts.

On the other hand, a faith tradition is much more than a discrete set of ideas, beliefs, or even organizational structures. It is deeply rooted in individuals' daily experiences, a way of life held together by a variety of complex person-to-person interactions. Sociologists and anthropologists have attempted to explore these human dimensions through surveys and ethnographies, and writers have attempted to capture them in literature.

This localized or individualized approach yields piecemeal, sometimes contradictory representations of what it means to be a Latter-day Saint. For instance, Eliza Roxcy Snow and Ann Eliza Webb were both wives of Brigham Young, but in her public discourse Eliza defended the Church's institution of plural marriage, while Ann Eliza published an exposé describing abuse and heartbreak.[1] A survey of Latter-day Saint teenagers in the United States will paint a different picture of faith compared to an ethnography of mature Latter-day Saint women in Botswana. Yet these focused, particularistic studies are just as authentic as sweeping theological or historical overviews. The gospel of Christ does not exist in the abstract. It only becomes real as it sounds in the ears of individuals who desire to hear it, and only comes forth as these individuals bend their lives to its call.

I'm just one Latter-day Saint. In some ways, my life could be seen as highly typical, and in other ways, it could be seen as highly anomalous. I don't claim to embody an entire religious tradition or represent an entire community of believers. Yet I hope that the letters, lectures, and essays in this book can speak in a useful way about the meaning of a life of faith in Christ and ongoing restoration of Christ's pattern. They tell stories about crossing divides in a world full of daunting separations.

This project of bridging gaps and traversing difficult terrain is at the heart of the Latter-day Saint experience. Our scriptures, oral traditions, and histories tell numerous stories of exodus, migration, and estrangement (sometimes self-inflicted). And yet along with traditions of exile and renunciation, Latter-day Saints are also eagerly engaged with the world, seeing in life's ordinary conundrums the patterns for becoming like our Heavenly Mother and Heavenly Father. Our practical theology blurs the boundaries between the sacred and the profane, the ethereal and the quotidian. "To be queens and priestesses we must be business women," declared Eliza R. Snow in 1872, as she called on her fellow Relief Society sisters not only to be generous and moral but also to acquire more education and perfect domestic duties into an art.[2]

To live a Latter-day Saint life is to wrestle with life's contradictions and challenges, not necessarily with the aim of always coming out "on top," but of getting to somewhere new. As we struggle to cross canyons and ford streams, we grow in capability and confidence. Here I speak metaphorically, although I do like hiking. We often valorize the physical struggles of early pioneers in nineteenth-century America—fleeing mobs, walking across the Great Plains, eating thistles while the early crops were in the ground—but we should remember that they also struggled with significant cultural, moral, and intellectual challenges. How did white settlers relate to the native peoples into whose homeland they had come as refugees? How did they treat those who did not share their faith? How did Latter-day Saints of color who endured prejudice and discrimination maintain their hope for Zion? What did it mean to say that God was no respecter of persons, that "all [were] alike unto God" (2 Nephi 26:33)?

Such questions remain deeply relevant today. In the globalized world of the twenty-first century, in which people's everyday lives unfold on a larger and more diverse stage, Jesus Christ's teachings on loving our neighbors as ourselves, giving up our riches to nurture the poor, and treating strangers who have met with grief as if they were the Savior himself are daunting.[3] At times, the call to follow Jesus seems nearly impossible. But now is not the time to ignore our covenants or lose our pioneering spirit. Now is the time to frame up the handcarts and go marching up the hill—some must push, and some must pull.

"There are no atheists in foxholes," the saying goes. I tried to come up with a similarly pithy saying about "members of The Church of Jesus Christ of Latter-day Saints" and cancer, but failed. "There are no prophets in prognosis"? (Not really sure what this means, though the alliteration is nice.) What I would say is that an encounter with cancer pulls a bit of the veil from one's eyes. One can suddenly see, very clearly, the presence of death. Death will come to all of us eventually, but most are used to thinking of it as far, far away. Now death is an open door I walk past every day. Sometimes I cannot help but ask questions such as: *Will I live to see my credit card expire? Will I be brave like my mother? Do I have faith to be healed? Shall I take up that two-year term on the Faculty Staffing Committee? Will I be around when the Shoot graduates from high school? Should I put Joseph's phone number down as the parent contact because it is more permanent?*

Before the veil separating life and what lies beyond, there is stillness, though the storms of everyday life may rage around. Sometimes, God speaks to us out of the stillness. At other times, we may shout into it and hear nothing return. Into this stillness I have deposited many whispered prayers. I have lain on my bed, repeating in my head words given to me by my Auntie Sharen: "Breathe in love; breathe out love." I feel my chest rise and fall. I visualize my mother's face and see her smiling. I wonder where she is and what she is doing. But I do not wish to join her now.

Though I have hope, and determined reliance on God's promises, I can't know for certain how much time I have ahead of me, whether years or decades. But I will give thanks for each new day. I will fight with every breath, will cling to every skein of faith, to stay here with my children. At the same time, I know I will always be sending them away from me, across many divides, so they may come to know life's dimensions through their own experience. I must also let go and leave us all in God's hands.

A Latter-day Saint life inevitably leads to separations and journeys. We are always venturing out into other spaces and coming to terms with difference. I wouldn't say we're particularly good at it, but we're always doing it, and so we should always expect to find ourselves on steep learning curves. Our shared stories point to the value of leaving home and starting anew, over and over again. Our past history has taught us what it means to make crossings over prairies, rivers, mountains, jungles, and seas. Future challenges will test whether we are able to make similar crossings over cultures, languages, racial divides, national borders, worldviews, and time. A gospel that is true is a gospel that will withstand and adapt to such rigorous tests. The question is whether we will be courageous and hardy enough to undertake the new treks the gospel requires. With all my heart, I pray that we will. Shoulders to the wheel!

In solidarity,
Melissa

ACKNOWLEDGMENTS

The genesis of this book was the kindness of an old friend. As I faced surgery and an uncertain diagnosis for colon cancer, I contemplated the possibility of never having serious conversations with my children about their faith, their university courses of study, big life milestones, and other grown-up topics. It was sobering. My college friend Erin McPhie reached out. She offered to gather my personal writings together into a website. Her daughter Emily was a web design whiz, and Erin said she would pay the hosting fee. I gratefully accepted. One funny thing was that Erin insisted that the writings on the website include our family's annual Christmas letters. I'd always enjoyed writing these and populating the margins with silly illustrations, but had always thought of them as ephemera, without any real literary value. However, I began to see that if you combined these semiautobiographical letters with memoir, lectures to students, and essays on faith, someone reading through the website (like my kids) would get a fairly comprehensive picture of my worldview. Then I began to think: Why not turn this into a book? I am grateful to Erin and Emily for launching this literary lifeboat in a time of need.

I am also very grateful to scholars, editors, and other professionals working with the Neal A. Maxwell Institute for Religious Scholarship and

Deseret Book who have supported this book since its inception, including Blair Hodges, Tona Hangen, Rosalynde Welch, Miranda Wilcox, Morgan Davis, Spencer Fluhman, Jeremy King, Kristine Haglund, David Holland, Phil Barlow, Lisa Roper, Sheri Dew, and Heather Ward. During the copyediting and typesetting phase I was especially grateful for the artful competence and sharp eyes of Emily Strong and Shirley Ricks of the BYU Religious Studies Center. One of the book's peer reviewers remained anonymous but gave invaluable feedback that greatly improved the organization of the book in particular. Of course, I recognize that "organized" is not really the best word to describe this book, with its overlapping timelines, mixed genres and media, and shifting audiences. This unwieldiness perfectly reflects my life's realities, but it is not very tidy. For this messiness, and any other flaws in the book, I am solely responsible.

I am indebted to many friends and family members who were sounding boards for drafts of the manuscript or its component parts, including Charity Shumway, Tanya Samu, Erin McPhie, Emily McPhie, Emily Bates, Randall Paul, Amy Hoyt, Laurel Thatcher Ulrich, Patrick Mason, Graci Kim Cribbens, Ally Isom, Holly Miller Jones, Carolina Allen, Bill Turnbull, Julia Chiou, Rachel Rueckert, Carol Ann Litster, Mei Li Inouye, Emily Inouye Huey, Emily Mitarai, Sharyn Wada Inouye, Benjamin Inouye, Mark Lambert, Mika Inouye Lambert, Cathy Tibbitts, Warren Sanji Inouye, Charles Shirō Inouye, Ann Takasaki, Alex Alton, Phil McMullin, Joy McMullin, Jolayne Eastman, Kerry McMullin, and Lisa McMullin Horvath. I am deeply grateful to my father, Warren Inouye, and my stepmother, Cathy Tibbetts, for their care and support. I am especially thankful to my late mother, Susan Lew Inouye, for her love and good example, and to her mother, Marjorie Ju Lew, for her loving care for me, my siblings, my father, and my children all these years. Finally, I am grateful to my husband Joseph McMullin for being not only a dependable editor and constructive critic of this book, but also a major character (and frequent source of comic relief) within its pages. He is one of the best examples I have of my faith's good fruits.

NOTES

Introduction

1. This is a reference to *The Hitchhiker's Guide to the Galaxy* by Douglas Adams, in which a supercomputer named Deep Thought works to generate the "Answer to the Ultimate Question of Life, the Universe, and Everything" for 7.5 million years and comes up with the answer: 42.

2. My hair fell out when I was twenty-seven. It's called alopecia areata. It was semitraumatic for about a month and a half as I met with doctors, learned that my hair would probably never come back, and tried various headscarves and hats to cover up. Then I got lazy. Now my casual look is bald without shaving, and my dressy look is bald with shaving.

3. While the official name of my church is The Church of Jesus Christ of Latter-day Saints, and while members of this church are Latter-day Saints, since the earliest years of our history in the mid-1800s, we have often been referred to as "Mormons" by those not of our faith (probably because of our distinctive new book of scripture, the Book of Mormon). Historically, members and leaders of The Church of Jesus Christ of Latter-day Saints have also referred to themselves as "Mormons" and to their faith tradition as "Mormonism." In October 2018, President Russell M. Nelson called on Latter-day Saints to use only the official name of the Church, and to discontinue use of nicknames. In my own writing in this book, I have adhered to the Church's newly revised style guide. However, when quoting what other people have said, I have accurately transcribed the words that they used.

4. In general, I will use pseudonyms for nonfamily who are not already comfortably engaged in speaking, teaching, or publishing in the public domain.

5. Latter-day Saints in greater China generally see the Tomb-Sweeping Festival as a wonderful opportunity to remember family members, tell family history stories, and celebrate the eternal connections that bind the generations together. In the past, and perhaps in some places in the present, some

NOTES

American church leaders and members (including, at one time, my recently returned-missionary self) felt uneasy about participation in this holiday on the grounds that it historically constituted worship of ancestors. However, the general view within Chinese wards today, which I now share, is that burning incense is a culturally appropriate gesture of respect, comparable to placing flowers on a Western grave.

PART 1: GOING PLACES

Long Departures, Long Returns

1. I imagine this reflection was somewhat parallel in sentiment (though much smaller in scale) to Moses's reaction when he saw all the worlds and all the children of God that have been and ever will be (Pearl of Great Price, Moses 1:10).

PART 2: STAYING HOME

Introduction to Part 2

1. Jonathan Stapley and Kristine Wright, "Female Ritual Healing in Mormonism," *Journal of Mormon History* 37, no. 1 (2011): 1–85.

To the Bean

1. In June 2003 I gave a speech at the "Class Day" ceremony for my university graduation, standing on the steps of Memorial Church.

The Sweaty Sprout

1. This is a reference to the book of Job, where Job says, "The Lord giveth, and the Lord taketh away."

Dispatch from Dissertation Research

1. To learn more about the True Jesus Church and the history of modern China, see Melissa Wei-Tsing Inouye, *China and the True Jesus: Charisma and Organization in a Chinese Christian Church* (New York: Oxford University Press, 2019).

Newsletter 2010

1. A reference to the Harry Potter book series by J. K. Rowling.
2. Shirley O. Corriher, *CookWise: The Hows and Whys of Successful Cooking* (New York: William Morrow Cookbooks, 1997).

PART 3: THINKING THINGS THROUGH

Toxic Religion? The Parable of the Pan

1. "Plural Marriage in Kirtland and Nauvoo," lds.org, https://www.lds.org/topics/plural-marriage-in-kirtland-and-nauvoo.

2. This "mechanical/manufactured" metaphor is one way of visualizing the role of religious traditions. The "Rotten Things Rotten, Good Things Good" letter to "E." at the end of this book takes the opposite tack.

Conversations Are Like Casseroles

1. "The whole gamut of human endeavor is now open to women. There is not anything that you cannot do if you will set your mind to it. You can include in the dream of the woman you would like to be a picture of one qualified to serve society and make a significant contribution to the world of which she will be a part." Gordon B. Hinckley, "How Can I Become the Woman of Whom I Dream?" General Young Women meeting, April 2001. https://www.lds.org/ensign/2001/05/how-can-i-become-the-woman-of-whom-i-dream.

2. These dynamics are complex. In recent years, more and more Latter-day Saint women are expressing a desire to be more involved in church leadership. Jana Riess's forthcoming survey of millennial Latter-day Saints, *The Next Mormons: How Millennials Are Changing the LDS Church* (New York: Oxford University Press, 2019), shows that views of American Latter-day Saints on gender and sexuality are shifting significantly, particularly among women. A 2014 study of American Latter-day Saints found that "Mormon women are overwhelmingly opposed to women as (lay) priests, but Mormon men have more mixed views: 90 percent of Mormon women as compared to 52 percent of Mormon men. In short, Mormons, especially Mormon women, appear to be the only substantial holdouts against the growing and substantial consensus across the religious spectrum in favor of women playing a fuller role in church leadership." Robert D. Putnam and David E. Campbell, *American Grace: How Religion Divides and Unites Us* (New York: Simon & Schuster, 2010), 244. Outside the United States, things become even more complex. In general, women in countries of the global South are more conservative than women in developed Western countries with regard to issues of gender and sexuality.

3. See the Foundation's website at http://religious-diplomacy.org.

Electric (Mutual) Joy

1. 6 November 2016, "Elder Christofferson Says Handbook Changes regarding Same-Sex Marriages Help Protect Children," https://www.lds.org/church/news/elder-christofferson-says-handbook-changes-regarding-same-sex-marriages-help-protect-children.

2. "Tom Christofferson interview from Rational Faiths," https://wheatandtares.org/2015/11/07/tom-christofferson-transcript/. Tom Christofferson is an actively practicing Latter-day Saint. Tom's expressions of love and affection for his church and his brother are laid out alongside his candid accounts of the many difficulties that LGBTQ Latter-day Saints face with regard to church policies and culture in his new book, *That We May Be One: A Gay Mormon's Perspective on Faith and Family* (Salt Lake City: Deseret Book, 2017).

3. Thanks to Kristine Haglund and Jonathan Stapley for sharing the following quotation from George Q. Cannon, then First Counselor in the First Presidency, showing a range of approaches to policies on children's baptism within church history: "In some minds there seems to be an idea that there should be a different form of blessing for children born of non-members and for those who are identified with the Church; and it is from such sources that in the case of children belonging to members of the Church 'the blessings of Abraham, Isaac and Jacob' and all the attendant favors are frequently conferred upon the child. This is all wrong. If we take the example of our Lord and Redeemer, who is our pattern and whose example we cannot too closely follow, we find that He blessed all who were brought to Him. We have no hint that He asked whose children they were, or the standing or faith of their parents. His remark was, 'Suffer little children, and forbid them not, to come unto me, for of such is the Kingdom of Heaven'; and He laid His hands upon them and blessed them. All little children, no matter what their parentage may be, are innocent in the sight of heaven, and they should be received as such and blessed as such." The Editor [George Q. Cannon], "Topics of the Times," *Juvenile Instructor* 34 (1 March 1899): 137–38; reprinted in *Latter-day Saints' Millennial Star* 61 (30 March 1899), 198–99; *Latter-day Saints' Southern Star* 1 (29 April 1899): 170.

4. In a 2012 general conference talk titled "Protect the Children," Elder Dallin H. Oaks affirmed the gravity of psychological or emotional harm to children: "When we consider the dangers from which children should be protected, we should also include psychological abuse. Parents or other caregivers or teachers or peers who demean, bully, or humiliate children or youth can inflict harm more permanent than physical injury. Making a child or youth feel worthless, unloved, or unwanted can inflict serious and long-lasting injury on his or her emotional well-being and development." https://www.lds.org/general-conference/2012/10/protect-the-children.

What Ana Said

1. Claudia Goldin and Cecilia Rouse, "Orchestrating Impartiality: The Impact of 'Blind' Auditions on Female Musicians," http://gap.hks.harvard.edu/orchestrating-impartiality-impact-"blind"-auditions-female-musicians.
2. "The Family: A Proclamation to the World," *Ensign*, November 2010, 129.
3. Mormon Land podcast: "Researcher Jana Riess discusses survey that reveals why LDS young people leave, why they stay and how they differ." https://www.sltrib.com/religion/2018/03/07/mormon-land-researcher-jana-riess-discusses-survey-that-reveals-why-lds-young-people-leave-why-they-stay-and-how-they-differ/.
4. As President Gordon B. Hinckley acknowledged in 2003, some Latter-day Saint women, no matter how righteous, willing, capable, or attractive, never have the opportunity to marry. Gordon B. Hinckley, "To the Women of the

NOTES

Church," https://www.lds.org/general-conference/2003/10/to-the-women-of -the-church.

5. Neil L. Andersen, "Come unto Him," *Ensign*, May 2009, 78.

6. This particular convention was introduced in 1946 but had still not been uniformly implemented as late as the mid-1950s. First Presidency circular to stake presidents and bishops, 2 May 1946, First Presidency Circular Letters, Church History Library. "Passing the Sacrament: Highest Authority to Be Recognized First," *Messenger*, no. 1 (January 1956): 1. See Jonathan Stapley's *Power of Godliness* (New York: Oxford University Press, 2018), 97, for an extensive discussion of the history of the administration of the sacrament ordinance.

7. This is a reference to the talk by Dallin H. Oaks in April 2014 general conference, "The Keys and Authority of the Priesthood," *Ensign*, May 2014, in which he said that priesthood is the authority to do God's work. For instance, when girls and boys go on a mission, they are set apart to preach the gospel and, Elder Oaks said, "given priesthood authority to perform a priesthood function." When the Primary president or Primary teachers are set apart to their callings in the Church, those sisters and brothers exercise "priesthood authority in performing her or his assigned duties" (p. 51).

8. Understandings of priesthood authority have changed dramatically over the course of Old and New Testament history and even in our church's short history. Latter-day Saints believe in ongoing revelation. It's not my place to declare that future changes are or are not off God's table. The historical record shows dynamism.

9. See Neylan McBaine, *Women at Church: Magnifying LDS Women's Local Impact* (Sandy, UT: Greg Kofford Books, 2014). This widely acclaimed book articulates why so many women feel pain at church, proposes solutions that uphold existing church policies, and shares many real-world examples of how local units and leaders are already thinking and acting creatively.

10. In the past, beginning with Emma Smith and continuing into the late nineteenth century at least, the president of the Relief Society was called for life, like an apostle, and was addressed as "President." Another solution, which I think is actually better, though less likely, is to do away with all titles altogether and to simply call all church members and leaders "sister" and "brother" (as the founding prophet Joseph Smith was often called "Brother Joseph").

11. David G. Stewart Jr. and Matthew Martinich, *Reaching the Nations: International LDS Church Growth Almanac, 2014 Edition* (Henderson, NV: Cumorah Foundation, 2013).

12. My thanks to Randall Paul for his cogent thinking on this issue, which I have paraphrased in this paragraph.

13. "The Origin of Man," *Improvement Era*, November 1909, 78; "Mother in Heaven," Gospel Topics, topics.lds.org.

14. Erastus Snow, in *Journal of Discourses,* 26 vols. (London: Latter-day Saints' Book Depot, 1854–86), 266; cited in Fiona and Terryl Givens, *The Christ Who Heals* (Salt Lake City: Deseret Book, 2017), 11.

15. Givens and Givens, *Christ Who Heals,* 12.

16. David L. Paulsen and Martin Pulido, "A Mother There: A Survey of Historical Teachings about Mother in Heaven," *BYU Studies* 50, no. 1 (2011): 77–78. Some of the article's many quotations from Latter-day Saints of God as Heavenly Father and Heavenly Mother also appear in the opening paragraphs of *Christ Who Heals,* by Givens and Givens.

17. John A. Widtsoe, "Everlasting Motherhood," *Millennial Star,* 10 May 1928, 298.

18. James E. Talmage, "The Philosophical Basis of Mormonism," *Improvement Era,* September 1915, 950.

19. Brigham Young, *Discourses of Brigham Young,* ed. John A. Widtsoe (Salt Lake City: Deseret Book, 1954), 51.

20. "The Family: A Proclamation to the World."

21. For example, see Jennifer Maddy, "Kylie's Parents," *Friend,* FJ2.

22. M. Russell Ballard, "The Trek Continues!," *Ensign,* November 2017, 106.

23. Pseudonym.

24. Ballard, "Trek Continues!," 106.

25. Certainly women do give counsel in talks and lessons, make decisions within auxiliaries, and can command personal respect from members of the community. However, the point of this essay is to show that the balance of institutional power within official Church structures is overwhelmingly male (i.e., very imbalanced). This is why it attracts notice even from Primary children.

The Problem We Want to Have

1. Tarienne Mitchell, archivist, Church History Library, "Blacks in Church History: Research Guide," https://history.lds.org/article/blacks-in-church-history -research-guide.

2. Dieter F. Uchtdorf, "The Merciful Obtain Mercy," *Ensign,* May 2012, 75.

3. Ian Linden, *Global Catholicism: Diversity and Change Since Vatican II* (New York: Columbia University Press, 2009); Pew Research Center, "Global Christianity," http://www.pewforum.org/interactives/global-christianity/# /global,ALL.

4. Laurel Thatcher Ulrich, *A House Full of Females* (New York: Knopf, 2017); Kathryn Daynes, *More Wives Than One* (Urbana: University of Illinois Press, 2001); "Plural Marriage in Kirtland and Nauvoo," https://www.lds.org/topics /plural-marriage-in-kirtland-and-nauvoo; "Plural Marriage in The Church of Jesus Christ of Latter-day Saints," Gospel Topics, topics.lds.org.

5. "Plural Marriage in Kirtland and Nauvoo."

6. "The Manifesto and the End of Plural Marriage," https://www.lds.org/topics /the-manifesto-and-the-end-of-plural-marriage.

7. "Manifesto and the End of Plural Marriage."

8. Doctrine and Covenants Official Declaration 1; "Plural Marriage in The Church of Jesus Christ of Latter-day Saints."

9. Plural marriage is still practiced, however, in current temple sealing policies.

10. On this topic, Melissa Proctor's article, "Babies, Bodies, and Birth Control," *Dialogue* 36, no. 3 (2003): 159–75, is the most comprehensive on the subject.

11. George Q. Cannon, *Deseret Weekly*, October 1894, 739; reprinted in *Gospel Truth* (Salt Lake City: Deseret Book, 1987), 379.

12. "Birth Control," *Relief Society Magazine*, July 1916, 364.

13. "Birth Control," 365.

14. "Birth Control," Gospel Topics, topics.lds.org.

15. "Chastity," Gospel Topics, topics.lds.org. The second paragraph of this article states: "Physical intimacy between husband and wife is beautiful and sacred. It is ordained of God for the creation of children and for the expression of love within marriage."

16. Latter-day Saints refer to the Lord's supper rite as the sacrament. See William Hartley, "Ordained and Acting Teachers in the Lesser Priesthood, 1851–1883," *BYU Studies* 16, no. 3 (1976): 375–98; and Jonathan Stapley, *The Power of Godliness* (New York: Oxford University Press, 2018).

17. "Articles and Covenants," in Joseph Smith Papers D1, Documents, Vol. 1: July 1828–June 1831, ed. Michael Hubbard MacKay, Gerrit J. Dirkmaat, Grant Underwood, Robert J. Woodford, and William G. Hartley (Salt Lake City: Church Historian's Press, 2013), 124 (Doctrine and Covenants 20:40, 58); see Stapley, *Power of Godliness*, 95.

18. Hartley, "Ordained and Acting Teachers," 395.

19. Aaronic Priesthood Manual 2 (n.p.: The Church of Jesus Christ of Latter-day Saints, 1993), 72–73; see Stapley, *Power of Godliness*, 97.

20. Aaronic Priesthood Manual 2, 72–73; see Stapley, *Power of Godliness*, 97.

21. See H. Michael Marquardt, comp., *Early Patriarchal Blessings of the Church of Jesus Christ of Latter-day Saints* (Salt Lake City: Smith–Pettit Foundation, 2007), 19, 56, 104, 147; Jonathan Stapley and Kristine Wright, "Female Ritual Healing in Mormonism," *Journal of Mormon History* 37, no. 1 (2011): 4.

22. Joseph Smith, sermon, 28 April 1842, in Jill Mulvay Derr, Carol Cornwall Madsen, Kate Holbrook, et al., eds., *The First Fifty Years of Relief Society* (Salt Lake City: Church Historian's Press, 2016), 54–59; Stapley, *Power of Godliness*, 84.

23. Derr et al., *First Fifty Years of Relief Society*, introduction (online), https://www.churchhistorianspress.org/the-first-fifty-years-of-relief-society/front-matter/introduction.

24. The healing ministrations of Zina D. H. Young and Eliza R. Snow, along with many other Latter-day Saint women, are chronicled in the forthcoming volume 2 of the new official Church history, *Saints*.

25. Stapley and Wright, "Female Ritual Healing in Mormonism," 1–85; Derr et al., *First Fifty Years of Relief Society*, introduction (online), https://www.churchhistorianspress.org/the-first-fifty-years-of-relief-society/front-matter/introduction.

26. Derr et al., *First Fifty Years of Relief Society*, part 4.8 (online). https://www.church
historianspress.org/the-first-fifty-years-of-relief-society/part-4/4-8.
27. Stapley, *Power of Godliness*, 101.
28. See Joseph F. Smith's description of healing George Romney with Smith's
wives the year before Smith passed away. [Joseph F. Smith], Sermon at the
Funeral of Joseph H. Grant, "Editor's Table," *Improvement Era*, February 1918,
355; Stapley and Wright, "Female Ritual Healing," 53–64; Stapley, *Power of
Godliness*, 91.
29. Relief Society, *Handbook of the Relief Society of The Church of Jesus Christ
of Latter-day Saints* (Salt Lake City: General Board of Relief Society, 1949),
82–83; this section was removed in the correlated version of the Relief Society
Handbook of 1968. See Stapley and Wright, "Female Ritual Healing," 81–82.
30. See the recent film, *Jane and Emma* (2018), for an exploration of the two wom-
en's friendship.
31. My thanks to Janan Graham-Russell for bringing this 1836 source to my attention. Joseph Smith, "Letter to Oliver Cowdery, circa 9 April 1836," http://
www.josephsmithpapers.org/paper-summary/letter-to-oliver-cowdery-circa
-9-april-1836/1; "Joseph Smith and His Papers: An Introduction," http://www
.josephsmithpapers.org/articles/joseph-smith-and-his-papers-an-introduction.
32. Paul Reeve, *Religion of a Different Color* (New York: Oxford University Press,
2015).
33. "Race and the Priesthood," Gospel Topics, topics.lds.org.
34. "As we look to the future, one of the most important effects of the revelation
on the priesthood is its divine call to abandon attitudes of prejudice against
any group of God's children. Racism is probably the most familiar source
of prejudice today, and we are all called to repent of that." Dallin H. Oaks,
"President Oaks Remarks at Worldwide Priesthood Celebration," https://
www.mormonnewsroom.org/article/president-oaks-remarks-worldwide
priesthood-celebration.
35. Mitchell, "Blacks in Church History: Research Guide."
36. "Manifesto and the End of Plural Marriage."
37. Patrick Mason has also expressed this idea. He has advocated "the restoration
of the Restoration" as a pathway forward into the twenty-first century.
38. Dieter F. Uchtdorf, "Come Join with Us," *Ensign*, November 2013, 22.
39. M. Russell Ballard, "Precious Gifts from God," *Ensign*, May 2018, 9.
40. L. Frank Baum, *The Wonderful Wizard of Oz* (Chicago: George M. Hill, 1900).
In this classic American children's novel and later musical film, the great and
powerful "Wizard of Oz" turns out to be an illusion, controlled by a "humbug"
(impostor) hiding behind a screen.
41. "Racism, sexism, and nationalism" are worldly attitudes that M. Russell Ballard
said the Latter-day Saints should eliminate from among their fellowship. "The
Trek Continues!," *Ensign*, November 2017, 106.

42. This is an idea developed by Armand Mauss in his book, *The Angel and the Beehive: The Mormon Struggle with Assimilation* (Urbana: University of Illinois Press, 1994).
43. Andrew H. Hedges, Alex D. Smith, and Brent M. Rogers, eds., *Journals, Volume 3: May 1843–June 1844*, vol. 3 of the Journals series of *The Joseph Smith Papers*, edited by Ronald K. Esplin and Matthew J. Grow (Salt Lake City: Church Historian's Press, 2015), 55 and 66.
44. I am teaching my children to protect themselves in such instances, which unfortunately have been known to occur repeatedly in church contexts. Abuse in any context is unacceptable; https://www.lds.org/get-help/abuse?cid=rdb_v_abuse.
45. Russell M. Nelson, "Revelation for the Church, Revelation for Our Lives," *Ensign*, May 2018, 95.
46. D. Todd Christofferson, "The Doctrine of Christ," *Ensign*, May 2012, 89; the longer quotation is: "Even the President of the Church, himself, may not always be 'moved upon by the Holy Ghost,' when he addresses the people. This has happened about matters of doctrine (usually of a highly speculative character) where subsequent Presidents of the Church and the peoples themselves have felt that in declaring the doctrine, the announcer was not 'moved upon by the Holy Ghost.' How shall the Church know when these adventurous expeditions of the brethren into these highly speculative principles and doctrines meet the requirements of the statutes that the announcers thereof have been 'moved upon by the Holy Ghost'? The Church will know by the testimony of the Holy Ghost in the body of the members, whether the brethren in voicing their views are 'moved upon by the Holy Ghost'; and in due time that knowledge will be made manifest." Christofferson, "Doctrine of Christ," 90, quoting J. Reuben Clark, "When Are Church Leaders' Words Entitled to Claim of Scripture?" *Church News*, 31 July 1954, 9–10.
47. Ballard, "Precious Gifts from God," 9.

The Trouble with Revolutions

1. Pei-Kai Cheng and Michael Lestz, eds., *The Search for Modern China: A Documentary Collection* (New York: W. W. Norton, 1999), 198.

Civilization = Organization?

1. Emperor of the early Ming dynasty, lived from 1360 to 1424, famous for commissioning a huge "treasure fleet" of giant ships that sailed to various far-flung kingdoms, including some in East Africa, to demonstrate China's wealth and power.
2. Emperor of the Qing dynasty during the height of its power, lived from 1711 to 1799, a member of the "Manchu" ethnic group that ruled China as a multi-ethnic empire (including Manchus, Mongols, Han Chinese, and numerous other minority peoples). The Manchu-led Qing dynasty overthrew the native Ming dynasty in 1644 and was itself overthrown in the Chinese Revolution

of 1911. The Qing dynasty was one of several Chinese dynasties established by foreign conquest. The Manchu homeland is a region that now comprises northeastern China.

3. An imperial academy staffed by the empire's brightest and most promising young scholars.
4. The source for the entire discussion of the Complete Library of the Four Treasuries in this lecture is F. W. Mote, *Imperial China* (Cambridge, MA: Harvard University Press, 2003), 923–28.
5. The native Han Chinese Ming dynasty (1368–1644) fell to the foreign Manchu Qing dynasty (1644–1911).
6. *The Analects*, XV:24, online at the Chinese Text Project, http://ctext.org/analects /wei-ling-gong.
7. *The Analects*, XII:19, http://ctext.org/analects/yan-yuan.
8. *The Analects*, VII:30, https://ctext.org/analects/shu-er.
9. Personal name of the founder of the Ming dynasty, lived from 1328 to 1398.
10. *The Analects*, II:4, http://ctext.org/analects/wei-zheng.

Rich Entanglements

1. Personal name of the founder of the Ming dynasty, lived from 1328 to 1398.
2. Reign name of the emperor of the Qing dynasty at the height of its power. Qianlong reigned 1735–1796.
3. Public Service Announcement for University Students: Avoid the Cardinal Sins—that is, the three egregious grammatical errors most commonly made by students. They are as follows: apostrophe misuse, run-on sentences, and sentence fragments.
4. F. W. Mote, *Imperial China* (Cambridge, MA: Harvard University Press, 2003), 588–90.

PART 4: GETTING DISEMBOWELED

FOLFOX

1. A combination of drugs used to target colorectal cancer.

400 Meters; 6 Miles

1. Chinese term for maternal grandmother.

PART 5: LOOKING TO THE FUTURE

A Letter to My Not-Yet-Teenage Children

1. Actually, it feels more than discouraging. It feels soul-crushing. Nevertheless, on this topic, read Laurel Thatcher Ulrich, "Lusterware," in *A Thoughtful Faith: Essays on Belief by Mormon Scholars*, ed. Philip Barlow (Centerville, UT: Canon Press, 1986).
2. See M. Russell Ballard's call to "eliminate any prejudice, including racism, sexism, and nationalism." "The Trek Continues!," *Ensign*, November 2017, 106.

3. Neill F. Marriott, "What Shall We Do?," *Ensign*, May 2016, 11.

4. "Race and the Priesthood," Gospel Topics, topics.lds.org.

5. Brigham Young, *Journal of Discourses*, 7:290–91 (9 October 1859), archived online in BYU Digital Collections, https://contentdm.lib.byu.edu/digital/collection/JournalOfDiscourses3/id/2854.

6. Bruce R. McConkie, *Mormon Doctrine* (Salt Lake City: Bookcraft, 1966), 527–28.

7. "Race and the Priesthood."

8. Dallin H. Oaks, "President Oaks Remarks at Worldwide Priesthood Celebration," https://www.mormonnewsroom.org/article/president-oaks-remarks-worldwide-priesthood-celebration.

9. The text of Sister Burch's remarks at the 2016 Mormon History Association Women's History breakfast can be found at https://www.mormonwomenshistoryinitiative.org/mwhit-breakfast-2016.html.

10. Eugene England, "Why the Church Is as True as the Gospel," http://www.eugeneengland.org/why-the-church-is-as-true-as-the-gospel.

11. President Russell M. Nelson offered a similar promise in his first major address as the new President of the Church in the April 2018 general conference. "Revelation for the Church, Revelation for Our Lives," *Ensign*, May 2018, 93–96.

12. The Chinese revolutionary Sun Yat-sen (1866–1925) famously said on his deathbed, "The Revolution is not yet complete. Comrades still need to work hard!" See also a talk by President Dieter F. Uchtdorf in which he affirms that "the Restoration is an ongoing process. . . . It includes 'all that God has revealed, all that He does now reveal,' and the 'many great and important things' that 'He will yet reveal.'" Uchtdorf, "Are You Sleeping through the Restoration?," *Ensign*, May 2014, 59.

Rotten Things Rotten, Good Things Good

1. See the essay, "Toxic Religion: The Parable of the Pan," for an "inorganic" metaphor to describe the Latter-day Saint tradition.

2. See Laurel Thatcher Ulrich, *A House Full of Females: Plural Marriage and Women's Rights in Early Mormonism, 1835–1870* (New York: Knopf, 2017). Also note contemporary organizations such as Big Ocean Women and Mormon Women for Ethical Government.

3. In a similar vein, see Caroline Kline's doctoral dissertation comparing the experiences of Latter-day Saint women on a global scale, working with women in Botswana and Mexico and women of color in the US. Caroline Kline, "Navigating Mormonism's Gendered Theology and Practice: Mormon Women in a Global Context" (PhD dissertation, Claremont Graduate University, 2018).

4. Patrick Q. Mason's book, *Planted: Belief and Belonging in an Age of Doubt* (Provo, UT: Neal A. Maxwell Institute for Religious Scholarship; Salt Lake City: Deseret Book, 2015), is part of the BYU Maxwell Institute's Living Faith series; it is a fantastic discussion of faith, doubt, and being "rooted" in Christ.

5. Pseudonym.

6. Another pithy aphorism coined by my Uncle Charles.

7. The fear narrative doesn't work, but the triumphalist one isn't much better. You definitely shouldn't choose to be a Latter-day Saint because we're just about to conquer the world, because we're not. According to the Pew Research Center's statistics on world religion, about 31.2 percent (2.2 billion) of the world's population is Christian, about half (1.1 billion) of whom are Catholic. There are 1.8 billion Muslims (24 percent), 1 billion Hindus (15 percent), and 500 million Buddhists (7 percent). In terms of numbers, we are a tiny scratch on the surface of humanity, especially if you think historically. Though organizationally energetic and overflowing with theological certitude, we are undeniably small in proportion to all people and all religions. A little humility is in order. However, we are indeed poised to live up to Jesus's biblical prescriptions to be salt, or leaven—something very small that makes a big difference. Pew Research Center, "The Changing Global Religious Landscape," April 2017, http://assets.pewresearch.org/wp-content/uploads/sites/11/2017/04/07092755/FULL-REPORT-WITH-APPENDIXES-A-AND-B-APRIL-3.pdf.

8. These are all actual people I've encountered at church.

On Fear

1. "Pink Sausage" became one of Sprout's permanent nicknames, because he got so red when he cried. There's a good reason the Japanese word for "baby" is akachan ("the little red one").

2. Chinese name for grandmother.

3. This divine vulnerability is a clear result of our Heavenly Parents' gift of agency to their children. As recorded in the Book of Moses in the Pearl of Great Price, when God beheld all humanity and wept, Enoch asked why. In Moses 7:32–33, God responded: "Behold these thy brethren [and sisters]; they are the workmanship of mine own hands, and I gave unto them their knowledge, in the day I created them; and in the Garden of Eden, gave I unto [men and women] [their] agency; and unto thy brethren [and sisters] have I said, and also given commandment, that they should love one another, and that they should choose me, their Father; but behold, they are without affection, and they hate their own blood."

Conclusion

1. Eliza R. Snow, plural wife of both Joseph Smith and Brigham Young, features prominently in Laurel Thatcher Ulrich, *A House Full of Females: Plural Marriage and Women's Rights in Early Mormonism, 1835–1870* (New York: Alfred A. Knopf, 2017). Near the end of her life, she participated in an "indignation meeting," vehemently refuting criticisms of plural marriage as degrading and oppressive to women (377–79). Ann Eliza Young, *Wife No. 19, or the Story of a Life in Bondage, Being a Complete Exposé of Mormonism and Revealing the*

Sorrows, Sacrifices and Suffering of Women in Polygamy (Hartford, CT: Dustin, Gilman, 1875).

2. Eliza R. Snow, "An Elevation So High Above the Ordinary," 11 October 1872, in Jennifer Reeder and Kate Holbrook, eds., *At the Pulpit: 185 Years of Discourses by Latter-day Saint Women* (Salt Lake City: The Church Historian's Press, 2017).

3. Mark 12:30–31; 10:21–22; Matthew 25:40–45. Shortly before his death, Joseph Smith asked John Taylor to sing a favorite hymn, "A Poor Wayfaring Man of Grief," depicting many of these scenarios.

MELISSA WEI-TSING INOUYE is a senior lecturer in Asian Studies at the University of Auckland. She received her PhD in East Asian languages and civilizations from Harvard University. Dr. Inouye's research includes the history of Chinese Christianity, moral ideology in modern China, global charismatic religious movements, and women and religion. Her book *China and the True Jesus: Charisma and Organization in a Chinese Christian Church* was published by Oxford University Press in January 2019. She leads the Global Mormon Studies Research Network and is a recipient of the University of Auckland's highest award for teaching at the early career stage.

She served in the Taiwan Kaohsiung Mission from 2000 to 2002, was a temple worker in the Boston Massachusetts Temple, and has served in many callings in Primary, Young Women, and Public Affairs. A member of the advisory board of the Neal A. Maxwell Institute for Religious Scholarship at Brigham Young University, Dr. Inouye is committed to the mutually reinforcing relationship between faith and learning. Her writings on Latter-day Saint life and faith have been published online and in print in Patheos, the *Washington Post*, *Meridian Magazine*, *Square Two*, and the *Ensign*. She and her husband Joseph have four noisy and joyful children, botanically nicknamed Bean, Sprout, Leaf, and Shoot.